Robert Browning

MEN AND WOMEN
AND OTHER POEMS

Edited, with an introduction
and notes, by
J. W. HARPER
Senior Lecturer in English and Related Studies
in the University of York

DENT: LONDON, MELBOURNE AND TORONTO
EVERYMAN'S LIBRARY

© Introduction and notes,
J. M. Dent & Sons Ltd, 1975
All rights reserved
Made in Great Britain
by
Richard Clay (The Chaucer Press) Ltd, Bungay, Suffolk
for
J. M. DENT & SONS LTD
Aldine House, 33 Welbeck St, London W1M 8LX
First published 1975
Reprinted 1977, 1980, 1982

No. 427 Hardback ISBN 0 460 10427 6
No. 1427 Paperback ISBN 0 460 11427 1

CONTENTS

Contents

Contents

NOTE ON THE TEXT

In the collected editions which appeared during his lifetime Browning made many changes in the order, grouping, and text of his poems. The final arrangement and revised text is that of the collected edition of 1888–9 in sixteen volumes. A thorough discussion of the problems of editing Browning's texts is found in the Introduction to Volume I of the new *Complete Works of Robert Browning*, edited by King, Honan, Peckham, and Pitts, currently in progress, which is cited in the Bibliography.

The Everyman University Library edition is based on the texts of the earliest published editions, apart from a few corrections of obvious errors subsequently made by Browning and indicated in the notes. The arrangement of the poems following *Men and Women* is chronological.

INTRODUCTION

When Robert and Elizabeth Barrett Browning made what was to prove their final visit to England in the summer of 1855, their principal purpose was to see Browning's new book, *Men and Women*, through the press. Though the works of this devoted couple had been before the public for about the same length of time, their public reputations during their long Italian exile had been very different. Mrs Browning was one of the most famous writers of the age. She had been seriously considered for the laureateship in 1850, and *Aurora Leigh*, shortly to be published, went through edition after edition. Browning, by contrast, had been consistently neglected by the public and the critics; and when he began to assemble the poems for what was to become the volumes of *Men and Women*, he was specifically aiming at the popular success which had eluded him, thinking (as he said in one of his letters) of 'a first step towards popularity for me—lyrics with more music and painting than before, so as to get people to hear and see'. The poems destined for these two volumes were gradually written during the Brownings' happiest period in Florence, the most richly productive period of Browning's life, and those who saw the work in manuscript were enthusiastic. Mrs Browning thought the new poems 'magnificent'; Browning's friend Milsand found them 'superhuman'. And during that London summer, while the book was in the hands of the printers, Browning wrote the splendid afterthought 'One Word More', the dedication to his wife which he had long meditated, in which he emphasized the dramatic quality of the whole work:

> Love, you saw me gather men and women,
> Live or dead as fashioned by my fancy,
> Enter each and all, and use their service,
> Speak from every mouth,—the speech, a poem.
> Hardly shall I tell my joys and sorrows,
> Hopes and fears, belief and disbelieving:
> I am mine and yours—the rest be all men's,
> Karshish, Cleon, Norbert and the fifty.
> Let me speak this once in my true person . . .

The great book, one of the finest single creations of Victorian literature, was complete, and the Brownings settled back comfortably to await the result. As Dean DeVane put it, 'the British public was on trial'.[1]

The story of that trial has been often told, but perhaps never quite accurately, and a reading of the reviews which appeared in the winter of 1855–6[2] provides a fascinating episode in the history of literary taste. *The Athenaeum* reviewed the book on the day of its publication, 17 November 1855, and set the tone for much of what was to follow: 'These volumes contain some fifty poems, which will make the least imaginative man think, and the least thoughtful man grieve. Who will not grieve over energy wasted and power misspent,—over fancies chaste and noble, so overhung by the "seven veils" of obscurity, that we can oftentimes be only sure that fancies exist?' Other reviewers' comments were similar: 'It is really high time that this sort of thing should, if possible, be stopped . . .', 'Perversity, carelessness, and bad taste. . . '. Browning's bitter disappointment is chronicled in his letters, and for some time he wrote hardly anything at all.

Yet this was not really the fiasco that it seemed to the poet at the time. The more considerable reviewers—David Masson, John Forster, George Eliot—saw the merits of the book and praised it intelligently. And every one of the unfavourable reviews contained fulsome recognition of the poet's great talent: that in *Fraser's Magazine*, concluding several hundred words of faultfinding with the startling assertion that Browning stood second only to Tennyson among the poets of the age. Posterity can see a dual significance in William Morris's enthusiastic praise in *The Oxford and Cambridge Magazine*; for Browning's poetry was warmly received by both the artists of the Pre-Raphaelite movement and by intelligent young readers at the universities, by those who would influence the taste of the next decade. This was the new poetry, and the enthusiasm of the young was to prove more significant than the objections of conventional reviewers to Browning's obscurity, his roughness, the occasional harshness of his humour and the general novelty of his manner. Thus the 'apparent failure' of *Men and Women* actually laid the groundwork for the comparative success of the selection from Browning's work which appeared only a few years later, for the acclaim which greeted *Dramatis Personae* in 1864 (a book which no one today would regard as superior to its predecessor), and for the public triumph of *The Ring and the Book* in 1868. *Men and*

Women, generally regarded by later readers as Browning's best single book, finally established his reputation.

But the excellence of *Men and Women* is that of maturity rather than of novelty. Nothing that is present here had not been present in Browning's previous writings, and every tendency which he was to develop in the future is here forecast. That he did not regard this book as in any sense a unity is shown by his complete rearrangement of his poems for the collected editions which appeared in his later years, where 'Men and Women' became a separate section, a category of his verse in which only eight poems from the original book were included, together with others from other publications. The rest of the original *Men and Women* were distributed under the headings 'Dramatic Lyrics' and 'Dramatic Romances', and this is now the traditional arrangement for collected editions of Browning's poems. In the poet's mind a 'Men and Women' piece had become a type of poem.

Much of Browning's verse in *Men and Women* is devoted to love poetry, to what his Victorian readers particularly valued and what Sir Henry Jones called 'the richest vein of pure ore in his verse'. This vein of ore apparently seems less rich to the present age, probably because Browning's love poetry, for all its vast variety, is based upon certain personal doctrines, most centrally the belief that the experience of personal love is equivalent to a revelation of the divine nature. Love is indubitable, revelatory, and the climactic experience of life, and here the central text is the poem 'Saul', where in section XVIII David is inspired by his self-sacrificing love for the dying king to a vision of the future Redeemer. Similarly, in *The Ring and the Book* the Pope is saved from despair by his love for his conception of the dead Pompilia. In the poems concerning sexual love the same assumption underlies the whole conception, as in one of the most famous pieces in *Men and Women*, 'By the Fireside', where 'one moment, one and infinite' gives meaning and unity to the whole past and future lives of the lovers. Only an acceptance of Browning's exigent claims for the power and full meaning of love saves the once widely admired 'Evelyn Hope' from appearing to be the pathetic self-delusions of a dotard.

But precisely because of the extravagant value which Browning assigned to human love, he was obsessed by instances of its failure. This no doubt offers a partial explanation of his life-time habit of writing poems in pairs. To a mind sufficiently flexible to see both sides of every question (and Browning lost such flexibility only late in life) the simple ecstasy of 'Meeting at Night' simply must transpose into the complex tone of 'Parting at Morning', 'One Way of Love' balances 'Another Way of Love', 'Love in a Life' must be elaborated by 'Life in a Love', and thus the serene statement of 'By the Fireside' must be confronted by 'Two in the Campagna' and the doctrine completely tested by the full range of human experience.

Haunted as he was by humanity's incessant failure to achieve its highest mode of being, Browning became an acute analyst of the 'sex war', the differing attitudes of male and female towards sexual love; and he is remarkable among male poets in being able to write convincingly from the woman's point of view. 'A Lovers' Quarrel' may be seen as providing a generic title for much of his verse. Love being such an overpowering experience, its greatest danger is the temptation to self-abnegation which it creates. Thus in 'A Woman's Last Word' the woman bows her being to her husband; but her last word is 'that will be tomorrow', which shows that she *has* a personality which is being unfairly suppressed. The masculine tendency is to elevate the feminine opposite into an unapproachable ideal which ceases to be human and which thus creates demands which no mere human can meet. 'Any Wife to Any Husband' adumbrates this theme; but here Browning's most profound statement is the later symbolic poem 'Numpholeptos', which thoroughly puzzled his contemporaries but which perhaps contains his clearest vision of the agonizing difficulties which plague the loves of men and women.

The most difficult and debated symbolic poem in *Men and Women* itself is the enigmatic 'Childe Roland to the Dark Tower Came'; perhaps Browning's most 'modern' poem in that it provokes as much discussion in our day as it did in 1855, even if the questions which it raises have subtly changed with the passage of time. But 'Childe Roland', the poem which its writer alleged came to him in 'a kind of dream', actually belongs to a very broad strand of Browning's writing which forms as important an element in his work as his love poetry, and its full impact can be felt only by a reader who is aware of its context. Many of Browning's most frequently anthologized poems—'Incident in the French Camp', 'How They Brought the Good News from Ghent to Aix,' 'Count Gismond'—are poems celebrating a heroism based upon a simple acceptance of duty, and the character of Caponsacchi in *The Ring and the Book* illustrates this theme as well. Browning's heroes do not 'reason why'; they seize unreflectingly upon the task at hand and find in the thrill of the challenge and the excitement of the battle a sufficient justification of life, content to leave the final reward to God. So widespread is this theme in Browning that the sensations of strenuosity and breathless rush may seem the chief characteristics of his poetry, and the famous 'Prospice' enthusiastically celebrates death as the final battle whose favourable result to the brave can be confidently predicted. The most sophisticated and satisfying of these poems is 'A Grammarian's Funeral' in *Men and Women*, in which an early humanist's lifetime of devotion to the elucidation of the classical languages is elevated to the plane of heroic self-sacrifice which surely must find its due reward in heaven:

> Was it not great? did not he throw on God,
>   (He loves the burthen)——
> God's task to make the heavenly period
> Perfect the earthen?

This is the 'philosophy of the imperfect' which Browning shared with Ruskin and others amongst his contemporaries: the view that life can only be truly lived in the endeavour to encompass a task that is beyond one's powers; so that failure is predestined and yet, paradoxically, proves to be the greatest success, in that man fully tests, extends, and ultimately transcends his limitations in the excitement of the struggle. As Andrea del Sarto puts it

> Ah, but a man's reach should exceed his grasp,
> Or what's a heaven for?

Andrea recognizes his own failure but at the same time sees how he might have succeeded, and his question is the question which the whole line of Browning's heroes ask with complete confidence.

All except Childe Roland. This whole conception of heroism is based upon a very simple faith, thus one which is readily susceptible of doubt; and the feeling that 'the prize is in the process', that the excitement of the moment of crisis is a sufficient basis for life, is subject to changes of mood, to the ebb and flow of psychic energy. Thus Roland is haunted by the question which Browning's other simple-minded heroes never ask: when the crucial trial finally faces him, will he be fit? And though 'Childe Roland to the Dark Tower Came' contains the usual features of Browning's heroic narratives—the challenge, the quest, the intense visceral combat, and the final heroic resolution:

> Dauntless the slug-horn to my lips I set
> And blew: 'Childe Roland to the Dark Tower Came.'

—the response to this desperate triumph of courage is a shattering silence; as it must be, on this side of the tomb. 'Childe Roland' contains the complete obverse of Browning's customary view of life: the world turned to a trackless and horrifying wasteland. Yet since, as has been shown by several critical analyses, it is composed almost entirely out of elements elsewhere present in his work, it suggests the extent to which his poetry is a poetry of tension between what he desperately willed to believe and what he subconsciously knew and feared.

'Childe Roland', of course, is a dramatic monologue, but that is not the category in which we are inclined to place it. All of these poems are dramatic, as Browning reminds us in 'One Word More'. And here with 'Fra Lippo Lippi' and 'Andrea del Sarto' he presents us with a pair of masterpieces which are the culmination of his previous work in this genre which he made so peculiarly his own. *Men and Women* also contains a brilliant poem, 'Bishop Blougram's Apology', which forecasts the new and more intricate way in which this form was to be developed. As a third variety of the poetry of *Men and Women*, the type of poem by which Browning principally influenced the development of modern poetry, the dramatic monologue requires separate consideration.

In the fascinating discussion of poetic art in his early poem *Sordello* Browning indicated that he viewed the dramatic mode as an inferior form of literature. But since the world was, he felt, not yet ready for the highest mode, lyric, or complete self-expression, he cultivated the dramatic form and made himself its complete master (the dramatic monologues of Tennyson make an interesting comparison). In the dramatic monologue the poet disappears behind his creation and the presentation of an alien self becomes the whole subject of the poem. Karshish, Cleon, Norbert and the fifty take the stage in turn and we have, not actual drama, but 'action in character rather than character in action', as Browning once expressed it, adding that apart from the development of a soul, 'little else is worth study'.

This poetry is based upon certain assumptions about human personality: that each personality contains a central core which constitutes the individual's essential nature, and that this core continually reveals itself to the acute observer in the smallest gestures and tricks of phrase, so that it is quite possible to come to know another person to his very depths.[3] One can analyse and catalogue the technical devices by which Browning explores his *personæ* and turns them inside out for our delectation;[4] but though his character studies are usually drawn from the Renaissance, the early Christian era, and his own day, each of his men and women is in some important sense unique, their very language being subtly varied to bring out the essence of their individuality.

As has recently been argued, the primary purpose of Browning's dramatic monologues is not a moral judgment of the character presented;[5] but this observation is worth making not because no moral judgment is made but because, on the contrary, such judgment is so obvious in the earlier poems in this genre that it can hardly be regarded as constituting their purpose. Fra Lippo Lippi is *l'homme moyen sensuel* who happens to be an artistic genius and whose immense vitality enables him to raise his art above the unfavourable circumstances in which he finds himself. Andrea del Sarto, seemingly so much more fortunate and talented, is a pathetic failure, sympathetic because of the self-knowledge which he has attained. The Bishop of St. Praxed's is a disgusting, though amusing, old rogue. 'Pictor Ignotus' is a coward, the Duke of Ferrara an egoistical villain, Johannes Agricola and Porphyria's lover are mad. The moral reactions which we register are not the meanings of these poems but only aspects of their total meaning. But as Browning elaborated the technique of the dramatic monologue, the way in which moral judgment is present in the poem becomes increasingly complicated and confusing. 'Bishop Blougram's Apology' begins the series of what has come to be called 'casuistical monologues' ('Mr. Sludge, the Medium', 'Prince Hohenstiel-Schwangau', 'Fifine at the Fair', etc.) in which the arguments become progressively lengthier and more tortuous, the points at issue more subtle, and the tasks of judging the speakers and grasping the poem's purpose increasingly puzzling.

Donald Smalley's discovery of Browning's essay on Chatterton,[6] long lost among the anonymous book reviews in *The Foreign Quarterly Review*, gives us, as Professor Smalley's introduction shows, the chance to observe one of the poet's casuistical monologues in the making, for here we can see adumbrated the four essential characteristics of Browning's unique form. Each of these poems is obviously a genuine 'apology' for the life of the speaker, delivered with considerable moral earnestness. Yet at the same time, each is an exposure of the speaker's fundamental weakness or baseness, as indicated by the 'give-away' which is invariably present, usually at the end (Blougram, the poet informs us extra-dramatically, 'believed, say, half he spoke' and ignored 'certain hell-deep instincts'). We may also observe that upon logical grounds the casuist is irrefutable. But at the same time each of these monologues contains a central passage of lyrical poetry which suddenly rises above the grey argument and seems to give us the essential clue to what the protagonist really wishes he could be or believe:

> Just when we are safest, there's a sunset-touch,
> A fancy from a flower-bell, someone's death,
> A chorus-ending from Euripides,—
> And that's enough for fifty hopes and fears
> As old and new at once as Nature's self,
> To rap and knock and enter in our soul,
> Take hands and dance there, a fantastic ring,
> Round the ancient idol, on his base again,—
> The grand Perhaps!

Thus we have a rather confusing collection of generalizations. Apparently it is possible to sympathize with the casuist while knowing him to be despicable and to understand that his self-defence is sophistical while being unable to refute it. No one had ever written poetry like this before. Except, at moments, Shakespeare.

What was Browning's intention in cultivating this genre and in bringing it to such a perverse perfection? The intention of a dramatic monologue, enriched with the elaborate techniques brought to the form, would appear to be the total exposition of a personality, a venture into what Santayana called 'literary psychology', that imaginative penetration of an alien being of which we are sometimes capable, which enables us to know another person as well as, in our clear-sightedly introspective moments, we know ourselves. Thus conceived, dramatic monologue would be an independent and gratuitous form of literature, the product solely of the joy of its own inspiration. It would be art for art's sake.

In reading dramatic monologue, however, we are always

inclined to wonder about the principle of selection. Why has the poet chosen this particular man or woman at this particular moment? Is it really because of disinterested delight in the *haecceitas* of that being, its ultimate principle of individuality; or has the poet made his selection from some personal motive? Are these particular men and women actually in some way illustrations of his personal philosophy?

In *Dramatis Personae* Browning included a bizarre narrative poem called 'Gold Hair: A Story of Pornic', the story of a beautiful and apparently saintly girl who died young, and on her death-bed asked only that she be allowed to keep her long yellow hair intact. She was buried as she wished, but a later disturbance of her tomb revealed that her anxiety about her hair had been due to her miserly hoarding of a large store of gold which she had hidden there. And Browning is unusually explicit in drawing his moral:

> Why I deliver this horrible verse?
>   As the text of a sermon which now I preach:
> Evil or good may be better or worse
>   In the human heart, but the mixture of each
> Is a marvel and a curse.
>
> The candid incline to surmise of late
>   That the Christian faith proves false, I find;
> For our Essays-and-Reviews' debate
>   Begins to tell on the public mind,
> And Colenso's words have weight.
>
> I still, to suppose it true, for my part,
>   See reasons and reasons; this, to begin:
> 'Tis the faith that launched point-blank her dart
>   At the head of a lie—taught Original Sin,
> The Corruption of Man's Heart.

'The corruption of man's heart': this is really what these casuistical poems, and the whole series of dramatic monologues which precede them, are basically concerned with. They are concerned for the most part (and there are several exceptions which convey the positive side of Browning's vision of mankind's moral life) with the rise, growth, and triumph of moral evil in the human mind. In 'The Critic as Artist' Oscar Wilde made one of the most profound observations about Browning when he remarked that what fascinated this poet was not thought itself but the process by which thought moves. This is a perfect description of the dramatic monologue as Browning developed it; for the 'process by which thought moves', as he shows (and here he is dangerously close to epiphenomenology), is a process which moves independently of the human will; and it is in this cancerous growth that evil is born and develops. Browning was widely celebrated amongst his contemporaries for his 'solution' to the problem of physical evil (such questions as why a just God allows the Lisbon Cathedral to collapse on the heads of the worshippers on Easter Day, etc.), and this 'solution' has long been consigned to the dustbins which historians keep for earnestly inscribed but ultimately useless waste-paper. But the analysis of the process of moral evil he made the essence of his own unique form of poetry, and he was clear in his denunciation of man's ratiocinative intellect as the corrupting organ. His casuistical poems are ingeniously elaborate analyses of men and women who are essentially good at heart but have gone wrong in the head. For all its variety, its exuberance, and its grotesque fun, Browning's Inferno is as populous as Dante's.

The three types of poetry which have been considered—love poetry, poems of heroic action, and dramatic monologues—do not exhaust the richness of *Men and Women*. There are other ways to divide the contents of the book in order to get a sense of its scope. There are the poems on art, such as 'A Toccata of Galuppi's' and 'Master Hugues of Saxe-Gotha'; there are the religious monologues 'Cleon' and 'Karshish'; there are grotesqueries such as 'The Heretic's Tragedy', and with 'In a Balcony' one further testimony to Browning's inability to write a play. Despite its total devotion to the dramatic mode—'poetry always dramatic in principle, and so many utterances of so many imaginary persons, not mine', as he described it in 1867—the book is remarkable for its variety, and its central position in his life's work makes it the book which most readers of Browning have always preferred. The deliberately flaunted eccentricities and the promethean grandeurs of the early poems have been outgrown, and in 1855 Browning had not yet begun the task of his later years, the endeavour, encouraged by the adulation of the Browning Society, to solve the problems of the universe in blank verse. This was Browning's central statement, and some readers saw it as such. Dante Gabriel Rossetti acquired the volumes at once and wrote almost immediately to a friend: 'What a magnificent series is *Men and Women*! Of course you have it half by heart ere this.' Largely unknown to Browning in his initial disappointment, it was the presence of such reactions as this, beneath the reviewer level but far more significant in the long run, which showed that the British reading public, confronted by the mature fruits of Browning's art, actually emerged successfully from its trial; though the results were not fully apparent for another decade.

1. *A Browning Handbook*, p. 25.

2. These are available in Litzinger and Smalley (eds), *Browning: The Critical Heritage*.

3. See the discussion in J. Hillis Miller, *The Disappearance of God* (Cambridge, Mass., 1963).

4. As has been done by Park Honan in *Browning's Characters* (New Haven and London, 1961).

5. See Robert Langbaum, *The Poetry of Experience: The Dramatic Monologue in Modern Literary Tradition* (London, 1957).

6. Donald Smalley (ed.), *Browning's Essay on Chatterton* (Cambridge, Mass., 1948).

SELECT BIBLIOGRAPHY

TEXTS

Browning's Essay on Chatterton, ed. D. Smalley (Cambridge, Mass., 1948).

The Complete Works of Robert Browning, ed. R. King, P. Honan, M. Peckham and G. Pitts, 13 vols (Athens, Ohio, 1969 onwards).

The Letters of Robert Browning and Elizabeth Barrett Browning, 1845–1846, ed. E. Kintner, 2 vols (Cambridge, Mass., 1969).

The Letters of Robert Browning, Collected by Thomas J. Wise, ed. T. L. Hood (New Haven, Conn., 1933).

BIOGRAPHICAL AND CRITICAL STUDIES

L. N. Broughton, C. S. Northrup, R. Pearsall, *Robert Browning: A Bibliography, 1830–1950* (Ithaca, N.Y., 1953).

William Clyde DeVane, *A Browning Handbook* (2nd edition, New York, 1955).

William Clyde DeVane, *Browning's Parleyings: The Autobiography of a Mind* (2nd edition, New York, 1964).

B. Litzinger and D. Smalley (eds.), *Browning: The Critical Heritage* (London, 1970).

Herbert F. Tucker, *Browning's Beginnings* (Minneapolis, 1980).

J. R. Watson (ed.), *Browning: 'Men and Women' and Other Poems: A Casebook* (London, 1974).

(The following books contain collections of modern critical studies of Browning's work.)

Isobel Armstrong (ed.), *Writers and their Backgrounds: Robert Browning* (London, 1974).

Philip Drew (ed.), *Robert Browning: A Collection of Critical Essays* (London, 1966).

B. Litzinger and K. L. Knickerbocker (eds.), *The Browning Critics* (Lexington, Kentucky, 1965).

Clarence Tracy (ed.), *Browning's Mind and Art* (Edinburgh and London, 1968).

MEN AND WOMEN

LOVE AMONG THE RUINS.

I. WHERE the quiet-coloured end of evening smiles
        Miles and miles
  On the solitary pastures where our sheep
        Half-asleep
  Tinkle homeward thro' the twilight, stray or stop
        As they crop—

II. Was the site once of a city great and gay,
        (So they say)
  Of our country's very capital, its prince
        Ages since   10
  Held his court in, gathered councils, wielding far
        Peace or war.

III. Now—the country does not even boast a tree,
        As you see,
  To distinguish slopes of verdure, certain rills
        From the hills
  Intersect and give a name to (else they run
        Into one)

IV. Where the domed and daring palace shot its spires
        Up like fires   20
  O'er the hundred-gated circuit of a wall
        Bounding all,
  Made of marble, men might march on nor be prest,
        Twelve abreast.

V. And such plenty and perfection, see, of grass
        Never was!
  Such a carpet as, this summer-time, o'erspreads
        And embeds
  Every vestige of the city, guessed alone,
        Stock or stone—   30

VI. Where a multitude of men breathed joy and woe
　　　　Long ago;
　Lust of glory pricked their hearts up, dread of shame
　　　　Struck them tame;
　And that glory and that shame alike, the gold
　　　　Bought and sold.

VII. Now,—the single little turret that remains
　　　　On the plains,
　By the caper overrooted, by the gourd
　　　　Overscored,　　　　　　　　　　　　　　40
　While the patching houseleek's head of blossom winks
　　　　Through the chinks—

VIII. Marks the basement whence a tower in ancient time
　　　　Sprang sublime,
　And a burning ring all round, the chariots traced
　　　　As they raced,
　And the monarch and his minions and his dames
　　　　Viewed the games.

IX. And I know, while thus the quiet-coloured eve
　　　　Smiles to leave　　　　　　　　　　　50
　To their folding, all our many-tinkling fleece
　　　　In such peace,
　And the slopes and rills in undistinguished grey
　　　　Melt away—

X. That a girl with eager eyes and yellow hair
　　　　Waits me there
　In the turret, whence the charioteers caught soul
　　　　For the goal,
　When the king looked, where she looks now, breathless,
　　　dumb
　　　　Till I come.　　　　　　　　　　　　60

XI. But he looked upon the city, every side,
　　　　Far and wide,
　All the mountains topped with temples, all the glades'
　　　　Colonnades,
　All the causeys, bridges, aqueducts,—and then,
　　　　All the men!

2

XII. When I do come, she will speak not, she will stand,
        Either hand
    On my shoulder, give her eyes the first embrace
        Of my face,   70
    Ere we rush, ere we extinguish sight and speech
        Each on each.

XIII. In one year they sent a million fighters forth
        South and north,
    And they built their gods a brazen pillar high
        As the sky,
    Yet reserved a thousand chariots in full force—
        Gold, of course.

XIV. Oh, heart! oh, blood that freezes, blood that burns!
        Earth's returns   80
    For whole centuries of folly, noise and sin!
        Shut them in,
    With their triumphs and their glories and the rest.
        Love is best!

A LOVERS' QUARREL.

I.   OH, what a dawn of day!
     How the March sun feels like May!
        All is blue again
        After last night's rain,
     And the south dries the hawthorn-spray.
        Only, my Love's away!
     I'd as lief that the blue were grey.

II. Runnels, which rillets swell,
     Must be dancing down the dell
        With a foamy head   10
        On the beryl bed
     Paven smooth as a hermit's cell;
        Each with a tale to tell,
     Could my Love but attend as well.

III. Dearest, three months ago!
     When we lived blocked-up with snow,—

3

When the wind would edge
In and in his wedge,
In, as far as the point could go—
Not to our ingle, though,
Where we loved each the other so!

20

IV. Laughs with so little cause!
We devised games out of straws.
We would try and trace
One another's face
In the ash, as an artist draws;
Free on each other's flaws,
How we chattered like two church daws!

V. What's in the " Times "?—a scold
At the emperor deep and cold;
He has taken a bride
To his gruesome side,
That's as fair as himself is bold:
There they sit ermine-stoled,
And she powders her hair with gold.

30

VI. Fancy the Pampas' sheen!
Miles and miles of gold and green
Where the sun-flowers blow
In a solid glow,
And to break now and then the screen—
Black neck and eyeballs keen,
Up a wild horse leaps between!

40

VII. Try, will our table turn?
Lay your hands there light, and yearn
Till the yearning slips
Thro' the finger tips
In a fire which a few discern,
And a very few feel burn,
And the rest, they may live and learn!

VIII. Then we would up and pace,
For a change, about the place,
Each with arm o'er neck.
'Tis our quarter-deck,
We are seamen in woeful case,
Help in the ocean-space!
Or, if no help, we'll embrace.

50

IX. See, how she looks now, drest
In a sledging-cap and vest.
'Tis a huge fur cloak—
Like a reindeer's yoke
Falls the lappet along the breast:
Sleeves for her arms to rest,
Or to hang, as my Love likes best.   60

X. Teach me to flirt a fan
As the Spanish ladies can,
Or I tint your lip
With a burnt stick's tip
And you turn into such a man!
Just the two spots that span
Half the bill of the young male swan.   70

XI. Dearest, three months ago
When the mesmeriser Snow
With his hand's first sweep
Put the earth to sleep,
'Twas a time when the heart could show
All—how was earth to know,
'Neath the mute hand's to-and-fro!

XII. Dearest, three months ago
When we loved each other so,
Lived and loved the same   80
Till an evening came
When a shaft from the Devil's bow
Pierced to our ingle-glow,
And the friends were friend and foe!

XIII. Not from the heart beneath—
'Twas a bubble born of breath
Neither sneer nor vaunt,
Nor reproach nor taunt.
See a word, how it severeth!
Oh, power of life and death   90
In the tongue, as the Preacher saith!

XIV. Woman, and will you cast
For a word, quite off at last,
Me, your own, your you,—
Since, as Truth is true,

5

I was you all the happy past—
 Me do you leave aghast
With the memories we amassed?

xv. Love, if you knew the light
That your soul casts in my sight,
 How I look to you
 For the pure and true,
And the beauteous and the right,—
 Bear with a moment's spite
When a mere mote threats the white!

idealises her

xvi. What of a hasty word?
Is the fleshly heart not stirred
 By a worm's pin-prick
 Where its roots are quick?
See the eye, by a fly's foot blurred—
 Ear, when a straw is heard
Scratch the brain's coat of curd!

xvii. Foul be the world or fair,
More or less, how can I care?
 'Tis the world the same
 For my praise or blame,
And endurance is easy there.
 Wrong in the one thing rare—
Oh, it is hard to bear!

xviii. Here's the spring back or close,
When the almond-blossom blows;
 We shall have the word
 In that minor third
There is none but the cuckoo knows—
 Heaps of the guelder-rose!
I must bear with it, I suppose.

xix. Could but November come,
Were the noisy birds struck dumb
 At the warning slash
 Of his driver's-lash—
I would laugh like the valiant Thumb
 Facing the castle glum
And the giant's fee-faw-fum!

100

110

120

130

xx. Then, were the world well stript
 Of the gear wherein equipped
  We can stand apart,
  Heart dispense with heart
In the sun, with the flowers unnipped,—
  Oh, the world's hangings ripped,
We were both in a bare-walled crypt!   *140*

xxi. Each in the crypt would cry
 " But one freezes here! and why?
  When a heart as chill
  At my own would thrill
Back to life, and its fires out-fly?
  Heart, shall we live or die?
The rest, . . . settle it by and by!"

xxii. So, she'd efface the score,
 And forgive me as before.
  Just at twelve o'clock   *150*
  I shall hear her knock
In the worst of a storm's uproar—
  I shall pull her through the door—
I shall have her for evermore!

EVELYN HOPE.

i. Beautiful Evelyn Hope is dead!
 Sit and watch by her side an hour.
That is her book-shelf, this her bed;
 She plucked that piece of geranium-flower,
Beginning to die too, in the glass.
 Little has yet been changed, I think—
The shutters are shut, no light may pass
 Save two long rays thro' the hinge's chink.

ii. Sixteen years old when she died!
 Perhaps she had scarcely heard my name— *10*
It was not her time to love: beside,
 Her life had many a hope and aim,
Duties enough and little cares,
 And now was quiet, now astir—
Till God's hand beckoned unawares,
 And the sweet white brow is all of her.

III. Is it too late then, Evelyn Hope?
  What, your soul was pure and true,
The good stars met in your horoscope,
  Made you of spirit, fire and dew—   *20*
And just because I was thrice as old,
  And our paths in the world diverged so wide,
Each was nought to each, must I be told?
  We were fellow mortals, nought beside?

IV. No, indeed! for God above
  Is great to grant, as mighty to make,
And creates the love to reward the love,—
  I claim you still, for my own love's sake!
Delayed it may be for more lives yet,
  Through worlds I shall traverse, not a few—   *30*
Much is to learn and much to forget
  Ere the time be come for taking you.

V. But the time will come,—at last it will,
  When, Evelyn Hope, what meant, I shall say,
In the lower earth, in the years long still,
  That body and soul so pure and gay?
Why your hair was amber, I shall divine,
  And your mouth of your own geranium's red—
And what you would do with me, in fine,
  In the new life come in the old one's stead.   *40*

VI. I have lived, I shall say, so much since then,
  Given up myself so many times,
Gained me the gains of various men,
  Ransacked the ages, spoiled the climes;
Yet one thing, one, in my soul's full scope,
  Either I missed or itself missed me—
And I want and find you, Evelyn Hope!
  What is the issue? let us see!

VII. I loved you, Evelyn, all the while;
  My heart seemed full as it could hold—   *50*
There was place and to spare for the frank young smile
  And the red young mouth and the hair's young gold.
So, hush,—I will give you this leaf to keep—
  See, I shut it inside the sweet cold hand.
There, that is our secret! go to sleep;
  You will wake, and remember, and understand.

UP AT A VILLA—DOWN IN THE CITY.

(AS DISTINGUISHED BY AN ITALIAN PERSON OF QUALITY.)

I.

HAD I but plenty of money, money enough and to spare,
The house for me, no doubt, were a house in the city-square.
Ah, such a life, such a life, as one leads at the window there!

II.

Something to see, by Bacchus, something to hear, at least!
There, the whole day long, one's life is a perfect feast;
While up at a villa one lives, I maintain it, no more than a
    beast.

III.

Well, now, look at our villa! stuck like the horn of a bull
Just on a mountain's edge as bare as the creature's skull,
Save a mere shag of a bush with hardly a leaf to pull!
—I scratch my own, sometimes, to see if the hair's turned
    wool.   *10*

IV.

But the city, oh the city—the square with the houses!
    Why?
They are stone-faced, white as a curd, there's something to
    take the eye!
Houses in four straight lines, not a single front awry!
You watch who crosses and gossips, who saunters, who
    hurries by:
Green blinds, as a matter of course, to draw when the sun
    gets high;
And the shops with fanciful signs which are painted properly.

V.

What of a villa? Though winter be over in March by rights,
'Tis May perhaps ere the snow shall have withered well off
    the heights:
You've the brown ploughed land before, where the oxen
    steam and wheeze,
And the hills over-smoked behind by the faint grey olive trees. *20*

VI.

Is it better in May, I ask you? you've summer all at once;
In a day he leaps complete with a few strong April suns!
'Mid the sharp short emerald wheat, scarce risen three fingers
    well,
The wild tulip, at end of its tube, blows out its great red bell,
Like a thin clear bubble of blood, for the children to pick
    and sell.

VII.

Is it ever hot in the square? There's a fountain to spout
    and splash!
In the shade it sings and springs; in the shine such foam-bows
    flash
On the horses with curling fish-tails, that prance and paddle
    and pash
Round the lady atop in the conch—fifty gazers do not abash,
Though all that she wears is some weeds round her waist in
    a sort of sash!   *30*

VIII.

All the year long at the villa, nothing's to see though you
    linger,
Except yon cypress that points like Death's lean lifted fore-
    finger.
Some think fireflies pretty, when they mix in the corn and
    mingle,
Or thrid the stinking hemp till the stalks of it seem a-tingle.
Late August or early September, the stunning cicala is shrill,
And the bees keep their tiresome whine round the resinous
    firs on the hill.
Enough of the seasons,—I spare you the months of the fever
    and chill.

IX.

Ere opening your eyes in the city, the blessed church-bells
    begin:
No sooner the bells leave off, than the diligence rattles in:
You get the pick of the news, and it costs you never a pin.   *40*
By and by there's the travelling doctor gives pills, lets blood,
    draws teeth;

Or the Pulcinello-trumpet breaks up the market beneath.
At the post-office such a scene-picture—the new play, piping
    hot!
And a notice how, only this morning, three liberal thieves
    were shot.
Above it, behold the archbishop's most fatherly of rebukes,
And beneath, with his crown and his lion, some little new law
    of the Duke's!
Or a sonnet with flowery marge, to the Reverend Don So-
    and-so
Who is Dante, Boccaccio, Petrarca, Saint Jerome, and Cicero,
" And moreover," (the sonnet goes rhyming,) " the skirts of
    St. Paul has reached,
Having preached us those six Lent-lectures more unctuous
    than ever he preached."   *50*
Noon strikes,—here sweeps the procession! our Lady borne
    smiling and smart
With a pink gauze gown all spangles, and seven swords stuck
    in her heart!
Bang, whang, whang, goes the drum, *tootle-te-tootle* the fife;
No keeping one's haunches still: it's the greatest pleasure in
    life.

x.

But bless you, it's dear—it's dear! fowls, wine, at double the
    rate.
They have clapped a new tax upon salt, and what oil pays
    passing the gate
It's a horror to think of. And so, the villa for me, not the city!
Beggars can scarcely be choosers—but still—ah, the pity,
    the pity!
Look, two and two go the priests, then the monks with cowls
    and sandals,
And the penitents dressed in white shirts, a-holding the
    yellow candles.   *60*
One, he carries a flag up straight, and another a cross with
    handles,
And the Duke's guard brings up the rear, for the better
    prevention of scandals.
Bang, whang, whang, goes the drum, *tootle-te-tootle* the fife.
Oh, a day in the city-square, there is no such pleasure in life!

A WOMAN'S LAST WORD.

I. LET's contend no more, Love,
   Strive nor weep—
   All be as before, Love,
   —Only sleep!

II. What so wild as words are?
   —I and thou
   In debate, as birds are,
   Hawk on bough!

III. See the creature stalking
   While we speak—   *10*
   Hush and hide the talking,
   Cheek on cheek!

IV. What so false as truth is,
   False to thee?
   Where the serpent's tooth is,
   Shun the tree—

V. Where the apple reddens
   Never pry—
   Lest we lose our Edens,
   Eve and I!   *20*

VI. Be a god and hold me
   With a charm—
   Be a man and fold me
   With thine arm!

VII. Teach me, only teach, Love!
   As I ought
   I will speak thy speech, Love,
   Think thy thought—

VIII. Meet, if thou require it,
   Both demands,   *30*
   Laying flesh and spirit
   In thy hands!

    IX. That shall be to-morrow
           Not to-night:
        I must bury sorrow
           Out of sight.

    X. —Must a little weep, Love,
           —Foolish me!
        And so fall asleep, Love,
           Loved by thee.   *40*

FRA LIPPO LIPPI

I AM poor brother Lippo, by your leave!
You need not clap your torches to my face.
Zooks, what's to blame? you think you see a monk!
What, it's past midnight, and you go the rounds,
And here you catch me at an alley's end
Where sportive ladies leave their doors ajar.
The Carmine's my cloister: hunt it up,
Do,—harry out, if you must show your zeal,
Whatever rat, there, haps on his wrong hole,
And nip each softling of a wee white mouse,   *10*
Weke, weke, that's crept to keep him company!
Aha, you know your betters? Then, you'll take
Your hand away that's fiddling on my throat,
And please to know me likewise. Who am I?
Why, one, sir, who is lodging with a friend
Three streets off—he's a certain . . . how d'ye call?
Master—a . . . Cosimo of the Medici,
In the house that caps the corner. Boh! you were best!
Remember and tell me, the day you're hanged,
How you affected such a gullet's-gripe   *20*
But you, sir, it concerns you that your knaves
Pick up a manner nor discredit you.
Zooks, are we pilchards, that they sweep the streets
And count fair prize what comes into their net?
He's Judas to a tittle, that man is!
Just such a face! why, sir, you make amends.
Lord, I'm not angry! Bid your hangdogs go
Drink out this quarter florin to the health
Of the munificent House that harbours me

(And many more beside, lads! more beside!)   30
And all's come square again. I'd like his face—
His, elbowing on his comrade in the door
With the pike and lantern,—for the slave that holds
John Baptist's head a-dangle by the hair
With one hand (" look you, now," as who should say)
And his weapon in the other, yet unwiped!
It's not your chance to have a bit of chalk,
A wood-coal or the like? or you should see!
Yes, I'm the painter, since you style me so.
What, brother Lippo's doings, up and down,   40
You know them and they take you? like enough!
I saw the proper twinkle in your eye—
Tell you I liked your looks at very first.
Let's sit and set things straight now, hip to haunch.
Here's spring come, and the nights one makes up bands
To roam the town and sing out carnival,
And I've been three weeks shut within my mew,
A-painting for the great man, saints and saints
And saints again. I could not paint all night—
Ouf! I leaned out of window for fresh air.   50
There came a hurry of feet and little feet,
A sweep of lute-strings, laughs, and whifts of song,—
Flower o' the broom,
Take away love, and our earth is a tomb!
Flower o' the quince,
I let Lisa go, and what good's in life since?
Flower o' the thyme—and so on. Round they went.
Scarce had they turned the corner when a titter,
Like the skipping of rabbits by moonlight,—three slim
    shapes—
And a face that looked up . . . zooks, sir, flesh and blood, 60
That's all I'm made of! Into shreds it went,
Curtain and counterpane and coverlet,
All the bed furniture—a dozen knots,
There was a ladder! down I let myself,
Hands and feet, scrambling somehow, and so dropped,
And after them. I came up with the fun
Hard by St. Laurence, hail fellow, well met,—
Flower o' the rose
If I've been merry, what matter who knows?
And so as I was stealing back again   70
To get to bed and have a bit of sleep

Ere I rise up to-morrow and go work
On Jerome knocking at his poor old breast
With his great round stone to subdue the flesh,
You snap me of the sudden.   Ah, I see!
Though your eye twinkles still, you shake your head—
Mine's shaved,—a monk, you say—the sting's in that!
If Master Cosimo announced himself,
Mum's the word naturally; but a monk!
Come, what am I a beast for? tell us, now!   *80*
I was a baby when my mother died
And father died and left me in the street.
I starved there, God knows how, a year or two
On fig-skins, melon-parings, rinds and shucks,
Refuse and rubbish.   One fine frosty day
My stomach being empty as your hat,
The wind doubled me up and down I went.
Old Aunt Lapaccia trussed me with one hand,
(Its fellow was a stinger as I knew)
And so along the wall, over the bridge,   *90*
By the straight cut to the convent.   Six words, there,
While I stood munching my first bread that month:
" So, boy, you're minded," quoth the good fat father
Wiping his own mouth, 'twas refection-time,—
" To quit this very miserable world?
Will you renounce " . . . The mouthful of bread? thought I;
By no means!   Brief, they made a monk of me,
I did renounce the world, its pride and greed,
Palace, farm, villa, shop and banking-house,
Trash, such as these poor devils of Medici   *100*
Have given their hearts to—all at eight years old.
Well, sir, I found in time, you may be sure,
'Twas not for nothing—the good bellyful,
The warm serge and the rope that goes all round,
And day-long blessed idleness beside!
" Let's see what the urchin's fit for "—that came next.
Not overmuch their way, I must confess.
Such a to-do! they tried me with their books.
Lord, they'd have taught me Latin in pure waste!
Flower o' the clove,   *110*
All the Latin I construe is, " amo," I love !
But, mind you, when a boy starves in the streets
Eight years together, as my fortune was,
Watching folk's faces to know who will fling

The bit of half-stripped grape-bunch he desires,
And who will curse or kick him for his pains—
Which gentleman processional and fine,
Holding a candle to the Sacrament
Will wink and let him lift a plate and catch
The droppings of the wax to sell again,   120
Or holla for the Eight and have him whipped,—
How say I?—nay, which dog bites, which lets drop
His bone from the heap of offal in the street!
—The soul and sense of him grow sharp alike,
He learns the look of things, and none the less
For admonitions from the hunger-pinch.
I had a store o' such remarks, be sure,
Which, after I found leisure, turned to use:
I drew men's faces on my copy-books,
Scrawled them within the antiphonary's marge,   130
Joined legs and arms to the long music-notes,
Found nose and eyes and chin for A.s and B.s,
And made a string of pictures of the world
Betwixt the ins and outs of verb and noun,
On the wall, the bench, the door. The monks looked black.
" Nay," quoth the Prior, " turn him out, d'ye say?
In no wise. Lose a crow and catch a lark.
What if at last we get our man of parts,
We Carmelites, like those Camaldolese
And Preaching Friars, to do our church up fine   140
And put the front on it that ought to be!"
And hereupon they bade me daub away.
Thank you! my head being crammed, their walls a blank,
Never was such prompt disemburdening.
First, every sort of monk, the black and white,
I drew them, fat and lean: then, folks at church,
From good old gossips waiting to confess
Their cribs of barrel-droppings, candle-ends,—
To the breathless fellow at the altar-foot,
Fresh from his murder, safe and sitting there   150
With the little children round him in a row
Of admiration, half for his beard and half
For that white anger of his victim's son
Shaking a fist at him with one fierce arm,
Signing himself with the other because of Christ
(Whose sad face on the cross sees only this
After the passion of a thousand years)

Till some poor girl, her apron o'er her head
Which the intense eyes looked through, came at eve
On tip-toe, said a word, dropped in a loaf,   160
Her pair of ear-rings and a bunch of flowers
The brute took growling, prayed, and then was gone.
I painted all, then cried " 'tis ask and have—
Choose, for more's ready! "—laid the ladder flat,
And showed my covered bit of cloister-wall.
The monks closed in a circle and praised loud
Till checked, (taught what to see and not to see,
Being simple bodies) " that's the very man!
Look at the boy who stoops to pat the dog!
That woman's like the Prior's niece who comes   170
To care about his asthma: it's the life! "
But there my triumph's straw-fire flared and funked—
Their betters took their turn to see and say:
The Prior and the learned pulled a face
And stopped all that in no time. " How? what's here?
Quite from the mark of painting, bless us all!
Faces, arms, legs and bodies like the true
As much as pea and pea! it's devil's game!
Your business is not to catch men with show,
With homage to the perishable clay,   180
But lift them over it, ignore it all,
Make them forget there's such a thing as flesh.
Your business is to paint the souls of men—
Man's soul, and it's a fire, smoke . . . no it's not . . .
It's vapour done up like a new-born babe—
(In that shape when you die it leaves your mouth)
It's . . . well, what matters talking, it's the soul!
Give us no more of body than shows soul.
Here's Giotto, with his Saint a-praising God!
That sets you praising,—why not stop with him?   190
Why put all thoughts of praise out of our heads
With wonder at lines, colours, and what not?
Paint the soul, never mind the legs and arms!
Rub all out, try at it a second time.
Oh, that white smallish female with the breasts,
She's just my niece . . . Herodias, I would say,—
Who went and danced and got men's heads cut off—
Have it all out! " Now, is this sense, I ask?
A fine way to paint soul, by painting body
So ill, the eye can't stop there, must go further   200

17

And can't fare worse!   Thus, yellow does for white
When what you put for yellow's simply black,
And any sort of meaning looks intense
When all beside itself means and looks nought.
Why can't a painter lift each foot in turn,
Left foot and right foot, go a double step,
Make his flesh liker and his soul more like,
Both in their order?   Take the prettiest face,
The Prior's niece . . . patron-saint—is it so pretty
You can't discover if it means hope, fear,   *210*
Sorrow or joy? won't beauty go with these?
Suppose I've made her eyes all right and blue,
Can't I take breath and try to add life's flash
And then add soul and heighten them threefold?
Or say there's beauty with no soul at all—
(I never saw it—put the case the same—)
If you get simple beauty and nought else,
You get about the best thing God invents,—
That's somewhat.   And you'll find the soul you have missed,
Within yourself when you return Him thanks!   *220*
" Rub all out! " well, well, there's my life, in short,
And so the thing has gone on ever since.
I'm grown a man no doubt, I've broken bounds—
You should not take a fellow eight years old
And make him swear to never kiss the girls—
I'm my own master, paint now as I please—
Having a friend, you see, in the Corner-house!
Lord, its fast holding by the rings in front—
Those great rings serve more purposes than just
To plant a flag in, or tie up a horse!   *230*
And yet the old schooling sticks—the old grave eyes
Are peeping o'er my shoulder as I work,
The heads shake still—" it's Art's decline, my son!
You're not of the true painters, great and old:
Brother Angelico's the man, you'll find:
Brother Lorenzo stands his single peer.
Fag on at flesh, you'll never make the third! "
Flower o' the pine,
You keep your mistr . . . manners, and I'll stick to mine!
I'm not the third, then: bless us, they must know!   *240*
Don't you think they're the likeliest to know,
They, with their Latin? so I swallow my rage,
Clench my teeth, suck my lips in tight, and paint

18

To please them—sometimes do, and sometimes don't,
For, doing most, there's pretty sure to come
A turn—some warm eve finds me at my saints—
A laugh, a cry, the business of the world—
(*Flower o' the peach,*
Death for us all, and his own life for each !)
And my whole soul revolves, the cup runs o'er,⁣   250
The world and life's too big to pass for a dream,
And I do these wild things in sheer despite,
And play the fooleries you catch me at,
In pure rage! the old mill-horse, out at grass
After hard years, throws up his stiff heels so,
Although the miller does not preach to him
The only good of grass is to make chaff.
What would men have?   Do they like grass or no—
May they or mayn't they? all I want's the thing
Settled for ever one way: as it is,⁣   260
You tell too many lies and hurt yourself.
You don't like what you only like too much,
You do like what, if given you at your word,
You find abundantly detestable.
For me, I think I speak as I was taught—
I always see the Garden and God there
A-making man's wife—and, my lesson learned,
The value and significance of flesh,
I can't unlearn ten minutes afterward.
    You understand me: I'm a beast, I know.⁣   270
But see, now—why, I see as certainly
As that the morning-star's about to shine,
What will hap some day.   We've a youngster here
Comes to our convent, studies what I do,
Slouches and stares and lets no atom drop—
His name is Guidi—he'll not mind the monks—
They call him Hulking Tom, he lets them talk—
He picks my practice up—he'll paint apace,
I hope so—though I never live so long,
I know what's sure to follow.   You be judge!⁣   280
You speak no Latin more than I, belike—
However, you're my man, you've seen the world
—The beauty and the wonder and the power,
The shapes of things, their colours, lights and shades,
Changes, surprises,—and God made it all!
—For what? do you feel thankful, ay or no,

For this fair town's face, yonder river's line,
The mountain round it and the sky above,
Much more the figures of man, woman, child,
These are the frame to?   What's it all about?   *290*
To be passed o'er, despised? or dwelt upon,
Wondered at? oh, this last of course, you say.
But why not do as well as say,—paint these
Just as they are, careless what comes of it?
God's works—paint any one, and count it crime
To let a truth slip.   Don't object, " His works
Are here already—nature is complete:
Suppose you reproduce her—(which you can't)
There's no advantage! you must beat her, then."
For, don't you mark, we're made so that we love   *300*
First when we see them painted, things we have passed
Perhaps a hundred times nor cared to see;
And so they are better, painted—better to us,
Which is the same thing.   Art was given for that—
God uses us to help each other so,
Lending our minds out.   Have you noticed, now,
Your cullion's hanging face?   A bit of chalk,
And trust me but you should, though! How much more,
If I drew higher things with the same truth!
That were to take the Prior's pulpit-place,   *310*
Interpret God to all of you! oh, oh,
It makes me mad to see what men shall do
And we in our graves! This world's no blot for us,
Nor blank—it means intensely, and means good:
To find its meaning is my meat and drink.
" Ay, but you don't so instigate to prayer,"
Strikes in the Prior! " when your meaning's plain
It does not say to folks—remember matins—
Or, mind you fast next Friday."   Why, for this
What need of art at all?   A skull and bones,   *320*
Two bits of stick nailed cross-wise, or, what's best,
A bell to chime the hour with, does as well.
I painted a St. Laurence six months since
At Prato, splashed the fresco in fine style.
" How looks my painting, now the scaffold's down? "
I ask a brother: " Hugely," he returns—
" Already not one phiz of your three slaves
That turn the Deacon off his toasted side,
But's scratched and prodded to our heart's content,

The pious people have so eased their own   *330*
When coming to say prayers there in a rage.
We get on fast to see the bricks beneath.
Expect another job this time next year,
For pity and religion grow i' the crowd—
Your painting serves its purpose!" Hang the fools!

—That is—you'll not mistake an idle word
Spoke in a huff by a poor monk, God wot,
Tasting the air this spicy night which turns
The unaccustomed head like Chianti wine!
Oh, the church knows! don't misreport me, now!   *340*
It's natural a poor monk out of bounds
Should have his apt word to excuse himself:
And hearken how I plot to make amends.
I have bethought me: I shall paint a piece
. . . There's for you! Give me six months, then go, see
Something in Sant' Ambrogio's . . . (bless the nuns!
They want a cast of my office) I shall paint
God in the midst, Madonna and her babe,
Ringed by a bowery, flowery angel-brood,
Lilies and vestments and white faces, sweet   *350*
As puff on puff of grated orris-root
When ladies crowd to church at midsummer.
And then in the front, of course a saint or two—
Saint John, because he saves the Florentines,
Saint Ambrose, who puts down in black and white
The convent's friends and gives them a long day.
And Job, I must have him there past mistake,
The man of Uz, (and Us without the z,
Painters who need his patience). Well, all these
Secured at their devotions, up shall come   *360*
Out of a corner when you least expect,
As one by a dark stair into a great light,
Music and talking, who but Lippo! I!—
Mazed, motionless and moon-struck—I'm the man!
Back I shrink—what is this I see and hear?
I, caught up with my monk's things by mistake,
My old serge gown and rope that goes all round,
I, in this presence, this pure company!
Where's a hole, where's a corner for escape?
Then steps a sweet angelic slip of a thing   *370*
Forward, puts out a soft palm—" Not so fast!"
—Addresses the celestial presence, " nay—

21

He made you and devised you, after all,
Though he's none of you!   Could Saint John there, draw—
His camel-hair make up a painting-brush?
We come to brother Lippo for all that,
Iste perfecit opus !"   So, all smile—
I shuffle sideways with my blushing face
Under the cover of a hundred wings
Thrown like a spread of kirtles when you're gay   *380*
And play hot cockles, all the doors being shut,
Till, wholly unexpected, in there pops
The hothead husband!   Thus I scuttle off
To some safe bench behind, not letting go
The palm of her, the little lily thing
That spoke the good word for me in the nick,
Like the Prior's niece . . . Saint Lucy, I would say.
And so all's saved for me, and for the church
A pretty picture gained.   Go, six months hence!
Your hand, sir, and good-bye: no lights, no lights!   *390*
The street's hushed, and I know my own way back—
Don't fear me!   There's the grey beginning, Zooks!

A TOCCATA OF GALUPPI'S.

I.

Oh, Galuppi, Baldassaro, this is very sad to find!
I can hardly misconceive you; it would prove me deaf and
   blind;
But although I give you credit, 'tis with such a heavy mind!

II.

Here you come with your old music, and here's all the good
   it brings.
What, they lived once thus at Venice, where the merchants
   were the kings,
Where St. Marks is, where the Doges used to wed the sea
   with rings?

III.

Ay, because the sea's the street there; and 'tis arched by
   . . . what you call
. . . Shylock's bridge with houses on it, where they kept
   the carnival!
I was never out of England—it's as if I saw it all!

IV.

Did young people take their pleasure when the sea was
  warm in May? *10*
Balls and masks begun at midnight, burning ever to mid-day,
When they made up fresh adventures for the morrow, do
  you say?

V.

Was a lady such a lady, cheeks so round and lips so red,—
On her neck the small face buoyant, like a bell-flower on its
  bed,
O'er the breast's superb abundance where a man might base
  his head?

VI.

Well (and it was graceful of them) they'd break talk off and
  afford
—She, to bite her mask's black velvet, he to finger on his
  sword,
While you sat and played Toccatas, stately at the clavichord?

VII.

What? Those lesser thirds so plaintive, sixths diminished,
  sigh on sigh,
Told them something? Those suspensions, those solutions
  —" Must we die? " *20*
Those commiserating sevenths—" Life might last! we can
  but try! "

VIII.

" Were you happy? "—" Yes."—" And are you still as
  happy? "—" Yes—And you? "
—" Then more kisses "—" Did *I* stop them, when a million
  seemed so few? "
Hark—the dominant's persistence, till it must be answered
  to!

IX.

So an octave struck the answer. Oh, they praised you, I
  dare say!
" Brave Galuppi! that was music! good alike at grave and
  gay!
I can always leave off talking, when I hear a master play."

x.

Then they left you for their pleasure: till in due time, one
by one,
Some with lives that came to nothing, some with deeds as
well undone,
Death came tacitly and took them where they never see
the sun.

xi.

But when I sit down to reason,—think to take my stand nor
swerve   *30*
Till I triumph o'er a secret wrung from nature's close reserve,
In you come with your cold music, till I creep thro' every
nerve,

xii.

Yes, you, like a ghostly cricket, creaking where a house
was burned—
"Dust and ashes, dead and done with, Venice spent what
Venice earned!
The soul, doubtless, is immortal—where a soul can be dis-
cerned.

xiii.

"Yours for instance, you know physics, something of
geology,
Mathematics are your pastime; souls shall rise in their
degree;
Butterflies may dread extinction,—you'll not die, it cannot
be!

xiv.

"As for Venice and its people, merely born to bloom and
drop,
Here on earth they bore their fruitage, mirth and folly were
the crop,   *40*
What of soul was left, I wonder, when the kissing had to stop?

xv

"Dust and ashes!" So you creak it, and I want the heart
to scold.
Dear dead women, with such hair, too—what's become of all
the gold
Used to hang and brush their bosoms? I feel chilly and
grown old.

BY THE FIRE-SIDE.

I. How well I know what I mean to do
    When the long dark Autumn evenings come,
And where, my soul, is thy pleasant hue?
    With the music of all thy voices, dumb
In life's November too!

II. I shall be found by the fire, suppose,
    O'er a great wise book as beseemeth age,
While the shutters flap as the cross-wind blows,
    And I turn the page, and I turn the page,
Not verse now, only prose!   *10*

III. Till the young ones whisper, finger on lip,
    " There he is at it, deep in Greek—
Now or never, then, out we slip
    To cut from the hazels by the creek
A mainmast for our ship."

IV. I shall be at it indeed, my friends!
    Greek puts already on either side
Such a branch-work forth, as soon extends
    To a vista opening far and wide,
And I pass out where it ends.   *20*

V. The outside-frame like your hazel-trees—
    But the inside-archway narrows fast,
And a rarer sort succeeds to these,
    And we slope to Italy at last
And youth, by green degrees.

VI. I follow wherever I am led,
    Knowing so well the leader's hand—
Oh, woman-country, wooed, not wed,
    Loved all the more by earth's male-lands,
Laid to their hearts instead!   *30*

VII. Look at the ruined chapel again
    Half way up in the Alpine gorge.
Is that a tower, I point you plain,
    Or is it a mill or an iron forge
Breaks solitude in vain?

VIII. A turn, and we stand in the heart of things;
  The woods are round us, heaped and dim;
 From slab to slab how it slips and springs,
  The thread of water single and slim,
 Thro' the ravage some torrent brings!   *40*

IX. Does it feed the little lake below?
  That speck of white just on its marge
 Is Pella; see, in the evening glow
  How sharp the silver spear-heads charge
 When Alp meets Heaven in snow.

X. On our other side is the straight-up rock;
  And a path is kept 'twixt the gorge and it
 By boulder-stones where lichens mock
  The marks on a moth, and small ferns fit
 Their teeth to the polished block.   *50*

XI. Oh, the sense of the yellow mountain flowers,
  And the thorny balls, each three in one,
 The chestnuts throw on our path in showers,
  For the drop of the woodland fruit's begun
 These early November hours—

XII. That crimson the creeper's leaf across
  Like a splash of blood, intense, abrupt,
 O'er a shield, else gold from rim to boss,
  And lay it for show on the fairy-cupped
 Elf-needled mat of moss,   *60*

XIII. By the rose-flesh mushrooms, undivulged
  Last evening—nay, in to-day's first dew
 Yon sudden coral nipple bulged
  Where a freaked, fawn-coloured, flaky crew
 Of toad-stools peep indulged.

XIV. And yonder, at foot of the fronting ridge
  That takes the turn to a range beyond,
 Is the chapel reached by the one-arched bridge
  Where the water is stopped in a stagnant pond
 Danced over by the midge.   *70*

XV. The chapel and bridge are of stone alike,
  Blackish grey and mostly wet;
 Cut hemp-stalks steep in the narrow dyke.
  See here again, how the lichens fret
 And the roots of the ivy strike!

XVI. Poor little place, where its one priest comes
    On a festa-day, if he comes at all,
To the dozen folk from their scattered homes,
    Gathered within that precinct small
By the dozen ways one roams   *80*

XVII. To drop from the charcoal-burners' huts,
    Or climb from the hemp-dressers' low shed,
Leave the grange where the woodman stores his nuts,
    Or the wattled cote where the fowlers spread
Their gear on the rock's bare juts.

XVIII. It has some pretension too, this front,
    With its bit of fresco half-moon-wise
Set over the porch, art's early wont—
    'Tis John in the Desert, I surmise,
But has borne the weather's brunt—   *90*

XIX. Not from the fault of the builder, though,
    For a pent-house properly projects
Where three carved beams make a certain show,
    Dating—good thought of our architect's—
'Five, six, nine, he lets you know.

XX. And all day long a bird sings there,
    And a stray sheep drinks at the pond at times:
The place is silent and aware;
    It has had its scenes, its joys and crimes,
But that is its own affair.   *100*

XXI. My perfect wife, my Leonor,
    Oh, heart my own, oh, eyes, mine too,
Whom else could I dare look backward for,
    With whom beside should I dare pursue
The path grey heads abhor?

XXII. For it leads to a crag's sheer edge with them;
    Youth, flowery all the way, there stops—
Not they; age threatens and they contemn,
    Till they reach the gulf wherein youth drops,
One inch from our life's safe hem!   *110*

XXIII. With me, youth led—I will speak now,
    No longer watch you as you sit
Reading by fire-light, that great brow
    And the spirit-small hand propping it
Mutely—my heart knows how—

27

XXIV. When, if I think but deep enough,
    You are wont to answer, prompt as rhyme;
And you, too, find without a rebuff
    The response your soul seeks many a time
Piercing its fine flesh-stuff—   *120*

XXV. My own, confirm me! If I tread
    This path back, is it not in pride
To think how little I dreamed it led
    To an age so blest that by its side
Youth seems the waste instead!

XXVI. My own, see where the years conduct!
    At first, 'twas something our two souls
Should mix as mists do: each is sucked
    Into each now; on, the new stream rolls,
Whatever rocks obstruct.   *130*

XXVII. Think, when our one soul understands
    The great Word which makes all things new—
When earth breaks up and Heaven expands—
    How will the change strike me and you
In the House not made with hands?

XXVIII. Oh, I must feel your brain prompt mine,
    Your heart anticipate my heart,
You must be just before, in fine,
    See and make me see, for your part,
New depths of the Divine!   *140*

XXIX. But who could have expected this,
    When we two drew together first
Just for the obvious human bliss,
    To satisfy life's daily thirst
With a thing men seldom miss?

XXX. Come back with me to the first of all,
    Let us lean and love it over again—
Let us now forget and then recall,
    Break the rosary in a pearly rain,
And gather what we let fall!   *150*

XXXI. What did I say?—that a small bird sings
    All day long, save when a brown pair
Of hawks from the wood float with wide wings
    Strained to a bell: 'gainst the noon-day glare
You count the streaks and rings.

XXXII. But at afternoon or almost eve
  'Tis better; then the silence grows
To that degree, you half believe
  It must get rid of what it knows,
Its bosom does so heave.   *160*

XXXIII. Hither we walked, then, side by side,
  Arm in arm and cheek to cheek,
And still I questioned or replied,
  While my heart, convulsed to really speak,
Lay choking in its pride.

XXXIV. Silent the crumbling bridge we cross,
  And pity and praise the chapel sweet,
And care about the fresco's loss,
  And wish for our souls a like retreat,
And wonder at the moss.   *170*

XXXV. Stoop and kneel on the settle under—
  Look through the window's grated square:
Nothing to see! for fear of plunder,
  The cross is down and the altar bare,
As if thieves don't fear thunder.

XXXVI. We stoop and look in through the grate,
  See the little porch and rustic door,
Read duly the dead builder's date,
  Then cross the bridge we crossed before,
Take the path again—but wait!   *180*

XXXVII. Oh moment, one and infinite!
  The water slips o'er stock and stone;
The west is tender, hardly bright.
  How grey at once is the evening grown—
One star, the chrysolite!

XXXVIII. We two stood there with never a third,
  But each by each, as each knew well.
The sights we saw and the sounds we heard,
  The lights and the shades made up a spell
Till the trouble grew and stirred.   *190*

XXXIX. Oh, the little more, and how much it is!
  And the little less, and what worlds away!
How a sound shall quicken content to bliss,
  Or a breath suspend the blood's best play,
And life be a proof of this!

XL. Had she willed it, still had stood the screen
    So slight, so sure, 'twixt my love and her.
I could fix her face with a guard between,
    And find her soul as when friends confer,
Friends—lovers that might have been.   *200*

XLI. For my heart had a touch of the woodland time,
    Wanting to sleep now over its best.
Shake the whole tree in the summer-prime,
    But bring to the last leaf no such test.
" Hold the last fast ! " says the rhyme.

XLII. For a chance to make your little much,
    To gain a lover and lose a friend,
Venture the tree and a myriad such,
    When nothing you mar but the year can mend!
But a last leaf—fear to touch.   *210*

XLIII. Yet should it unfasten itself and fall
    Eddying down till it find your face
At some slight wind—(best chance of all!)
    Be your heart henceforth its dwelling-place
You trembled to forestal !

XLIV. Worth how well, those dark grey eyes,
    —That hair so dark and dear, how worth
That a man should strive and agonise,
    And taste a very hell on earth
For the hope of such a prize!   *220*

XLV. Oh, you might have turned and tried a man,
    Set him a space to weary and wear,
And prove which suited more your plan,
    His best of hope or his worst despair,
Yet end as he began.

XLVI. But you spared me this, like the heart you are,
    And filled my empty heart at a word.
If you join two lives, there is oft a scar,
    They are one and one, with a shadowy third;
One near one is too far.   *230*

XLVII. A moment after, and hands unseen
    Were hanging the night around us fast.
But we knew that a bar was broken between
    Life and life; we were mixed at last
In spite of the mortal screen.

XLVIII. The forests had done it; there they stood—
 We caught for a second the powers at play;
They had mingled us so, for once and for good,
 Their work was done—we might go or stay,
They relapsed to their ancient mood.   *240*

XLIX. How the world is made for each of us!
 How all we perceive and know in it
Tends to some moment's product thus,
 When a soul declares itself—to wit,
By its fruit—the thing it does!

L. Be Hate that fruit or Love that fruit,
 It forwards the General Deed of Man,
And each of the Many helps to recruit
 The life of the race by a general plan,
Each living his own, to boot.   *250*

LI. I am named and known by that hour's feat,
 There took my station and degree.
So grew my own small life complete
 As nature obtained her best of me—
One born to love you, sweet!

LII. And to watch you sink by the fire-side now
 Back again, as you mutely sit
Musing by fire-light, that great brow
 And the spirit-small hand propping it
Yonder, my heart knows how!   *260*

LIII. So the earth has gained by one man more,
 And the gain of earth must be Heaven's gain too,
And the whole is well worth thinking o'er
 When the autumn comes: which I mean to do
One day, as I said before.

ANY WIFE TO ANY HUSBAND.

I. My love, this is the bitterest, that thou
Who art all truth and who dost love me now
 As thine eyes say, as thy voice breaks to say—
Should'st love so truly and could'st love me still
A whole long life through, had but love its will,
 Would death that leads me from thee brook delay!

II. I have but to be by thee, and thy hand
   Would never let mine go, thy heart withstand
      The beating of my heart to reach its place.
   When should I look for thee and feel thee gone?　　10
   When cry for the old comfort and find none?
      Never, I know! Thy soul is in thy face.

III. Oh, I should fade—'tis willed so! might I save,
   Gladly I would, whatever beauty gave
      Joy to thy sense, for that was precious too.
   It is not to be granted. But the soul
   Whence the love comes, all ravage leaves that whole;
      Vainly the flesh fades—soul makes all things new.

IV. And 'twould not be because my eye grew dim
   Thou could'st not find the love there, thanks to Him　　20
      Who never is dishonoured in the spark
   He gave us from his fire of fires, and bade
   Remember whence it sprang nor be afraid
      While that burns on, though all the rest grow **dark**.

V. So, how thou would'st be perfect, white and clean
   Outside as inside, soul and soul's demesne
      Alike, this body given to show it by!
   Oh, three-parts through the worst of life's abyss,
   What plaudits from the next world after this,
      Could'st thou repeat a stroke and gain the sky!　　30

VI. And is it not the bitterer to think
   That, disengage our hands and thou wilt sink
      Although thy love was love in very deed?
   I know that nature! Pass a festive day
   Thou dost not throw its relic-flower away
      Nor bid its music's loitering echo speed.

VII. Thou let'st the stranger's glove lie where it fell;
   If old things remain old things all is well,
      For thou art grateful as becomes man best:
   And hadst thou only heard me play one tune,　　40
   Or viewed me from a window, not so soon
      With thee would such things fade as with the rest.

VIII. I seem to see! we meet and part: 'tis brief:
   The book I opened keeps a folded leaf,

The very chair I sat on, breaks the rank;
That is a portrait of me on the wall—
Three lines, my face comes at so slight a call;
And for all this, one little hour's to thank.

IX. But now, because the hour through years was fixed,
Because our inmost beings met and mixed,   *50*
Because thou once hast loved me—wilt thou dare
Say to thy soul and Who may list beside,
" Therefore she is immortally my bride,
Chance cannot change that love, nor time impair.

X. " So, what if in the dusk of life that's left,
I, a tired traveller, of my sun bereft,
Look from my path when, mimicking the same,
The fire-fly glimpses past me, come and gone?
—Where was it till the sunset? where anon
It will be at the sunrise! what's to blame? "   *60*

XI. Is it so helpful to thee? canst thou take
The mimic up, nor, for the true thing's sake,
Put gently by such efforts at a beam?
Is the remainder of the way so long
Thou need'st the little solace, thou the strong?
Watch out thy watch, let weak ones doze and dream!

XII. " —Ah, but the fresher faces! Is it true,"
Thou'lt ask, " some eyes are beautiful and new?
Some hair,—how can one choose but grasp such
     wealth?
And if a man would press his lips to lips   *70*
Fresh as the wilding hedge-rose-cup there slips
The dew-drop out of, must it be by stealth?

XIII. " It cannot change the love kept still for Her,
Much more than, such a picture to prefer
Passing a day with, to a room's bare side.
The painted form takes nothing she possessed,
Yet while the Titian's Venus lies at rest
A man looks. Once more, what is there to chide?

XIV. So must I see, from where I sit and watch,
My own self sell myself, my hand attach   *80*

Its warrant to the very thefts from me—
Thy singleness of soul that made me proud,
Thy purity of heart I loved aloud,
    Thy man's truth I was bold to bid God see!

xv. Love so, then, if thou wilt! Give all thou canst
Away to the new faces—disentranced—
    (Say it and think it) obdurate no more,
Re-issue looks and words from the old mint—
Pass them afresh, no matter whose the print
    Image and superscription once they bore!   *90*

xvi. Re-coin thyself and give it them to spend,—
It all comes to the same thing at the end,
    Since mine thou wast, mine art, and mine shalt be,
Faithful or faithless, sealing up the sum
Or lavish of my treasure, thou must come
    Back to the heart's place here I keep for thee!

xvii. Only, why should it be with stain at all?
Why must I, 'twixt the leaves of coronal,
    Put any kiss of pardon on thy brow?
Why need the other women know so much   *100*
And talk together, " Such the look and such
    The smile he used to love with, then as now!"

xviii. Might I die last and shew thee! Should I find
Such hardship in the few years left behind,
    If free to take and light my lamp, and go
Into thy tomb, and shut the door and sit
Seeing thy face on those four sides of it
    The better that they are so blank, I know!

xix. Why, time was what I wanted, to turn o'er
Within my mind each look, get more and more   *110*
    By heart each word, too much to learn at first,
And join thee all the fitter for the pause
'Neath the low door-way's lintel. That were cause
    For lingering, though thou calledst, if I durst!

xx. And yet thou art the nobler of us two.
What dare I dream of, that thou canst not do,
    Outstripping my ten small steps with one stride?
I'll say then, here's a trial and a task—
Is it to bear?—if easy, I'll not ask—
    Though love fail, I can trust on in thy pride.   *120*

XXI. Pride?—when those eyes forestal the life behind
　　The death I have to go through!—when I find,
　　　Now that I want thy help most, all of thee!
　　What did I fear?　Thy love shall hold me fast
　　Until the little minute's sleep is past
　　　And I wake saved.—And yet, it will not be!

AN EPISTLE

CONTAINING THE STRANGE MEDICAL EXPERIENCE OF KARSHISH, THE ARAB PHYSICIAN.

KARSHISH, the picker-up of learning's crumbs,
The not-incurious in God's handiwork
(This man's-flesh He hath admirably made,
Blown like a bubble, kneaded like a paste,
To coop up and keep down on earth a space
That puff of vapour from his mouth, man's soul)
—To Abib, all-sagacious in our art,
Breeder in me of what poor skill I boast,
Like me inquisitive how pricks and cracks
Befall the flesh through too much stress and strain,　　*10*
Whereby the wily vapour fain would slip
Back and rejoin its source before the term,—
And aptest in contrivance, under God,
To baffle it by deftly stopping such:—
The vagrant Scholar to his Sage at home
Sends greeting (health and knowledge, fame with peace),
Three samples of true snake-stone—rarer still,
One of the other sort, the melon-shaped,
(But fitter, pounded fine, for charms than drugs)
And writeth now the twenty-second time.　　　*20*

　My journeyings were brought to Jericho,
Thus I resume.　Who studious in our art
Shall count a little labour unrepaid?
I have shed sweat enough, left flesh and bone
On many a flinty furlong of this land.
Also the country-side is all on fire
With rumours of a marching hitherward—
Some say Vespasian cometh, some, his son.
A black lynx snarled and pricked a tufted ear;

Lust of my blood inflamed his yellow balls: 30
I cried and threw my staff and he was gone.
Twice have the robbers stripped and beaten me,
And once a town declared me for a spy,
But at the end, I reach Jerusalem,
Since this poor covert where I pass the night,
This Bethany, lies scarce the distance thence
A man with plague-sores at the third degree
Runs till he drops down dead.   Thou laughest here!
'Sooth, it elates me, thus reposed and safe,
To void the stuffing of my travel-scrip   40
And share with thee whatever Jewry yields.
A viscid choler is observable
In tertians, I was nearly bold to say,
And falling-sickness hath a happier cure
Than our school wots of: there's a spider here
Weaves no web, watches on the ledge of tombs,
Sprinkled with mottles on an ash-grey back;
Take five and drop them . . . but who knows his mind,
The Syrian run-a-gate I trust this to?
His service payeth me a sublimate   50
Blown up his nose to help the ailing eye.
Best wait: I reach Jerusalem at morn,
There set in order my experiences,
Gather what most deserves and give thee all—
Or I might add, Judea's gum-tragacanth
Scales off in purer flakes, shines clearer-grained,
Cracks 'twixt the pestle and the porphyry,
In fine exceeds our produce.   Scalp-disease
Confounds me, crossing so with leprosy—
Thou hadst admired one sort I gained at Zoar—   60
But zeal outruns discretion.   Here I end.

Yet stay: my Syrian blinketh gratefully,
Protesteth his devotion is my price—
Suppose I write what harms not, though he steal?
I half resolve to tell thee, yet I blush,
What set me off a-writing first of all.
An itch I had, a sting to write, a tang!
For, be it this town's barrenness—or else
The Man had something in the look of him—
His case has struck me far more than 'tis worth.   70
So, pardon if—(lest presently I lose

In the great press of novelty at hand
The care and pains this somehow stole from me)
I bid thee take the thing while fresh in mind,
Almost in sight—for, wilt thou have the truth?
The very man is gone from me but now,
Whose ailment is the subject of discourse.
Thus then, and let thy better wit help all.

   'Tis but a case of mania—subinduced
By epilepsy, at the turning-point   *80*
Of trance prolonged unduly some three days,
When by the exhibition of some drug
Or spell, exorcisation, stroke of art
Unknown to me and which 'twere well to know,
The evil thing out-breaking all at once
Left the man whole and sound of body indeed,—
But, flinging, so to speak, life's gates too wide,
Making a clear house of it too suddenly,
The first conceit that entered pleased to write
Whatever it was minded on the wall   *90*
So plainly at that vantage, as it were,
(First come, first served) that nothing subsequent
Attaineth to erase the fancy-scrawls
Which the returned and new-established soul
Hath gotten now so thoroughly by heart
That henceforth she will read or these or none.
And first—the man's own firm conviction rests
That he was dead (in fact they buried him)
That he was dead and then restored to life
By a Nazarene physician of his tribe: *100*
—'Sayeth, the same bade " Rise," and he did rise.
" Such cases are diurnal," thou wilt cry.
Not so this figment!—not, that such a fume,
Instead of giving way to time and health,
Should eat itself into the life of life,
As saffron tingeth flesh, blood, bones and all!
For see, how he takes up the after-life.
The man—it is one Lazarus a Jew,
Sanguine, proportioned, fifty years of age,
The body's habit wholly laudable,   *110*
As much, indeed, beyond the common health
As he were made and put aside to show.
Think, could we penetrate by any drug

And bathe the wearied soul and worried flesh,
And bring it clear and fair, by three days sleep!
Whence has the man the balm that brightens all?
This grown man eyes the world now like a child.
Some elders of his tribe, I should premise,
Led in their friend, obedient as a sheep,
To bear my inquisition.   While they spoke,   120
Now sharply, now with sorrow,—told the case,—
He listened not except I spoke to him,
But folded his two hands and let them talk,
Watching the flies that buzzed: and yet no fool.
And that's a sample how his years must go.
Look if a beggar, in fixed middle-life,
Should find a treasure, can he use the same
With straightened habits and with tastes starved small
And take at once to his impoverished brain
The sudden element that changes things,   130
—That sets the undreamed-of rapture at his hand,
And puts the cheap old joy in the scorned dust?
Is he not such an one as moves to mirth—
Warily parsimonious, when's no need,
Wasteful as drunkenness at undue times?
All prudent counsel as to what befits
The golden mean, is lost on such an one.
The man's fantastic will is the man's law.
So here—we'll call the treasure knowledge, say—
Increased beyond the fleshy faculty—   140
Heaven opened to a soul while yet on earth,
Earth forced on a soul's use while seeing Heaven.
The man is witless of the size, the sum,
The value in proportion of all things,
Or whether it be little or be much.
Discourse to him of prodigious armaments
Assembled to besiege his city now,
And of the passing of a mule with gourds—
'Tis one!   Then take it on the other side,
Speak of some trifling fact—he will gaze rapt   150
With stupor at its very littleness—
(Far as I see) as if in that indeed
He caught prodigious import, whole results;
And so will turn to us the bystanders
In ever the same stupor (note this point)
That we too see not with his opened eyes!

38

Wonder and doubt come wrongly into play,
Preposterously, at cross purposes.
Should his child sicken unto death,—why, look
For scarce abatement of his cheerfulness,　　　　160
Or pretermission of his daily craft—
While a word, gesture, glance, from that same child
At play or in the school or laid asleep,
Will start him to an agony of fear,
Exasperation, just as like! demand
The reason why—" 'tis but a word," object—
" A gesture "—he regards thee as our lord
Who lived there in the pyramid alone,
Looked at us, dost thou mind, when being young
We both would unadvisedly recite　　　　170
Some charm's beginning, from that book of his,
Able to bid the sun throb wide and burst
All into stars, as suns grown old are wont.
Thou and the child have each a veil alike
Thrown o'er your heads from under which ye both
Stretch your blind hands and trifle with a match
Over a mine of Greek fire, did ye know!
He holds on firmly to some thread of life—
(It is the life to lead perforcedly)
Which runs across some vast distracting orb　　　　180
Of glory on either side that meagre thread,
Which, conscious of, he must not enter yet—
The spiritual life around the earthly life!
The law of that is known to him as this—
His heart and brain move there, his feet stay here.
So is the man perplext with impulses
Sudden to start off crosswise, not straight on,
Proclaiming what is Right and Wrong across—
And not along—this black thread through the blaze—
" It should be " balked by " here it cannot be."　　　　190
And oft the man's soul springs into his face
As if he saw again and heard again
His sage that bade him " Rise " and he did rise.
Something—a word, a tick of the blood within
Admonishes—then back he sinks at once
To ashes, that was very fire before,
In sedulous recurrence to his trade
Whereby he earneth him the daily bread—
And studiously the humbler for that pride,

Professedly the faultier that he knows 200
God's secret, while he holds the thread of life.
Indeed the especial marking of the man
Is prone submission to the Heavenly will—
Seeing it, what it is, and why it is.
'Sayeth, he will wait patient to the last
For that same death which will restore his being
To equilibrium, body loosening soul
Divorced even now by premature full growth:
He will live, nay, it pleaseth him to live
So long as God please, and just how God please. 210
He even seeketh not to please God more
(Which meaneth, otherwise) than as God please.
Hence I perceive not he affects to preach
The doctrine of his sect whate'er it be—
Make proselytes as madmen thirst to do.
How can he give his neighbour the real ground,
His own conviction? ardent as he is—
Call his great truth a lie, why still the old
" Be it as God please " reassureth him.
I probed the sore as thy disciple should— 220
" How, beast," said I, " this stolid carelessness
Sufficeth thee, when Rome is on her march
To stamp out like a little spark thy town,
Thy tribe, thy crazy tale and thee at once? "
He merely looked with his large eyes on me.
The man is apathetic, you deduce?
Contrariwise he loves both old and young,
Able and weak—affects the very brutes
And birds—how say I? flowers of the field—
As a wise workman recognises tools 230
In a master's workshop, loving what they make.
Thus is the man as harmless as a lamb:
Only impatient, let him do his best,
At ignorance and carelessness and sin—
An indignation which is promptly curbed.
As when in certain travels I have feigned
To be an ignoramus in our art
According to some preconceived design,
And happed to hear the land's practitioners
Steeped in conceit sublimed by ignorance, 240
Prattle fantastically on disease,
Its cause and cure—and I must hold my peace!

Thou wilt object—why have I not ere this
Sought out the sage himself, the Nazarene
Who wrought this cure, enquiring at the source,
Conferring with the frankness that befits?
Alas! it grieveth me, the learned leech
Perished in a tumult many years ago,
Accused,—our learning's fate,—of wizardry.
Rebellion, to the setting up a rule   250
And creed prodigious as described to me.
His death which happened when the earthquake fell
(Prefiguring, as soon appeared, the loss
To occult learning in our lord the sage .
That lived there in the pyramid alone)
Was wrought by the mad people—that's their wont—
On vain recourse, as I conjecture it,
To his tried virtue, for miraculous help—
How could he stop the earthquake?   That's their way!
The other imputations must be lies: 260
But take one—though I loathe to give it thee,
In mere respect to any good man's fame!
(And after all our patient Lazarus
Is stark mad—should we count on what he says?
Perhaps not—though in writing to a leech
'Tis well to keep back nothing of a case.)
This man so cured regards the curer then,
As—God forgive me—who but God himself,
Creater and Sustainer of the world,
That came and dwelt in flesh on it awhile!   270
—'Sayeth that such an One was born and lived,
Taught, healed the sick, broke bread at his own house,
Then died, with Lazarus by, for ought I know,
And yet was . . . what I said nor choose repeat,
And must have so avouched himself, in fact,
In hearing of this very Lazarus
Who saith—but why all this of what he saith?
Why write of trivial matters, things of price
Calling at every moment for remark?
I noticed on the margin of a pool   280
Blue-flowering borage, the Aleppo sort,
Aboundeth, very nitrous.   It is strange!

Thy pardon for this long and tedious case,
Which, now that I review it, needs must seem

Unduly dwelt on, prolixly set forth.
Nor I myself discern in what is writ
Good cause for the peculiar interest
And awe indeed this man has touched me with.
Perhaps the journey's end, the weariness
Had wrought upon me first. I met him thus—   290
I crossed a ridge of short sharp broken hills
Like an old lion's cheek-teeth. Out there came
A moon made like a face with certain spots
Multiform, manifold, and menacing:
Then a wind rose behind me. So we met
In this old sleepy town at unaware,
The man and I. I send thee what is writ.
Regard it as a chance, a matter risked
To this ambiguous Syrian—he may lose,
Or steal, or give it thee with equal good.   300
Jerusalem's repose shall make amends
For time this letter wastes, thy time and mine,
Till when, once more thy pardon and farewell!

The very God! think, Abib; dost thou think?
So, the All-Great, were the All-Loving too—
So, through the thunder comes a human voice
Saying, " O heart I made, a heart beats here!
Face, my hands fashioned, see it in myself.
Thou hast no power nor may'st conceive of mine,
But love I gave thee, with Myself to love,   310
And thou must love me who have died for thee! "
The madman saith He said so: it is strange.

MESMERISM.

I. ALL I believed is true!
    I am able yet
    All I want to get
By a method as strange as new:
Dare I trust the same to you?

II. If at night, when the doors are shut,
    And the wood-worm picks,
    And the death-watch ticks,
And the bar has a flag of smut,
And a cat's in the water-butt—   10

III. And the socket floats and flares,
      And the house-beams groan,
      And a foot unknown
  Is surmised on the garret-stairs,
  And the locks slip unawares—

IV. And the spider, to serve his ends,
      By a sudden thread,
      Arms and legs outspread,
  On the table's midst descends,
  Comes to find, God knows what friends!—   *20*

V. If since eve drew in, I say,
      I have sate and brought
      (So to speak) my thought
  To bear on the woman away,
  Till I felt my hair turn grey—

VI. Till I seemed to have and hold
      In the vacancy
      'Twixt the wall and me,
  From the hair-plait's chestnut gold
  To the foot in its muslin fold—   *30*

VII. Have and hold, then and there,
      Her, from head to foot,
      Breathing and mute,
  Passive and yet aware,
  In the grasp of my steady stare—

VIII. Hold and have, there and then,
      All her body and soul
      That completes my Whole,
  All that women add to men,
  In the clutch of my steady ken—   *40*

IX. Having and holding, till
      I imprint her fast
      On the void at last
  As the sun does whom he will
  By the calotypist's skill—

X. Then,—if my heart's strength serve.
      And through all and each
      Of the veils I reach
  To her soul and never swerve,
  Knitting an iron nerve—   *50*

XI. Commanding that to advance
　　　And inform the shape
　　　Which has made escape
　And before my countenance
　Answers me glance for glance—

XII. I, still with a gesture fit
　　　Of my hands that best
　　　Do my soul's behest,
　Pointing the power from it,
　While myself do steadfast sit—　　　　　*60*

XIII. Steadfast and still the same
　　　On my object bent
　　　While the hands give vent
　To my ardour and my aim
　And break into very flame—

XIV. Then, I reach, I must believe,
　　　Not her soul in vain,
　　　For to me again
　It reaches, and past retrieve
　Is wound in the toils I weave—　　　　　*70*

XV. And must follow as I require
　　　As befits a thrall,
　　　Bringing flesh and all,
　Essence and earth-attire,
　To the source of the tractile fire—

XVI. Till the house called hers, not mine,
　　　With a growing weight
　　　Seems to suffocate
　If she break not its leaden line
　And escape from its close confine—　　　*80*

XVII. Out of doors into the night!
　　　On to the maze
　　　Of the wild wood-ways,
　Not turning to left or right
　From the pathway, blind with sight—

XVIII. Making thro' rain and wind
　　　O'er the broken shrubs,
　　　'Twixt the stems and stubs,
　With a still composed strong mind,
　Not a care for the world behind—　　　*90*

XIX. Swifter and still more swift,
      As the crowding peace
      Doth to joy increase
In the wide blind eyes uplift,
Thro' the darkness and the drift!

XX. While I—to the shape, I too
      Feel my soul dilate
      Nor a whit abate
And relax not a gesture due
As I see my belief come true—   *100*

XXI. For there! have I drawn or no
      Life to that lip?
      Do my fingers dip
In a flame which again they throw
On the cheek that breaks a-glow?

XXII. Ha! was the hair so first?
      What, unfilleted,
      Made alive and spread
Through the void with a rich outburst,
Chestnut gold-interspersed!   *110*

XXIII. Like the doors of a casket-shrine,
      See, on either side,
      Her two arms divide
Till the heart betwixt makes sign,
Take me, for I am thine!

XXIV. Now—now—the door is heard
      Hark! the stairs and near—
      Nearer—and here—
Now! and at call the third
She enters without a word.   *120*

XXV. On doth she march and on
      To the fancied shape—
      It is past escape
Herself, now—the dream is done
And the shadow and she are one.

XXVI. First I will pray. Do Thou
      That ownest the soul,
      Yet wilt grant controul
To another nor disallow
For a time, restrain me now!   *130*

XXVII. I admonish me while I may,
  Not to squander guilt,
  Since require Thou wilt
At my hand its price one day!
What the price is, who can say?

A SERENADE AT THE VILLA

I. THAT was I, you heard last night
  When there rose no moon at all,
Nor, to pierce the strained and tight
  Tent of heaven, a planet small:
Life was dead, and so was light.

II. Not a twinkle from the fly,
  Not a glimmer from the worm.
When the crickets stopped their cry,
  When the owls forbore a term,
You heard music; that was I.   10

III. Earth turned in her sleep with pain,
  Sultrily suspired for proof:
In at heaven, and out again,
  Lightning!—where it broke the roof,
Bloodlike, some few drops of rain.

IV. What they could my words expressed,
  O my love, my all, my one!
Singing helped the verses best,
  And when singing's best was done,
To my lute I left the rest.   20

V. So wore night; the east was grey,
  White the broad-faced hemlock flowers;
Soon would come another day;
  Ere its first of heavy hours
Found me, I had past away.

VI. What became of all the hopes,
  Words and song and lute as well?
Say, this struck you—" When life gropes
  Feebly for the path where fell
Light last on the evening slopes,   30

VII. " One friend in that path shall be
 To secure my steps from wrong;
One to count night day for me,
 Patient through the watches long,
Serving most with none to see."

VIII. Never say—as something bodes—
 " So the worst has yet a worse!
When life halts 'neath double loads,
 Better the task-master's curse
Than such music on the roads!   *40*

IX. " When no moon succeeds the sun,
 Nor can pierce the midnight's tent
Any star, the smallest one,
 While some drops, where lightning went,
Show the final storm begun—

X. " When the fire-fly hides its spot,
 When the garden-voices fail
In the darkness thick and hot,—
 Shall another voice avail,
That shape be where those are not?   *50*

XI. " Has some plague a longer lease
 Proffering its help uncouth?
Can't one even die in peace?
 As one shuts one's eyes on youth,
Is that face the last one sees? "

XII. Oh, how dark your villa was,
 Windows fast and obdurate!
How the garden grudged me grass
 Where I stood—the iron gate
Ground its teeth to let me pass!   *60*

MY STAR.

ALL that I know
 Of a certain star,
Is, it can throw
 (Like the angled spar)
Now a dart of red,
 Now a dart of blue,
Till my friends have said
 They would fain see, too,

My star that dartles the red and the blue!
Then it stops like a bird,—like a flower, hangs furled;   *10*
  They must solace themselves with the Saturn above it.
What matter to me if their star is a world?
  Mine has opened its soul to me; therefore I love it.

INSTANS TYRANNUS.

I. OF the million or two, more or less,
    I rule and possess,
    One man, for some cause undefined,
    Was least to my mind.

II. I struck him, he grovelled of course—
    For, what was his force?
    I pinned him to earth with my weight
    And persistence of hate—
    And he lay, would not moan, would not curse,
    As if lots might be worse.   *10*

III. " Were the object less mean, would he stand
    At the swing of my hand!
    For obscurity helps him and blots
    The hole where he squats."
    So I set my five wits on the stretch
    To inveigle the wretch.
    All in vain! gold and jewels I threw,
    Still he couched there perdue.
    I tempted his blood and his flesh,
    Hid in roses my mesh,   *20*
    Choicest cates and the flagon's best spilth—
    Still he kept to his filth!

IV. Had he kith now or kin, were access
    To his heart, if I press—
    Just a son or a mother to seize—
    No such booty as these!
    Were it simply a friend to pursue
    'Mid my million or two,
    Who could pay me in person or pelf
    What he owes me himself.   *30*
    No! I could not but smile through my chafe—
    For the fellow lay safe

As his mates do, the midge and the nit,
—Through minuteness, to wit.
Then a humour more great took its place
At the thought of his face,
The droop, the low cares of the mouth,
The trouble uncouth

v. 'Twixt the brows, all that air one is fain
   To put out of its pain—   40
   And, no, I admonished myself,
   " Is one mocked by an elf,
   Is one baffled by toad or by rat?
   The gravamen's in that!
   How the lion, who crouches to suit
   His back to my foot,
   Would admire that I stand in debate!
   But the Small is the Great
   If it vexes you,—that is the thing!
   Toad or rat vex the King?   50
   Though I waste half my realm to unearth
   Toad or rat, 'tis well worth! "

vi. So I soberly laid my last plan
   To extinguish the man.
   Round his creep-hole,—with never a break
   Ran my fires for his sake;
   Over-head, did my thunders combine
   With my under-ground mine:
   Till I looked from my labour content
   To enjoy the event.   60

vii. When sudden. . . . how think ye, the end?
   Did I say " without friend? "
   Say rather, from marge to blue marge
   The whole sky grew his targe
   With the sun's self for visible boss,
   While an Arm ran across
   Which the earth heaved beneath like a breast
   Where the wretch was safe prest!
   Do you see? just my vengeance complete,
   The man sprang to his feet,   70
   Stood erect, caught at God's skirts and prayed!
   —So, *I* was afraid!

A PRETTY WOMAN.

I. THAT fawn-skin-dappled hair of hers,
      And the blue eye
      Dear and dewy,
    And that infantine fresh air of hers!

II. To think men cannot take you, Sweet.
       And enfold you,
       Ay, and hold you,
     And so keep you what they make you, Sweet!

III. You like us for a glance, you know—
        For a word's sake,   *10*
        Or a sword's sake,
      All's the same, whate'er the chance, you know.

IV. And in turn we make you ours, we say—
       You and youth too,
       Eyes and mouth too,
     All the face composed of flowers, we say.

V. All's our own, to make the most of, Sweet—
      Sing and say for,
      Watch and pray for,
    Keep a secret or go boast of, Sweet.   *20*

VI. But for loving, why, you would not, Sweet,
       Though we prayed you,
       Paid you, brayed you
     In a mortar—for you could not, Sweet.

VII. So, we leave the sweet face fondly there—
        Be its beauty
        Its sole duty!
      Let all hope of grace beyond, lie there!

VIII. And while the face lies quiet there,
         Who shall wonder   *30*
         That I ponder
       A conclusion? I will try it there.

IX. As,—why must one, for the love forgone,
      Scout mere liking?
      Thunder-striking
Earth,—the heaven, we looked above for, gone!

X. Why with beauty, needs there money be—
      Love with liking?
      Crush the fly-king
In his gauze, because no honey bee?   *40*

XI. May not liking be so simple-sweet,
      If love grew there
      'Twould undo there
All that breaks the cheek to dimples sweet?

XII. Is the creature too imperfect, say?
      Would you mend it
      And so end it?
Since not all addition perfects aye!

XIII. Or is it of its kind, perhaps,
      Just perfection—   *50*
      Whence, rejection
Of a grace not to its mind, perhaps?

XIV. Shall we burn up, tread that face at once
      Into tinder,
      And so hinder
Sparks from kindling all the place at once?

XV. Or else kiss away one's soul on her?
      Your love-fancies!—
      A sick man sees
Truer, when his hot eyes roll on her!   *60*

XVI. Thus the craftsman thinks to grace the rose,—
      Plucks a mould-flower
      For his gold flower,
Uses fine things that efface the rose.

XVII. Rosy rubies make its cup more rose,
      Precious metals
      Ape the petals,—
Last, some old king locks it up, morose!

XVIII. Then, how grace a rose?   I know a way!
   Leave it rather.   *70*
   Must you gather?
  Smell, kiss, wear it—at last, throw away!

"CHILDE ROLAND TO THE DARK TOWER CAME."
(See Edgar's Song in "LEAR.")

I.

MY first thought was, he lied in every word,
 That hoary cripple, with malicious eye
 Askance to watch the working of his lie
On mine, and mouth scarce able to afford
Suppression of the glee that pursed and scored
 Its edge at one more victim gained thereby.

II.

What else should he be set for, with his staff?
 What, save to waylay with his lies, ensnare
 All travellers that might find him posted there,
And ask the road?   I guessed what skull-like laugh   *10*
Would break, what crutch 'gin write my epitaph
 For pastime in the dusty thoroughfare,

III.

If at his counsel I should turn aside
 Into that ominous tract which, all agree,
 Hides the Dark Tower.   Yet acquiescingly
I did turn as he pointed; neither pride
Nor hope rekindling at the end descried,
 So much as gladness that some end should be.

IV.

For, what with my whole world-wide wandering,
 What with my search drawn out thro' years, my hope   *20*
 Dwindled into a ghost not fit to cope
With that obstreperous joy success would bring,—
I hardly tried now to rebuke the spring
 My heart made, finding failure in its scope.

V.

As when a sick man very near to death
 Seems dead indeed, and feels begin and end
 The tears and takes the farewell of each friend,

And hears one bid the other go, draw breath
Freelier outside, (" since all is o'er," he saith,
   " And the blow fall'n no grieving can amend ")   *30*

VI.

While some discuss if near the other graves
   Be room enough for this, and when a day
   Suits best for carrying the corpse away,
With care about the banners, scarves and staves,—
And still the man hears all, and only craves
   He may not shame such tender love and stay.

VII.

Thus, I had so long suffered in this quest,
   Heard failure prophesied so oft, been writ
   So many times among " The Band "—to wit,
The knights who to the Dark Tower's search addressed   *40*
Their steps—that just to fail as they, seemed best,
   And all the doubt was now—should I be fit.

VIII.

So, quiet as despair, I turned from him,
   That hateful cripple, out of his highway
   Into the path he pointed.   All the day
Had been a dreary one at best, and dim
Was settling to its close, yet shot one grim
   Red leer to see the plain catch its estray.

IX.

For mark! no sooner was I fairly found
   Pledged to the plain, after a pace or two,   *50*
   Than pausing to throw backward a last view
To the safe road, 'twas gone! grey plain all round!
Nothing but plain to the horizon's bound.
   I might go on; nought else remained to do.

X.

So on I went.   I think I never saw
   Such starved ignoble nature; nothing throve:
   For flowers—as well expect a cedar grove!
But cockle, spurge, according to their law
Might propagate their kind, with none to awe,
   You'd think: a burr had been a treasure-trove.   *60*

XI.

No! penury, inertness, and grimace,
  In some strange sort, were the land's portion.   "See
  Or shut your eyes "—said Nature peevishly—
" It nothing skills: I cannot help my case:
The Judgment's fire alone can cure this place,
  Calcine its clods and set my prisoners free."

XII.

If there pushed any ragged thistle-stalk
  Above its mates, the head was chopped—the bents
  Were jealous else.   What made those holes and rents
In the dock's harsh swarth leaves—bruised as to baulk   *70*
All hope of greenness? 'tis a brute must walk
  Pashing their life out, with a brute's intents.

XIII.

As for the grass, it grew as scant as hair
  In leprosy—thin dry blades pricked the mud
  Which underneath looked kneaded up with blood,
One stiff blind horse, his every bone a-stare,
Stood stupified, however he came there—
  Thrust out past service from the devil's stud!

XIV.

Alive? he might be dead for all I know,
  With that red gaunt and colloped neck a-strain,   *80*
  And shut eyes underneath the rusty mane.
Seldom went such grotesqueness with such woe:
I never saw a brute I hated so—
  He must be wicked to deserve such pain.

XV.

I shut my eyes and turned them on my heart.
  As a man calls for wine before he fights,
  I asked one draught of earlier, happier sights
Ere fitly I could hope to play my part.
Think first, fight afterwards—the soldier's art:
  One taste of the old times sets all to rights!   *90*

XVI.

Not it!   I fancied Cuthbert's reddening face
  Beneath its garniture of curly gold,
  Dear fellow, till I almost felt him fold

An arm in mine to fix me to the place,
That way he used.   Alas! one night's disgrace!
   Out went my heart's new fire and left it cold.

XVII.

Giles, then, the soul of honour—there he stands
   Frank as ten years ago when knighted first.
   What honest men should dare (he said) he durst.
Good—but the scene shifts—faugh! what hangman's hands *100*
Pin to his breast a parchment? his own bands
   Read it.   Poor traitor, spit upon and curst!

XVIII.

Better this present than a past like that—
   Back therefore to my darkening path again.
   No sound, no sight as far as eye could strain.
Will the night send a howlet or a bat?
I asked: when something on the dismal flat
   Came to arrest my thoughts and change their train.

XIX.

A sudden little river crossed my path
   As unexpected as a serpent comes.   *110*
   No sluggish tide congenial to the glooms—
This, as it frothed by, might have been a bath
For the fiend's glowing hoof—to see the wrath
   Of its black eddy bespate with flakes and spumes.

XX.

So petty yet so spiteful! all along,
   Low scrubby alders kneeled down over it;
   Drenched willows flung them headlong in a fit
Of mute despair, a suicidal throng:
The river which had done them all the wrong,
   Whate'er that was, rolled by, deterred no whit.   *120*

XXI.

Which, while I forded,—good saints, how I feared
   To set my foot upon a dead man's cheek,
   Each step, or feel the spear I thrust to seek
For hollows, tangled in his hair or beard!
—It may have been a water-rat I speared,
   But, ugh; it sounded like a baby's shriek.

XXII.

Glad was I when I reached the other bank.
  Now for a better country. Vain presage!
  Who were the strugglers, what war did they wage
Whose savage trample thus could pad the dank   *130*
Soil to a plash? toads in a poisoned tank,
  Or wild cats in a red-hot iron cage—

XXIII.

The fight must so have seemed in that fell cirque.
  What kept them there, with all the plain to choose?
  No foot-print leading to that horrid mews,
None out of it: mad brewage set to work
Their brains, no doubt, like galley-slaves the Turk
  Pits for his pastime, Christians against Jews.

XXIV.

And more than that—a furlong on—why, there!
  What bad use was that engine for, that wheel,   *140*
  Or brake, not wheel—that harrow fit to reel
Men's bodies out like silk? with all the air
Of Tophet's tool, on earth left unaware,
  Or brought to sharpen its rusty teeth of steel.

XXV.

Then came a bit of stubbed ground, once a wood,
  Next a marsh, it would seem, and now mere earth
  Desperate and done with; (so a fool finds mirth,
Makes a thing and then mars it, till his mood
Changes and off he goes!) within a rood
  Bog, clay and rubble, sand and stark black dearth.   *150*

XXVI.

Now blotches rankling, coloured gay and grim,
  Now patches where some leanness of the soil's
  Broke into moss or substances like boils;
Then came some palsied oak, a cleft in him
Like a distorted mouth that splits its rim
  Gaping at death, and dies while it recoils.

XXVII.

And just as far as ever from the end!
  Nought in the distance but the evening, nought
  To point my footstep further! At the thought,

A great black bird, Apollyon's bosom-friend,   *160*
Sailed past, nor beat his wide wing dragon-penned
   That brushed my cap—perchance the guide I sought.

XXVIII.

For looking up, aware I somehow grew,
  'Spite of the dusk, the plain had given place
  All round to mountains—with such name to grace
Mere ugly heights and heaps now stol'n in view.
How thus they had surprised me,—solve it, you!
  How to get from them was no plainer case.

XXIX.

Yet half I seemed to recognise some trick
  Of mischief happened to me, God knows when—   *170*
  In a bad dream perhaps. Here ended, then,
Progress this way. When, in the very nick
Of giving up, one time more, came a click
  As when a trap shuts—you're inside the den!

XXX.

Burningly it came on me all at once,
  This was the place! those two hills on the right
  Crouched like two bulls locked horn in horn in fight—
While to the left, a tall scalped mountain . . . Dunce,
Fool, to be dozing at the very nonce,
  After a life spent training for the sight!   *180*

XXXI.

What in the midst lay but the Tower itself?
  The round squat turret, blind as the fool's heart,
  Built of brown stone, without a counterpart
In the whole world. The tempest's mocking elf
Points to the shipman thus the unseen shelf
  He strikes on, only when the timbers start.

XXXII.

Not see? because of night perhaps?—Why, day
  Came back again for that! before it left,
  The dying sunset kindled through a cleft:
The hills, like giants at a hunting, lay—   *190*
Chin upon hand, to see the game at bay,—
  " Now stab and end the creature—to the heft! "

XXXIII.

Not hear? when noise was everywhere? it tolled
  Increasing like a bell.   Names in my ears,
  Of all the lost adventurers my peers,—
How such a one was strong, and such was bold,
And such was fortunate, yet each of old
  Lost, lost! one moment knelled the woe of years.

XXXIV.

There they stood, ranged along the hill-sides—met
  To view the last of me, a living frame   *200*
  For one more picture; in a sheet of flame
I saw them and I knew them all.   And yet
Dauntless the slug-horn to my lips I set
  And blew.   "*Childe Roland to the Dark Tower came.*"

RESPECTABILITY.

I. DEAR, had the world in its caprice
    Deigned to proclaim " I know you both,
    Have recognised your plighted troth,
  Am sponsor for you—live in peace!"—
  How many precious months and years
    Of youth had passed, that speed so fast,
    Before we found it out at last,
  The world, and what it fears?

II. How much of priceless life were spent
    With men that every virtue decks,   *10*
    And women models of their sex,
  Society's true ornament,—
  Ere we dared wander, nights like this,
    Thro' wind and rain, and watch the Seine,
    And feel the Boulevart break again
  To warmth and light and bliss?

III. I know! the world proscribes not love;
    Allows my finger to caress
    Your lip's contour and downiness,
  Provided it supply a glove.   *20*
  The world's good word!—the Institute!
    Guizot receives Montalembert!
    Eh? down the court three lampions flare—
  Put forward your best foot!

A LIGHT WOMAN.

I. So far as our story approaches the end,
    Which do you pity the most of us three?—
My friend, or the mistress of my friend
    With her wanton eyes, or me?

II. My friend was already too good to lose,
    And seemed in the way of improvement yet,
When she crossed his path with her hunting-noose
    And over him drew her net.

III. When I saw him tangled in her toils,
    A shame, said I, if she adds just him   *10*
To her nine-and-ninety other spoils,
    The hundredth, for a whim!

IV. And before my friend be wholly hers,
    How easy to prove to him, I said,
An eagle's the game her pride prefers,
    Though she snaps at the wren instead!

V. So I gave her eyes my own eyes to take,
    My hand sought her as in earnest need,
And round she turned for my noble sake,
    And gave me herself indeed.   *20*

VI. The eagle am I, with my fame in the world,
    The wren is he, with his maiden face.
—You look away and your lip is curled?
    Patience, a moment's space!

VII. For see—my friend goes shaking and white;
    He eyes me as the basilisk:
I have turned, it appears, his day to night,
    Eclipsing his sun's disc.

VIII. And I did it, he thinks, as a very thief:
    " Though I love her—that he comprehends—   *30*
One should master one's passions, (love, in chief)
    And be loyal to one's friends! "

IX. And she,—she lies in my hand as tame
    As a pear hung basking over a wall;
Just a touch to try and off it came;
    'Tis mine,—can I let it fall?

X. With no mind to eat it, that's the worst!
    Were it thrown in the road, would the case assist?
'Twas quenching a dozen blue-flies' thirst
    When I gave its stalk a twist.   40

XI. And I,—what I seem to my friend, you see—
    What I soon shall seem to his love, you guess.
What I seem to myself, do you ask of me?
    No hero, I confess.

XII. 'Tis an awkward thing to play with souls,
    And matter enough to save one's own.
Yet think of my friend, and the burning coals
    He played with for bits of stone!

XIII. One likes to show the truth for the truth;
    That the woman was light is very true: 50
But suppose she says,—never mind that youth—
    What wrong have I done to you?

XIV. Well, any how, here the story stays,
    So far at least as I understand;
And, Robert Browning, you writer of plays,
    Here's a subject made to your hand!

THE STATUE AND THE BUST.

THERE's a palace in Florence, the world knows well,
And a statue watches it from the square,
And this story of both do the townsmen tell.

Ages ago, a lady there,
At the farthest window facing the east
Asked, " Who rides by with the royal air? "

The brides-maids' prattle around her ceased;
She leaned forth, one on either hand;
They saw how the blush of the bride increased—

They felt by its beats her heart expand— 10
As one at each ear and both in a breath
Whispered, " The Great-Duke Ferdinand."

That selfsame instant, underneath,
The Duke rode past in his idle way,
Empty and fine like a swordless sheath.

Gay he rode, with a friend as gay,
Till he threw his head back—" Who is she? "
—" A Bride the Riccardi brings home to-day."

Hair in heaps laid heavily
Over a pale brow spirit-pure— 20
Carved like the heart of the coal-black tree,

Crisped like a war-steed's encolure—
Which vainly sought to dissemble her eyes
Of the blackest black our eyes endure.

And lo, a blade for a knight's emprise
Filled the fine empty sheath of a man,—
The Duke grew straightway brave and wise.

He looked at her, as a lover can;
She looked at him, as one who awakes,—
The past was a sleep, and her life began. 30

As love so ordered for both their sakes,
A feast was held that selfsame night
In the pile which the mighty shadow makes.

(For Via Larga is three-parts light,
But the Palace overshadows one,
Because of a crime which may God requite!

To Florence and God the wrong was done,
Through the first republic's murder there
By Cosimo and his cursed son.)

The Duke (with the statue's face in the square) 40
Turned in the midst of his multitude
At the bright approach of the bridal pair.

Face to face the lovers stood
A single minute and no more,
While the bridegroom bent as a man subdued—

Bowed till his bonnet brushed the floor—
For the Duke on the lady a kiss conferred,
As the courtly custom was of yore.

In a minute can lovers exchange a word?
If a word did pass, which I do not think,   50
Only one out of the thousand heard.

That was the bridegroom.   At day's brink
He and his bride were alone at last
In a bed-chamber by a taper's blink.

Calmly he said that her lot was cast,
That the door she had passed was shut on her
Till the final catafalk repassed.

The world meanwhile, its noise and stir,
Through a certain window facing the east
She might watch like a convent's chronicler.   60

Since passing the door might lead to a feast,
And a feast might lead to so much beside,
He, of many evils, chose the least.

" Freely I choose too," said the bride—
" Your window and its world suffice."
So replied the tongue, while the heart replied—

" If I spend the night with that devil twice,
May his window serve as my loop of hell
Whence a damned soul looks on Paradise !

" I fly to the Duke who loves me well,   70
Sit by his side and laugh at sorrow
Ere I count another ave-bell.

" 'Tis only the coat of a page to borrow,
And tie my hair in a horse-boy's trim,
And I save my soul—but not to-morrow "—

(She checked herself and her eye grew dim)—
" My father tarries to bless my state:
I must keep it one day more for him.

" Is one day more so long to wait?
Moreover the Duke rides past, I know—   *80*
We shall see each other, sure as fate."

She turned on her side and slept. Just so!
So we resolve on a thing and sleep.
So did the lady, ages ago.

That night the Duke said, " Dear or cheap
As the cost of this cup of bliss may prove
To body or soul, I will drain it deep."

And on the morrow, bold with love,
He beckoned the bridegroom (close on call,
As his duty bade, by the Duke's alcove)   *90*

And smiled " 'Twas a very funeral
Your lady will think, this feast of ours,—
A shame to efface, whate'er befall!

" What if we break from the Arno bowers,
And let Petraja, cool and green,
Cure last night's fault with this morning's flowers? "

The bridegroom, not a thought to be seen
On his steady brow and quiet mouth,
Said, " Too much favour for me so mean!

" Alas! my lady leaves the south.   *100*
Each wind that comes from the Apennine
Is a menace to her tender youth.

" No way exists, the wise opine,
If she quits her palace twice this year,
To avert the flower of life's decline."

Quoth the Duke, " A sage and a kindly fear.
Moreover Petraja is cold this spring—
Be our feast to-night as usual here!"

And then to himself—" Which night shall bring
Thy bride to her lover's embraces, fool—
Or I am the fool, and thou art his king!

          110

" Yet my passion must wait a night, nor cool—
For to-night the Envoy arrives from France,
Whose heart I unlock with thyself, my tool.

" I need thee still and might miss perchance.
To-day is not wholly lost, beside,
With its hope of my lady's countenance—

" For I ride—what should I do but ride?
And passing her palace, if I list,
May glance at its window—well betide! "

          120

So said, so done: nor the lady missed
One ray that broke from the ardent brow,
Nor a curl of the lips where the spirit kissed.

Be sure that each renewed the vow,
No morrow's sun should arise and set
And leave them then as it left them now.

But next day passed, and next day yet,
With still fresh cause to wait one more
Ere each leaped over the parapet.

And still, as love's brief morning wore,
With a gentle start, half smile, half sigh,
They found love not as it seemed before.

          130

They thought it would work infallibly,
But not in despite of heaven and earth—
The rose would blow when the storm passed by.

Meantime they could profit in winter's dearth
By winter's fruits that supplant the rose:
The world and its ways have a certain worth!

And to press a point while these oppose
Were a simple policy—best wait,
And lose no friends and gain no foes.

          140

Meanwhile, worse fates than a lover's fate,
Who daily may ride and lean and look
Where his lady watches behind the grate!

And she—she watched the square like a book
Holding one picture and only one,
Which daily to find she undertook.

When the picture was reached the book was done,
And she turned from it all night to scheme
Of tearing it out for herself next sun.   *150*

Weeks grew months, years—gleam by gleam
The glory dropped from youth and love,
And both perceived they had dreamed a dream,

Which hovered as dreams do, still above,—
But who can take a dream for truth?
Oh, hide our eyes from the next remove!

One day as the lady saw her youth
Depart, and the silver thread that streaked
Her hair, and, worn by the serpent's tooth,

The brow so puckered, the chin so peaked,—   *160*
And wondered who the woman was,
So hollow-eyed and haggard-cheeked,

Fronting her silent in the glass—
" Summon here," she suddenly said,
" Before the rest of my old self pass,

" Him, the Carver, a hand to aid,
Who moulds the clay no love will change,
And fixes a beauty never to fade.

" Let Robbia's craft so apt and strange
Arrest the remains of young and fair,   *170*
And rivet them while the seasons range.

" Make me a face on the window there
Waiting as ever, mute the while,
My love to pass below in the square!

" And let me think that it may beguile
Dreary days which the dead must spend
Down in their darkness under the aisle—

" To say,—' What matters at the end?
I did no more while my heart was warm,
Than does that image, my pale-faced friend.'   *180*

" Where is the use of the lip's red charm,
The heaven of hair, the pride of the brow,
And the blood that blues the inside arm—

" Unless we turn, as the soul knows how,
The earthly gift to an end divine?
A lady of clay is as good, I trow."

But long ere Robbia's cornice, fine
With flowers and fruits which leaves enlace,
Was set where now is the empty shrine—

(With, leaning out of a bright blue space,   *190*
As a ghost might from a chink of sky,
The passionate pale lady's face—

Eyeing ever with earnest eye
And quick-turned neck at its breathless stretch,
Some one who ever passes by—)

The Duke sighed like the simplest wretch
In Florence, " So, my dream escapes!
Will its record stay? "   And he bade them fetch

Some subtle fashioner of shapes—
" Can the soul, the will, die out of a man   *200*
Ere his body find the grave that gapes?

" John of Douay shall work my plan,
Mould me on horseback here aloft,
Alive—(the subtle artisan!)

" In the very square I cross so oft!
That men may admire, when future suns
Shall touch the eyes to a purpose soft.

" While the mouth and the brow are brave in bronze—
Admire and say, ' When he was alive,
How he would take his pleasure once!'   210

" And it shall go hard but I contrive
To listen meanwhile and laugh in my tomb
At indolence which aspires to strive."

————

So! while these wait the trump of doom,
How do their spirits pass, I wonder,
Nights and days in the narrow room?

Still, I suppose, they sit and ponder
What a gift life was, ages ago,
Six steps out of the chapel yonder.

Surely they see not God, I know,   220
Nor all that chivalry of His,
The soldier-saints who, row on row,

Burn upward each to his point of bliss—
Since, the end of life being manifest,
He had cut his way thro' the world to this.

I hear your reproach—" But delay was best,
For their end was a crime!"—Oh, a crime will do
As well, I reply, to serve for a test,

As a virtue golden through and through,
Sufficient to vindicate itself   230
And prove its worth at a moment's view.

Must a game be played for the sake of pelf?
Where a button goes, 'twere an epigram
To offer the stamp of the very Guelph.

The true has no value beyond the sham.
As well the counter as coin, I submit,
When your table's a hat, and your prize, a dram.

Stake your counter as boldly every whit,
Venture as truly, use the same skill,
Do your best, whether winning or losing it,   240

If you choose to play—is my principle!
Let a man contend to the uttermost
For his life's set prize, be what it will!

The counter our lovers staked was lost
As surely as if it were lawful coin:
And the sin I impute to each frustrate ghost

Was, the unlit lamp and the ungirt loin,
Though the end in sight was a crime I say.
You of the virtue (we issue join)
How strive you?   *De te, fabula!*   *250*

LOVE IN A LIFE.

I. Room after room,
   I hunt the house through
   We inhabit together.
   Heart, fear nothing, for, heart, thou shalt find her,
   Next time, herself!—not the trouble behind her
   Left in the curtain, the couch's perfume!
   As she brushed it, the cornice-wreath blossomed anew,—
   Yon looking-glass gleamed at the wave of her feather.

II. Yet the day wears,
   And door succeeds door;   *10*
   I try the fresh fortune—
   Range the wide house from the wing to the centre,
   Still the same chance! she goes out as I enter.
   Spend my whole day in the quest,—who cares?
   But 'tis twilight, you see,—with such suites to explore,
   Such closets to search, such alcoves to importune!

LIFE IN A LOVE.

    Escape me?
    Never—
    Beloved!
While I am I, and you are you,
  So long as the world contains us both,
  Me the loving and you the loth,
While the one eludes, must the other pursue.

My life is a fault at last, I fear—
   It seems too much like a fate, indeed!
   Though I do my best I shall scarce succeed—   *10*
But what if I fail of my purpose here?
It is but to keep the nerves at strain,
   To dry one's eyes and laugh at a fall,
And baffled, get up to begin again,—
   So the chace takes up one's life, that's all.
While, look but once from your farthest bound,
   At me so deep in the dust and dark,
No sooner the old hope drops to ground
   Than a new one, straight to the self-same mark,
        I shape me—   *20*
        Ever
        Removed!

HOW IT STRIKES A CONTEMPORARY.

I ONLY knew one poet in my life:
And this, or something like it, was his way.

   You saw go up and down Valladolid,
A man of mark, to know next time you saw.
His very serviceable suit of black
Was courtly once and conscientious still,
And many might have worn it, though none did:
The cloak that somewhat shone and shewed the threads
Had purpose, and the ruff, significance.
He walked and tapped the pavement with his cane,   *10*
Scenting the world, looking it full in face,
An old dog, bald and blindish, at his heels.
They turned up, now, the alley by the church,
That leads no whither; now, they breathed themselves
On the main promenade just at the wrong time.
You'd come upon his scrutinising hat,
Making a peaked shade blacker than itself
Against the single window spared some house
Intact yet with its mouldered Moorish work,—
Or else surprise the ferrel of his stick   *20*
Trying the mortar's temper 'tween the chinks
Of some new shop a-building, French and fine.
He stood and watched the cobbler at his trade,

The man who slices lemons into drink,
The coffee-roaster's brazier, and the boys
That volunteer to help him turn its winch.
He glanced o'er books on stalls with half an eye,
And fly-leaf ballads on the vendor's string,
And broad-edge bold-print posters by the wall.
He took such cognisance of men and things,　　　　30
If any beat a horse, you felt he saw;
If any cursed a woman, he took note;
Yet stared at nobody,—they stared at him,
And found, less to their pleasure than surprise,
He seemed to know them and expect as much.
So, next time that a neighbour's tongue was loosed,
It marked the shameful and notorious fact,
We had among us, not so much a spy,
As a recording chief-inquisitor,
The town's true master if the town but knew!　　　40
We merely kept a Governor for form,
While this man walked about and took account
Of all thought, said, and acted, then went home,
And wrote it fully to our Lord the King
Who has an itch to know things, He knows why,
And reads them in His bed-room of a night.
Oh, you might smile! there wanted not a touch,
A tang of . . . well, it was not wholly ease
As back into your mind the man's look came—
Stricken in years a little,—such a brow　　　　50
His eyes had to live under!—clear as flint
On either side the formidable nose
Curved, cut, and coloured, like an eagle's claw.
Had he to do with A.'s surprising fate?
When altogether old B. disappeared
And young C. got his mistress,—was't our friend,
His letter to the King, that did it all?
What paid the bloodless man for so much pains?
Our Lord the King has favourites manifold,
And shifts his ministry some once a month;　　　60
Our city gets new Governors at whiles,—
But never word or sign, that I could hear,
Notified to this man about the streets
The King's approval of those letters conned
The last thing duly at the dead of night.
Did the man love his office? frowned our Lord,

Exhorting when none heard—" Beseech me not!
Too far above my people,—beneath Me!
I set the watch,—how should the people know?
Forget them, keep Me all the more in mind!"   70
Was some such understanding 'twixt the Two?

I found no truth in one report at least—
That if you tracked him to his home, down lanes
Beyond the Jewry, and as clean to pace,
You found he ate his supper in a room
Blazing with lights, four Titians on the wall,
And twenty naked girls to change his plate!
Poor man, he lived another kind of life
In that new, stuccoed, third house by the bridge,
Fresh-painted, rather smart than otherwise!   80
The whole street might o'erlook him as he sat,
Leg crossing leg, one foot on the dog's back,
Playing a decent cribbage with his maid
(Jacynth, you're sure her name was) o'er the cheese
And fruit, three red halves of starved winter-pears,
Or treat of radishes in April! nine—
Ten, struck the church clock, straight to bed went he.

My father, like the man of sense he was,
Would point him out to me a dozen times;
" St—St," he'd whisper, " the Corregidor!"   90
I had been used to think that personage
Was one with lacquered breeches, lustrous belt,
And feathers like a forest in his hat,
Who blew a trumpet and proclaimed the news,
Announced the bull-fights, gave each church its turn,
And memorized the miracle in vogue!
He had a great observance from us boys—
I was in error; that was not the man.

I'd like now, yet had haply been afraid,
To have just looked, when this man came to die,   100
And seen who lined the clean gay garret's sides
And stood about the neat low truckle-bed,
With the heavenly manner of relieving guard.
Here had been, mark, the general-in-chief,
Thro' a whole campaign of the world's life and death,
Doing the King's work all the dim day long,

In his old coat, and up to his knees in mud,
Smoked like a herring, dining on a crust,—
And now the day was won, relieved at once!
No further show or need for that old coat,   *110*
You are sure, for one thing!   Bless us, all the while
How sprucely we are dressed out, you and I!
A second, and the angels alter that.
Well, I could never write a verse,—could you?
Let's to the Prado and make the most of time.

THE LAST RIDE TOGETHER.

I. I SAID—Then, dearest, since 'tis so,
  Since now at length my fate I know,
  Since nothing all my love avails,
  Since all my life seemed meant for, fails,
    Since this was written and needs must be—
  My whole heart rises up to bless
  Your name in pride and thankfulness!
  Take back the hope you gave,—I claim
  Only a memory of the same,
    —And this beside, if you will not blame,   *10*
    Your leave for one more last ride with me.

II. My mistress bent that brow of hers,
  Those deep dark eyes where pride demurs
  When pity would be softening through,
  Fixed me a breathing-while or two
    With life or death in the balance—Right!
  The blood replenished me again:
  My last thought was at least not vain.
  I and my mistress, side by side
  Shall be together, breathe and ride,   *20*
  So one day more am I deified.
    Who knows but the world may end to-night?

III. Hush! if you saw some western cloud
  All billowy-bosomed, over-bowed
  By many benedictions—sun's
  And moon's and evening star's at once—
    And so, you, looking and loving best,
  Conscious grew, your passion drew
  Cloud, sunset, moonrise, star-shine too

Down on you, near and yet more near,   30
Till flesh must fade for heaven was here!—
Thus leant she and lingered—joy and fear!
    Thus lay she a moment on my breast.

IV. Then we began to ride. My soul
Smoothed itself out, a long-cramped scroll
Freshening and fluttering in the wind.
Past hopes already lay behind.
    What need to strive with a life awry?
Had I said that, had I done this,
So might I gain, so might I miss.   40
Might she have loved me? just as well
She might have hated,—who can tell?
Where had I been now if the worst befell?
    And here we are riding, she and I.

V. Fail I alone, in words and deeds?
Why, all men strive and who succeeds?
We rode; it seemed my spirit flew,
Saw other regions, cities new,
    As the world rushed by on either side.
I thought, All labour, yet no less   50
Bear up beneath their unsuccess.
Look at the end of work, contrast
The petty Done, the Undone vast,
This present of theirs with the hopeful past!
    I hoped she would love me.   Here we ride.

VI. What hand and brain went ever paired?
What heart alike conceived and dared?
What act proved all its thought had been?
What will but felt the fleshly screen?
    We ride and I see her bosom heave.   60
There's many a crown for who can reach.
Ten lines, a statesman's life in each!
The flag stuck on a heap of bones,
A soldier's doing! what atones?
They scratch his name on the Abbey-stones.
    My riding is better, by their leave.

VII. What does it all mean, poet? well,
Your brain's beat into rhythm—you tell
What we felt only; you expressed

73

You hold things beautiful the best,   70
   And pace them in rhyme so, side by side.
'Tis something, nay 'tis much—but then,
Have you yourself what's best for men?
Are you—poor, sick, old ere your time—
Nearer one whit your own sublime
Than we who never have turned a rhyme?
   Sing, riding's a joy! For me, I ride.

VIII. And you, great sculptor—so you gave
   A score of years to art, her slave,
   And that's your Venus—whence we turn   80
To yonder girl that fords the burn!
   You acquiesce and shall I repine?
What, man of music, you, grown grey
With notes and nothing else to say,
Is this your sole praise from a friend,
" Greatly his opera's strains intend,
But in music we know how fashions end! "
   I gave my youth—but we ride, in fine.

IX. Who knows what's fit for us? Had fate
   Proposed bliss here should sublimate   90
   My being; had I signed the bond—
Still one must lead some life beyond,
   —Have a bliss to die with, dim-descried.
This foot once planted on the goal,
This glory-garland round my soul,
Could I descry such? Try and test!
I sink back shuddering from the quest—
Earth being so good, would Heaven seem best?
   Now, Heaven and she are beyond this ride.

X. And yet—she has not spoke so long!   100
   What if Heaven be, that, fair and strong
   At life's best, with our eyes upturned
Whither life's flower is first discerned,
   We, fixed so, ever should so abide?
What if we still ride on, we two,
With life for ever old yet new,
Changed not in kind but in degree,
The instant made eternity,—
And Heaven just prove that I and she
   Ride, ride together, for ever ride?   110

THE PATRIOT.

AN OLD STORY.

I. IT was roses, roses, all the way,
   With myrtle mixed in my path like mad.
The house-roofs seemed to heave and sway
   The church-spires flamed, such flags they had,
A year ago on this very day!

II. The air broke into a mist with bells,
   The old walls rocked with the crowds and cries.
Had I said, "Good folks, mere noise repels—
   But give me your sun from yonder skies!"
They had answered, "And afterward, what else?"   10

III. Alack, it was I who leaped at the sun,
   To give it my loving friends to keep.
Nought man could do, have I left undone
   And you see my harvest, what I reap
This very day, now a year is run.

IV. There's nobody on the house-tops now—
   Just a palsied few at the windows set—
For the best of the sight is, all allow,
   At the Shambles' Gate—or, better yet,
By the very scaffold's foot, I trow.   20

V. I go in the rain, and, more than needs,
   A rope cuts both my wrists behind,
And I think, by the feel, my forehead bleeds,
   For they fling, whoever has a mind,
Stones at me for my year's misdeeds.

VI. Thus I entered Brescia, and thus I go!
   In such triumphs, people have dropped down dead.
"Thou, paid by the World,—what dost thou owe
   Me?" God might have questioned: but now instead
'Tis God shall requite! I am safer so.   30

MASTER HUGUES OF SAXE-GOTHA.

AN UNKNOWN MUSICIAN.

I. Hist, but a word, fair and soft!
    Forth and be judged, Master Hugues!
Answer the question I've put you so oft—
    What do you mean by your mountainous fugues?
See, we're alone in the loft,

II. I, the poor organist here,
    Hugues, the composer of note—
Dead, though, and done with, this many a year—
    Let's have a colloquy, something to quote,
Make the world prick up its ear!   10

III. See, the church empties a-pace.
    Fast they extinguish the lights—
Hallo, there, sacristan! five minutes' grace!
    Here's a crank pedal wants setting to rights,
Baulks one of holding the base.

IV. See, our huge house of the sounds
    Hushing its hundreds at once,
Bids the last loiterer back to his bounds
    —Oh, you may challenge them, not a response
Get the church saints on their rounds!   20

V. (Saints go their rounds, who shall doubt?
    —March, with the moon to admire,
Up nave, down chancel, turn transept about,
    Supervise all betwixt pavement and spire,
Put rats and mice to the rout—

VI. Aloys and Jurien and Just—
    Order things back to their place,
Have a sharp eye lest the candlesticks rust,
    Rub the church plate, darn the sacrament lace,
Clear the desk velvet of dust.)   30

VII. Here's your book, younger folks shelve!
    Played I not off-hand and runningly,
Just now, your masterpiece, hard number twelve?
    Here's what should strike,—could one handle it
        cunningly.
Help the axe, give it a helve!

VIII. Page after page as I played,
    Every bar's rest where one wipes
Sweat from one's brow, I looked up and surveyed
    O'er my three claviers, yon forest of pipes
Whence you still peeped in the shade.   *40*

IX. Sure you were wishful to speak,
    You, with brow ruled like a score,
Yes, and eyes buried in pits on each cheek.
    Like two great breves as they wrote them of yore
Each side that bar, your straight beak!

X. Sure you said—" Good, the mere notes!
    Still, couldst thou take my intent,
Know what procured me our Company's votes—
    Masters being lauded and sciolists shent,
Parted the sheep from the goats!"   *50*

XI. Well then, speak up, never flinch!
    Quick, ere my candle's a snuff
—Burnt, do you see? to its uttermost inch—
    I believe in you, but that's not enough.
Give my conviction a clinch!

XII. First you deliver your phrase
    —Nothing propound, that I see,
Fit in itself for much blame or much praise—
    Answered no less, where no answer needs be:
Off start the Two on their ways!   *60*

XIII. Straight must a Third interpose,
    Volunteer needlessly help—
In strikes a Fourth, a Fifth thrusts in his nose,
    So the cry's open, the kennel's a-yelp,
Argument's hot to the close!

XIV. One dissertates, he is candid—
    Two must discept,—has distinguished!
Three helps the couple, if ever yet man did:
    Four protests, Five makes a dart at the thing
        wished—
Back to One, goes the case bandied!   *70*

XV. One says his say with a difference—
    More of expounding, explaining!
All now is wrangle, abuse, and vociferance—

Now there's a truce, all's subdued, self-restrain-
ing—
Five, though, stands out all the stiffer hence.

XVI. One is incisive, corrosive—
Two retorts, nettled, curt, crepitant—
Three makes rejoinder, expansive, explosive—
Four overbears them all, strident and strepitant—
Five . . . O Danaides, O Sieve!　　　　　　　　*80*

XVII. Now, they ply axes and crowbars—
Now, they prick pins at a tissue
Fine as a skein of the casuist Escobar's
Worked on the bone of a lie. To what issue?
Where is our gain at the Two-bars?

XVIII. *Est fuga, volvitur rota !*
On we drift. Where looms the dim port?
One, Two, Three, Four, Five, contribute their quota—
Something is gained, if one caught but the import—
Show it us, Hugues of Saxe-Gotha!　　　　　　*90*

XIX. What with affirming, denying,
Holding, risposting, subjoining,
All's like . . . it's like . . . for an instance I'm
trying . . .
There! See our roof, its gilt moulding and groining
Under those spider-webs lying!

XX. So your fugue broadens and thickens,
Greatens and deepens and lengthens,
Till one exclaims—" But where's music, the dickens?
Blot ye the gold, while your spider-web strengthens,
Blacked to the stoutest of tickens?"　　　　　*100*

XXI. I for man's effort am zealous.
Prove me such censure's unfounded!
Seems it surprising a lover grows jealous—
Hopes 'twas for something his organ-pipes sounded,
Tiring three boys at the bellows?

XXII. Is it your moral of Life?
Such a web, simple and subtle,
Weave we on earth here in impotent strife,
Backward and forward each throwing his shuttle,
Death ending all with a knife?　　　　　　　*110*

XXIII. Over our heads Truth and Nature—
    Still our life's zigzags and dodges,
Ins and outs weaving a new legislature—
    God's gold just shining its last where that lodges,
Palled beneath Man's usurpature!

XXIV. So we o'ershroud stars and roses,
    Cherub and trophy and garland.
Nothings grow something which quietly closes
    Heaven's earnest eye,—not a glimpse of the far
        land
Gets through our comments and glozes.   *120*

XXV. Ah, but traditions, inventions,
    (Say we and make up a visage)
So many men with such various intentions
    Down the past ages must know more than this age!
Leave the web all its dimensions!

XXVI. Who thinks Hugues wrote for the deaf?
    Proved a mere mountain in labour?
Better submit—try again—what's the clef?
    'Faith, it's no trifle for pipe and for tabor—
Four flats—the minor in F.   *130*

XXVII. Friend, your fugue taxes the finger.
    Learning it once, who would lose it?
Yet all the while a misgiving will linger—
    Truth's golden o'er us although we refuse it—
Nature, thro' dust-clouds we fling her!

XXVIII. Hugues! I advise *meâ pœnâ*
    (Counterpoint glares like a Gorgon)
Bid One, Two, Three, Four, Five, clear the arena!
    Say the word, straight I unstop the Full-Organ,
Blare out the *mode Palestrina*.   *140*

XXIX. While in the roof, if I'm right there—
    . . . Lo, you, the wick in the socket!
Hallo, you sacristan, show us a light there!
    Down it dips, gone like a rocket!
What, you want, do you, to come unawares,
Sweeping the church up for first morning-prayers,
And find a poor devil at end of his cares
At the foot of your rotten-planked rat-riddled stairs?
    Do I carry the moon in my pocket?

BISHOP BLOUGRAM'S APOLOGY.

No more wine?   Then we'll push back chairs and talk.
A final glass for me, tho'; cool, i'faith!
We ought to have our Abbey back, you see.
It's different, preaching in basilicas,
And doing duty in some masterpiece
Like this of brother Pugin's, bless his heart!
I doubt if they're half baked, those chalk rosettes,
Ciphers and stucco-twiddlings everywhere;
It's just like breathing in a lime-kiln: eh?
These hot long ceremonies of our church   10
Cost us a little—oh, they pay the price,
You take me—amply pay it!   Now, we'll talk.

So, you despise me, Mr. Gigadibs.
No deprecation,—nay, I beg you, sir!
Beside 'tis our engagement: don't you know,
I promised, if you'd watch a dinner out,
We'd see truth dawn together?—truth that peeps
Over the glass's edge when dinner's done,
And body gets its sop and holds its noise
And leaves soul free a little.   Now's the time—   20
'Tis break of day!   You do despise me then.
And if I say, " despise me,"—never fear—
I know you do not in a certain sense—
Not in my arm-chair for example: here,
I well imagine you respect my place
(Status, *entourage*, worldly circumstance)
Quite to its value—very much indeed
—Are up to the protesting eyes of you
In pride at being seated here for once—
You'll turn it to such capital account!   30
When somebody, through years and years to come,
Hints of the bishop,—names me—that's enough—
" Blougram?   I knew him "—(into it you slide)
" Dined with him once, a Corpus Christi Day,
All alone, we two—he's a clever man—
And after dinner,—why, the wine you know,—
Oh, there was wine, and good!—what with the wine . . .
'Faith, we began upon all sorts of talk!

He's no bad fellow, Blougram—he had seen
Something of mine he relished—some review— 40
He's quite above their humbug in his heart,
Half-said as much, indeed—the thing's his trade—
I warrant, Blougram's sceptical at times—
How otherwise? I liked him, I confess!"
Che ch'è, my dear sir, as we say at Rome,
Don't you protest now! It's fair give and take;
You have had your turn and spoken your home-truths—
The hand's mine now, and here you follow suit.

    Thus much conceded, still the first fact stays—
You do despise me; your ideal of life 50
Is not the bishop's—you would not be I—
You would like better to be Goethe, now,
Or Buonaparte—or, bless me, lower still,
Count D'Orsay,—so you did what you preferred,
Spoke as you thought, and, as you cannot help,
Believed or disbelieved, no matter what,
So long as on that point, whate'er it was,
You loosed your mind, were whole and sole yourself.
—That, my ideal never can include,
Upon that element of truth and worth 60
Never be based! for say they make me Pope
(They can't—suppose it for our argument)
Why, there I'm at my tether's end—I've reached
My height, and not a height which pleases you.
An unbelieving Pope won't do, you say.
It's like those eerie stories nurses tell,
Of how some actor played Death on a stage
With pasteboard crown, sham orb, and tinselled dart,
And called himself the monarch of the world,
Then going in the tire-room afterward 70
Because the play was done, to shift himself,
Got touched upon the sleeve familiarly
The moment he had shut the closet door
By Death himself. Thus God might touch a Pope
At unawares, ask what his baubles mean,
And whose part he presumed to play just now?
Best be yourself, imperial, plain and true!

So, drawing comfortable breath again,
You weigh and find whatever more or less

I boast of my ideal realised   80
Is nothing in the balance when opposed
To your ideal, your grand simple life,
Of which you will not realise one jot.
I am much, you are nothing; you would be all,
I would be merely much—you beat me there.

No, friend, you do not beat me,—hearken why.
The common problem, yours, mine, every one's,
Is not to fancy what were fair in life
Provided it could be,—but, finding first
What may be, then find how to make it fair   90
Up to our means—a very different thing!
No abstract intellectual plan of life
Quite irrespective of life's plainest laws,
But one, a man, who is man and nothing more,
May lead within a world which (by your leave)
Is Rome or London—not Fool's-paradise.
Embellish Rome, idealise away,
Make Paradise of London if you can,
You're welcome, nay, you're wise.

                          A simile!   100
We mortals cross the ocean of this world
Each in his average cabin of a life—
The best's not big, the worst yields elbow-room.
Now for our six months' voyage—how prepare?
You come on shipboard with a landsman's list
Of things he calls convenient—so they are!
An India screen is pretty furniture,
A piano-forte is a fine resource,
All Balzac's novels occupy one shelf,
The new edition fifty volumes long;   110
And little Greek books with the funny type
They get up well at Leipsic fill the next—
Go on! slabbed marble, what a bath it makes!
And Parma's pride, the Jerome, let us add!
'Twere pleasant could Correggio's fleeting glow
Hang full in face of one where'er one roams;
Since he more than the others brings with him
Italy's self,—the marvellous Modenese!
Yet 'twas not on your list before, perhaps.
—Alas! friend, here's the agent . . . is't the name? 120

The captain, or whoever's master here—
You see him screw his face up; what's his cry
Ere you set foot on shipboard? " Six feet square! "
If you won't understand what six feet mean,
Compute and purchase stores accordingly—
And if in pique because he overhauls
Your Jerome, piano and bath, you come on board
Bare—why you cut a figure at the first
While sympathetic landsmen see you off;
Not afterwards, when, long ere half seas o'er,   *130*
You peep up from your utterly naked boards
Into some snug and well-appointed berth
Like mine, for instance (try the cooler jug—
Put back the other, but don't jog the ice)
And mortified you mutter " Well and good—
He sits enjoying his sea-furniture—
'Tis stout and proper, and there's store of it,
Though I've the better notion, all agree,
Of fitting rooms up! hang the carpenter,
Neat ship-shape fixings and contrivances—   *140*
I would have brought my Jerome, frame and all! "
And meantime you bring nothing: never mind—
You've proved your artist-nature: what you don't,
You might bring, so despise me, as I say.

Now come, let's backward to the starting place.
See my way: we're two college friends, suppose—
Prepare together for our voyage, then,
Each note and check the other in his work,—
Here's mine, a bishop's outfit; criticise!
What's wrong? why won't you be a bishop too?   *150*

Why, first, you don't believe, you don't and can't,
(Not statedly, that is, and fixedly
And absolutely and exclusively)
In any revelation called divine.
No dogmas nail your faith—and what remains
But say so, like the honest man you are?
First, therefore, overhaul theology!
Nay, I too, not a fool, you please to think,
Must find believing every whit as hard,
And if I do not frankly say as much,   *160*
The ugly consequence is clear enough.

Now, wait, my friend: well, I do not believe—
If you'll accept no faith that is not fixed,
Absolute and exclusive, as you say.
(You're wrong—I mean to prove it in due time)
Meanwhile, I know where difficulties lie
I could not, cannot solve, nor ever shall,
So give up hope accordingly to solve—
(To you, and over the wine). Our dogmas then
With both of us, tho' in unlike degree,   *170*
Missing full credence—overboard with them!
I mean to meet you on your own premise—
Good, there go mine in company with yours!

And now what are we? unbelievers both,
Calm and complete, determinately fixed
To-day, to-morrow, and for ever, pray?
You'll guarantee me that? Not so, I think.
In no-wise! all we've gained is, that belief,
As unbelief before, shakes us by fits,
Confounds us like its predecessor. Where's   *180*
The gain? how can we guard our unbelief,
Make it bear fruit to us?—the problem here.
Just when we are safest, there's a sunset-touch,
A fancy from a flower-bell, some one's death,
A chorus-ending from Euripides,—
And that's enough for fifty hopes and fears
As old and new at once as Nature's self,
To rap and knock and enter in our soul,
Take hands and dance there, a fantastic ring,
Round the ancient idol, on his base again,—   *190*
The grand Perhaps! we look on helplessly,—
There the old misgivings, crooked questions are—
This good God,—what he could do, if he would,
Would, if he could—then must have done long since:
If so, when, where, and how? some way must be,—
Once feel about, and soon or late you hit
Some sense, in which it might be, after all.
Why not, "The Way, the Truth, the Life?"

                         —That **way**
Over the mountain, which who stands upon
Is apt to doubt if it's indeed a road;   *200*
While if he views it from the waste itself,

Up goes the line there, plain from base to brow,
Not vague, mistakeable! what's a break or two
Seen from the unbroken desert either side?
And then (to bring in fresh philosophy)
What if the breaks themselves should prove at last
The most consummate of contrivances
To train a man's eye, teach him what is faith,—
And so we stumble at truth's very test?
What have we gained then by our unbelief   210
But a life of doubt diversified by faith,
For one of faith diversified by doubt?
We called the chess-board white,—we call it black.

" Well," you rejoin, " the end's no worse, at least,
We've reason for both colours on the board.
Why not confess, then, where I drop the faith
And you the doubt, that I'm as right as you? "

Because, friend, in the next place, this being so,
And both things even,—faith and unbelief
Left to a man's choice,—we'll proceed a step,   220
Returning to our image, which I like.

A man's choice, yes—but a cabin-passenger's—
The man made for the special life of the world—
Do you forget him?   I remember though!
Consult our ship's conditions and you find
One and but one choice suitable to all,
The choice that you unluckily prefer
Turning things topsy-turvy—they or it
Going to the ground.   Belief or unbelief
Bears upon life, determines its whole course,   230
Begins at its beginning.   See the world
Such as it is,—you made it not, nor I;
I mean to take it as it is,—and you
Not so you'll take it,—though you get nought else.
I know the special kind of life I like,
What suits the most my idiosyncrasy,
Brings out the best of me and bears me fruit
In power, peace, pleasantness, and length of days.
I find that positive belief does this
For me, and unbelief, no whit of this.   240
—For you, it does, however—that we'll try!

'Tis clear, I cannot lead my life, at least
Induce the world to let me peaceably,
Without declaring at the outset, " Friends,
I absolutely and peremptorily
Believe ! "—I say faith is my waking life.
One sleeps, indeed, and dreams at intervals,
We know, but waking's the main point with us,
And my provision's for life's waking part.
Accordingly, I use heart, head and hands   *250*
All day, I build, scheme, study and make friends;
And when night overtakes me, down I lie,
Sleep, dream a little, and get done with it,
The sooner the better, to begin afresh.
What's midnight's doubt before the dayspring's faith?
You, the philosopher, that disbelieve,
That recognise the night, give dreams their weight—
To be consistent you should keep your bed,
Abstain from healthy acts that prove you a man,
For fear you drowse perhaps at unawares !   *260*
And certainly at night you'll sleep and dream,
Live through the day and bustle as you please.
And so you live to sleep as I to wake,
To unbelieve as I to still believe ?
Well, and the common sense of the world calls you
Bed-ridden,—and its good things come to me.
Its estimation, which is half the fight,
That's the first cabin-comfort I secure—
The next . . . but you perceive with half an eye !
Come, come, it's best believing, if we can—   *270*
You can't but own that.

                    Next, concede again—
If once we choose belief, on all accounts
We can't be too decisive in our faith,
Conclusive and exclusive in its terms,
To suit the world which gives us the good things.
In every man's career are certain points
Whereon he dares not be indifferent;
The world detects him clearly, if he is,
As baffled at the game, and losing life.
He may care little or he may care much   *280*
For riches, honour, pleasure, work, repose,
Since various theories of life and life's

Success are extant which might easily
Comport with either estimate of these,
And whoso chooses wealth or poverty,
Labour or quiet, is not judged a fool
Because his fellows would choose otherwise.
We let him choose upon his own account
So long as he's consistent with his choice.
But certain points, left wholly to himself,   *290*
When once a man has arbitrated on,
We say he must succeed there or go hang.
Thus, he should wed the woman he loves most
Or needs most, whatsoe'er the love or need—
For he can't wed twice. Then, he must avouch
Or follow, at the least, sufficiently,
The form of faith his conscience holds the best,
Whate'er the process of conviction was.
For nothing can compensate his mistake
On such a point, the man himself being judge—   *300*
He cannot wed twice, nor twice lose his soul.

Well now—there's one great form of Christian faith
I happened to be born in—which to teach
Was given me as I grew up, on all hands,
As best and readiest means of living by;
The same on examination being proved
The most pronounced moreover, fixed, precise
And absolute form of faith in the whole world—
Accordingly, most potent of all forms
For working on the world. Observe, my friend,   *310*
Such as you know me, I am free to say,
In these hard latter days which hamper one,
Myself, by no immoderate exercise
Of intellect and learning, and the tact
To let external forces work for me,
Bid the street's stones be bread and they are bread,
Bid Peter's creed, or, rather, Hildebrand's,
Exalt me o'er my fellows in the world.
And make my life an ease and joy and pride,
It does so,—which for me's a great point gained,   *320*
Who have a soul and body that exact
A comfortable care in many ways.
There's power in me and will to dominate
Which I must exercise, they hurt me else:

In many ways I need mankind's respect,
Obedience, and the love that's born of fear:
While at the same time, there's a taste I have,
A toy of soul, a titillating thing,
Refuses to digest these dainties crude.
The naked life is gross till clothed upon: *330*
I must take what men offer, with a grace
As though I would not, could I help it, take!
A uniform to wear though over-rich—
Something imposed on me, no choice of mine;
No fancy-dress worn for pure fashion's sake
And despicable therefore! now men kneel
And kiss my hand—of course the Church's hand.
Thus I am made, thus life is best for me,
And thus that it should be I have procured;
And thus it could not be another way,   *340*
I venture to imagine.
                    You'll reply—
So far my choice, no doubt, is a success;
But were I made of better elements,
With nobler instincts, purer tastes, like you,
I hardly would account the thing success
Though it do all for me I say.
                              But, friend,
We speak of what is—not of what might be,
And how 'twere better if 'twere otherwise.
I am the man you see here plain enough—
Grant I'm a beast, why beasts must lead beasts' lives   *350*
Suppose I own at once to tail and claws—
The tailless man exceeds me; but being tailed
I'll lash out lion-fashion, and leave apes
To dock their stump and dress their haunches up.
My business is not to remake myself,
But make the absolute best of what God made.
Or—our first simile—though you proved me doomed
To a viler berth still, to the steerage-hole,
The sheep-pen or the pig-stye, I should strive
To make what use of each were possible;   *360*
And as this cabin gets upholstery,
That hutch should rustle with sufficient straw.

But, friend, I don't acknowledge quite so fast
I fail of all your manhood's lofty tastes

Enumerated so complacently,
On the mere ground that you forsooth can find
In this particular life I choose to lead
No fit provision for them. Can you not?
Say you, my fault is I address myself
To grosser estimators than I need,   370
And that's no way of holding up the soul—
Which, nobler, needs men's praise perhaps, yet knows
One wise man's verdict outweighs all the fools',—
Would like the two, but, forced to choose, takes that?
I pine among my million imbeciles
(You think) aware some dozen men of sense
Eye me and know me, whether I believe
In the last winking Virgin, as I vow,
And am a fool, or disbelieve in her
And am a knave,—approve in neither case,   380
Withhold their voices though I look their way:
Like Verdi when, at his worst opera's end
(The thing they gave at Florence,—what's its name?)
While the mad houseful's plaudits near out-bang
His orchestra of salt-box, tongs and bones,
He looks through all the roaring and the wreaths
Where sits Rossini patient in his stall.

    Nay, friend, I meet you with an answer here—
For even your prime men who appraise their kind
Are men still, catch a thing within a thing,   390
See more in a truth than the truth's simple self,
Confuse themselves. You see lads walk the street
Sixty the minute; what's to note in that?
You see one lad o'erstride a chimney-stack;
Him you must watch—he's sure to fall, yet stands!
Our interest's on the dangerous edge of things.
The honest thief, the tender murderer,
The superstitious atheist, demireps
That love and save their souls in new French books—
We watch while these in equilibrium keep   400
The giddy line midway: one step aside,
They're classed and done with. I, then, keep the line
Before your sages,—just the men to shrink
From the gross weights, coarse scales, and labels broad
You offer their refinement. Fool or knave?
Why needs a bishop be a fool or knave

When there's a thousand diamond weights between?
So I enlist them.   Your picked Twelve, you'll find,
Profess themselves indignant, scandalised
At thus being held unable to explain   410
How a superior man who disbelieves
May not believe as well: that's Schelling's way!
It's through my coming in the tail of time,
Nicking the minute with a happy tact.
Had I been born three hundred years ago
They'd say, "What's strange? Blougram of course believes;"
And, seventy years since, "disbelieves of course."
But now, "He may believe; and yet, and yet
How can he?"—All eyes turn with interest.
Whereas, step off the line on either side—   420
You, for example, clever to a fault,
The rough and ready man that write apace,
Read somewhat seldomer, think perhaps even less—
You disbelieve!   Who wonders and who cares?
Lord So-and-So—his coat bedropt with wax,
All Peter's chains about his waist, his back
Brave with the needlework of Noodledom,
Believes!   Again, who wonders and who cares?
But I, the man of sense and learning too,
The able to think yet act, the this, the that,   430
I, to believe at this late time of day!
Enough; you see, I need not fear contempt.

   —Except it's yours! admire me as these may,
You don't.   But what at least do you admire?
Present your own perfections, your ideal,
Your pattern man for a minute—oh, make haste!
Is it Napoleon you would have us grow?
Concede the means; allow his head and hand,
(A large concession, clever as you are)
Good!—In our common primal element   440
Of unbelief (we can't believe, you know—
We're still at that admission, recollect)
Where do you find—apart from, towering-o'er
The secondary temporary aims
Which satisfy the gross tastes you despise—
Where do you find his star?—his crazy trust
God knows through what or in what? it's alive
And shines and leads him and that's all we want.

Have we ought in our sober night shall point
Such ends as his were, and direct the means   *450*
Of working out our purpose straight as his,
Nor bring a moment's trouble on success,
With after-care to justify the same?
—Be a Napoleon and yet disbelieve!
Why, the man's mad, friend, take his light away.
What's the vague good of the world for which you'd dare
With comfort to yourself blow millions up?
We neither of us see it! we do see
The blown-up millions—spatter of their brains
And writhing of their bowels and so forth,   *460*
In that bewildering entanglement
Of horrible eventualities
Past calculation to the end of time!
Can I mistake for some clear word of God
(Which were my ample warrant for it all)
His puff of hazy instincts, idle talk,
" The state, that's I," quack-nonsense about kings,
And (when one beats the man to his last hold)
The vague idea of setting things to rights,
Policing people efficaciously,   *470*
More to their profit, most of all to his own;
The whole to end that dismallest of ends
By an Austrian marriage, cant to us the church,
And resurrection of the old *régime*.
Would I, who hope to live a dozen years,
Fight Austerlitz for reasons such and such?
No: for, concede me but the merest chance
Doubt may be wrong—there's judgment, life to come!
With just that chance, I dare not.   Doubt proves right?
This present life is all? you offer me   *480*
Its dozen noisy years with not a chance
That wedding an Arch-Duchess, wearing lace,
And getting called by divers new-coined names,
Will drive off ugly thoughts and let me dine,
Sleep, read and chat in quiet as I like!
Therefore, I will not.
                    Take another case;
Fit up the cabin yet another way.
What say you to the poet's? shall we write
Hamlets, Othellos—make the world our own,
Without a risk to run of either sort?   *490*

91

I can't!—to put the strongest reason first.
" But try," you urge, " the trying shall suffice:
The aim, if reached or not, makes great the life.
Try to be Shakspeare, leave the rest to fate! "
Spare my self-knowledge—there's no fooling me!
If I prefer remaining my poor self,
I say so not in self-dispraise but praise.
If I'm a Shakspeare, let the well alone—
Why should I try to be what now I am?
If I'm no Shakspeare, as too probable,———————————500
His power and consciousness and self-delight
And all we want in common, shall I find—
Trying for ever? while on points of taste
Wherewith, to speak it humbly, he and I
Are dowered alike—I'll ask you, I or he,
Which in our two lives realises most?
Much, he imagined—somewhat, I possess.
He had the imagination; stick to that!
Let him say " In the face of my soul's works
Your world is worthless and I touch it not———————510
Lest I should wrong them "—I withdraw my plea.
But does he say so? look upon his life!
Himself, who only can, gives judgment there.
He leaves his towers and gorgeous palaces
To build the trimmest house in Stratford town;
Saves money, spends it, owns the worth of things,
Giulio Romano's pictures, Dowland's lute;
Enjoys a show, respects the puppets, too,
And none more, had he seen its entry once,
Than " Pandulph, of fair Milan cardinal."———————520
Why then should I who play that personage,
The very Pandulph Shakspeare's fancy made,
Be told that had the poet chanced to start
From where I stand now (some degree like mine
Being just the goal he ran his race to reach)
He would have run the whole race back, forsooth,
And left being Pandulph, to begin write plays?
Ah, the earth's best can be but the earth's best!
Did Shakspeare live, he could but sit at home
And get himself in dreams the Vatican,———————530
Greek busts, Venetian paintings, Roman walls,
And English books, none equal to his own,
Which I read, bound in gold, (he never did).

—Terni and Naples' bay and Gothard's top—
Eh, friend?   I could not fancy one of these—
But, as I pour this claret, there they are—
I've gained them—crossed St. Gothard last July
With ten mules to the carriage and a bed
Slung inside; is my hap the worse for that?
We want the same things, Shakspeare and myself,   540
And what I want, I have: he, gifted more,
Could fancy he too had it when he liked,
But not so thoroughly that if fate allowed
He would not have it also in my sense.
We play one game.   I send the ball aloft
No less adroitly that of fifty strokes
Scarce five go o'er the wall so wide and high
Which sends them back to me: I wish and get.
He struck balls higher and with better skill,
But at a poor fence level with his head,   550
And hit—his Stratford house, a coat of arms,
Successful dealings in his grain and wool,—
While I receive heaven's incense in my nose
And style myself the cousin of Queen Bess.
Ask him, if this life's all, who wins the game?

    Believe—and our whole argument breaks up.
Enthusiasm's the best thing, I repeat;
Only, we can't command it; fire and life
Are all, dead matter's nothing; we agree:
And be it a mad dream or God's very breath,   560
The fact's the same,—belief's fire once in us,
Makes of all else mere stuff to show itself,
We penetrate our life with such a glow
As fire lends wood and iron—this turns steel,
That burns to ash—all's one, fire proves its power
For good or ill, since men call flare success.
But paint a fire, it will not therefore burn.
Light one in me, I'll find it food enough!
Why, to be Luther—that's a life to lead,
Incomparably better than my own.   570
He comes, reclaims God's earth for God, he says,
Sets up God's rule again by simple means,
Re-opens a shut book, and all is done.
He flared out in the flaring of mankind;
Such Luther's luck was—how shall such be mine?

If he succeeded, nothing's left to do:
And if he did not altogether—well,
Strauss is the next advance.   All Strauss should be
I might be also.   But to what result?
He looks upon no future: Luther did.   580
What can I gain on the denying side?
Ice makes no conflagration.   State the facts,
Read the text right, emancipate the world—
The emancipated world enjoys itself
With scarce a thank-you—Blougram told it first
It could not owe a farthing,—not to him
More than St. Paul! 'twould press its pay, you think?
Then add there's still that plaguey hundredth chance
Strauss may be wrong.   And so a risk is run—
For what gain? not for Luther's, who secured   590
A real heaven in his heart throughout his life,
Supposing death a little altered things!

" Ay, but since really I lack faith," you cry,
" I run the same risk really on all sides,
In cool indifference as bold unbelief.
As well be Strauss as swing 'twixt Paul and him.
It's not worth having, such imperfect faith,
Nor more available to do faith's work
Than unbelief like yours.   Whole faith, or none!"

Softly, my friend!   I must dispute that point.   600
Once own the use of faith, I'll find you faith.
We're back on Christian ground.   You call for faith;
I show you doubt, to prove that faith exists.
The more of doubt, the stronger faith, I say,
If faith o'ercomes doubt.   How I know it does?
By life and man's free will, God gave for that!
To mould life as we choose it, shows our choice:
That's our one act, the previous work's His own.
You criticise the soil? it reared this tree—
This broad life and whatever fruit it bears!   610
What matter though I doubt at every pore,
Head-doubts, heart-doubts, doubts at my fingers' ends,
Doubts in the trivial work of every day,
Doubts at the very bases of my soul
In the grand moments when she probes herself—
If finally I have a life to show,

The thing I did, brought out in evidence
Against the thing done to me underground
By Hell and all its brood, for ought I know?
I say, whence sprang this? shows it faith or doubt?   *620*
All's doubt in me; where's break of faith in this?
It is the idea, the feeling and the love
God means mankind should strive for and show forth,
Whatever be the process to that end,—
And not historic knowledge, logic sound,
And metaphysical acumen, sure!
" What think ye of Christ," friend? when all's done and said,
You like this Christianity or not?
It may be false, but will you wish it true?
Has it your vote to be so if it can?   *630*
Trust you an instinct silenced long ago
That will break silence and enjoin you love
What mortified philosophy is hoarse,
And all in vain, with bidding you despise?
If you desire faith—then you've faith enough.
What else seeks God—nay, what else seek ourselves?
You form a notion of me, we'll suppose,
On hearsay; it's a favourable one:
" But still " (you add), " there was no such good man,
Because of contradictions in the facts.   *640*
One proves, for instance, he was born in Rome,
This Blougram—yet throughout the tales of him
I see he figures as an Englishman."
Well, the two things are reconcileable.
But would I rather you discovered that
Subjoining—" Still, what matter though they be?
Blougram—concerns me nought, born here or there."

Pure faith indeed—you know not what you ask!
Naked belief in God the Omnipotent,
Omniscient, Omnipresent, sears too much   *650*
The sense of conscious creatures to be borne.
It were the seeing him, no flesh shall dare.
Some think, Creation's meant to show him forth:
I say, it's meant to hide him all it can,
And that's what all the blessed Evil's for.
Its use in time is to environ us,
Our breath, our drop of dew, with shield enough
Against that sight till we can bear its stress.

Under a vertical sun, the exposed brain
And lidless eye and disemprisoned heart   660
Less certainly would wither up at once
Than mind, confronted with the truth of Him.
But time and earth case-harden us to live;
The feeblest sense is trusted most; the child
Feels God a moment, ichors o'er the place,
Plays on and grows to be a man like us.
With me, faith means perpetual unbelief
Kept quiet like the snake 'neath Michael's foot
Who stands calm just because he feels it writhe.
Or, if that's too ambitious,—here's my box—   670
I need the excitation of a pinch
Threatening the torpor of the inside-nose
Nigh on the imminent sneeze that never comes.
" Leave it in peace " advise the simple folk—
Make it aware of peace by itching-fits,
Say I—let doubt occasion still more faith!

You'll say, once all believed, man, woman, child,
In that dear middle-age these noodles praise.
How you'd exult if I could put you back
Six hundred years, blot out cosmogony,   680
Geology, ethnology, what not,
(Greek endings, each the little passing-bell
That signifies some faith's about to die)
And set you square with Genesis again,—
When such a traveller told you his last news,
He saw the ark a-top of Ararat
But did not climb there since 'twas getting dusk
And robber-bands infest the mountain's foot!
How should you feel, I ask, in such an age,
How act? As other people felt and did;   690
With soul more blank than this decanter's knob,
Believe—and yet lie, kill, rob, fornicate
Full in belief's face, like the beast you'd be!

No, when the fight begins within himself,
A man's worth something.   God stoops o'er his head,
Satan looks up between his feet—both tug—
He's left, himself, in the middle: the soul wakes
And grows.   Prolong that battle through his life!
Never leave growing till the life to come!

Here, we've got callous to the Virgin's winks   **700**
That used to puzzle people wholesomely—
Men have outgrown the shame of being fools.
What are the laws of Nature, not to bend
If the Church bid them, brother Newman asks.
Up with the Immaculate Conception, then—
On to the rack with faith—is my advice!
Will not that hurry us upon our knees
Knocking our breasts, " It can't be—yet it shall!
Who am I, the worm, to argue with my Pope?
Low things confound the high things!" and so forth.   **710**
That's better than acquitting God with grace
As some folks do.   He's tried—no case is proved,
Philosophy is lenient—He may go!

You'll say—the old system's not so obsolete
But men believe still: ay, but who and where?
King Bomba's lazzaroni foster yet
The sacred flame, so Antonelli writes;
But even of these, what ragamuffin-saint
Believes God watches him continually,
As he believes in fire that it will burn,   **720**
Or rain that it will drench him?   Break fire's law,
Sin against rain, although the penalty
Be just singe or soaking?   No, he smiles;
Those laws are laws that can enforce themselves.

The sum of all is—yes, my doubt is great,
My faith's the greater—then my faith's enough.
I have read much, thought much, experienced much,
Yet would die rather than avow my fear
The Naples' liquefaction may be false,
When set to happen by the palace-clock   **730**
According to the clouds or dinner-time.
I hear you recommend, I might at least
Eliminate, decrassify my faith
Since I adopt it; keeping what I must
And leaving what I can—such points as this!
I won't—that is, I can't throw one away.
Supposing there's no truth in what I said
About the need of trials to man's faith,
Still, when you bid me purify the same,
To such a process I discern no end,   **740**
Clearing off one excrescence to see two;

There's ever a next in size, now grown as big,
That meets the knife—I cut and cut again!
First cut the Liquefaction, what comes last
But Fichte's clever cut at God himself?
Experimentalize on sacred things?
I trust nor hand nor eye nor heart nor brain
To stop betimes: they all get drunk alike.
The first step, I am master not to take.

You'd find the cutting-process to your taste   750
As much as leaving growths of lies unpruned,
Nor see more danger in it, you retort.
Your taste's worth mine; but my taste proves more wise
When we consider that the steadfast hold
On the extreme end of the chain of faith
Gives all the advantage, makes the difference,
With the rough purblind mass we seek to rule.
We are their lords, or they are free of us
Just as we tighten or relax that hold.
So, other matters equal, we'll revert   760
To the first problem—which if solved my way
And thrown into the balance turns the scale—
How we may lead a comfortable life,
How suit our luggage to the cabin's size.

Of course you are remarking all this time
How narrowly and grossly I view life,
Respect the creature-comforts, care to rule
The masses, and regard complacently
" The cabin," in our old phrase!   Well, I do.
I act for, talk for, live for this world now,   770
As this world calls for action, life and talk—
No prejudice to what next world may prove,
Whose new laws and requirements my best pledge
To observe them, is that I observe these now,
Doing hereafter what I do meanwhile.
Let us concede (gratuitously though)
Next life relieves the soul of body, yields
Pure spiritual enjoyments: well, my friend,
Why lose this life in the meantime, since its use
May be to make the next life more intense?   780

Do you know, I have often had a dream
(Work it up in your next month's article)

98

Of man's poor spirit in its progress still
Losing true life for ever and a day
Through ever trying to be and ever being
In the evolution of successive spheres,
Before its actual sphere and place of life,
Halfway into the next, which having reached,
It shoots with corresponding foolery
Halfway into the next still, on and off!   790
As when a traveller, bound from north to south,
Scouts fur in Russia—what's its use in France?
In France spurns flannel—where's its need in Spain?
In Spain drops cloth—too cumbrous for Algiers!
Linen goes next, and last the skin itself,
A superfluity at Timbuctoo.
When, through his journey, was the fool at ease?
I'm at ease now, friend—worldly in this world
I take and like its way of life; I think
My brothers who administer the means   800
Live better for my comfort—that's good too;
And God, if he pronounce upon it all,
Approves my service, which is better still.
If He keep silence,—why for you or me
Or that brute-beast pulled-up in to-day's " Times,"
What odds is't, save to ourselves, what life we lead?

You meet me at this issue—you declare,
All special pleading done with, truth is truth,
And justifies itself by undreamed ways.
You don't fear but it's better, if we doubt,   810
To say so, acting up to our truth perceived
However feebly. Do then,—act away!
'Tis there I'm on the watch for you!   How one acts
Is, both of us agree, our chief concern:
And how you'll act is what I fain would see
If, like the candid person you appear,
You dare to make the most of your life's scheme
As I of mine, live up to its full law
Since there's no higher law that counterchecks.
Put natural religion to the test   820
You've just demolished the revealed with—quick,
Down to the root of all that checks your will,
All prohibition to lie, kill, and thieve
Or even to be an atheistic priest!

Suppose a pricking to incontinence—
Philosophers deduce you chastity
Or shame, from just the fact that at the first
Whoso embraced a woman in the plain,
Threw club down, and forewent his brains beside,
So stood a ready victim in the reach   830
Of any brother-savage club in hand—
Hence saw the use of going out of sight
In wood or cave to prosecute his loves—
I read this in a French book t'other day.
Does law so analyzed coerce you much?
Oh, men spin clouds of fuzz where matters end,
But you who reach where the first thread begins,
You'll soon cut that!—which means you can, but won't
Through certain instincts, blind, unreasoned-out,
You dare not set aside, you can't tell why,   840
But there they are, and so you let them rule.
Then, friend, you seem as much a slave as I,
A liar, conscious coward and hypocrite,
Without the good the slave expects to get,
Suppose he has a master after all!
You own your instincts—why what else do I,
Who want, am made for, and must have a God
Ere I can be ought, do ought?—no mere name
Want, but the true thing with what proves its truth,
To wit, a relation from that thing to me,   850
Touching from head to foot—which touch I feel,
And with it take the rest, this life of ours!
I live my life here; yours you dare not live.

   Not as I state it, who (you please subjoin)
Disfigure such a life and call it names,
While, in your mind, remains another way
For simple men: knowledge and power have rights,
But ignorance and weakness have rights too.
There needs no crucial effort to find truth
If here or there or anywhere about—   860
We ought to turn each side, try hard and see,
And if we can't, be glad we've earned at least
The right, by one laborious proof the more,
To graze in peace earth's pleasant pasturage.
Men are not gods, but, properly, are brutes.
Something we may see, all we cannot see—

What need of lying? I say, I see all,
And swear to each detail the most minute,
In what I think a man's face—you, mere cloud:
I swear I hear him speak and see him wink,   *870*
For fear, if once I drop the emphasis,
Mankind may doubt if there's a cloud at all.
You take the simpler life—ready to see,
Willing to see—for no cloud's worth a face—
And leaving quiet what no strength can move,
And which, who bids you move? who has the right?
I bid you; but you are God's sheep, not mine—
" *Pastor est tui Dominus.*" You find
In these the pleasant pastures of this life
Much you may eat without the least offence,   *880*
Much you don't eat because your maw objects,
Much you would eat but that your fellow-flock
Open great eyes at you and even butt,
And thereupon you like your friends so much
You cannot please yourself, offending them—
Though when they seem exorbitantly sheep,
You weigh your pleasure with their butts and kicks
And strike the balance. Sometimes certain fears
Restrain you—real checks since you find them so—
Sometimes you please yourself and nothing checks;   *890*
And thus you graze through life with not one lie,
And like it best.

          But do you, in truth's name?
If so, you beat—which means—you are not I—
Who needs must make earth mine and feed my fill
Not simply unbutted at, unbickered with,
But motioned to the velvet of the sward
By those obsequious wethers' very selves.
Look at me, sir; my age is double yours.
At yours, I knew beforehand, so enjoyed,
What now I should be—as, permit the word,   *900*
I pretty well imagine your whole range
And stretch of tether twenty years to come.
We both have minds and bodies much alike.
In truth's name, don't you want my bishopric,
My daily bread, my influence and my state?
You're young, I'm old, you must be old one day;
Will you find then, as I do hour by hour,

Women their lovers kneel to, that cut curls
From your fat lap-dog's ears to grace a brooch—
Dukes, that petition just to kiss your ring—   910
With much beside you know or may conceive?
Suppose we die to-night: well, here am I,
Such were my gains, life bore this fruit to me,
While writing all the same my articles
On music, poetry, the fictile vase
Found at Albano, or Anacreon's Greek.
But you—the highest honour in your life,
The thing you'll crown yourself with, all your days,
Is—dining here and drinking this last glass
I pour you out in sign of amity   920
Before we part for ever. Of your power
And social influence, worldly worth in short,
Judge what's my estimation by the fact—
I do not condescend to enjoin, beseech,
Hint secresy on one of all these words!
You're shrewd and know that should you publish it
The world would brand the lie—my enemies first,
" Who'd sneer—the bishop's an arch-hypocrite,
And knave perhaps, but not so frank a fool,"
Whereas I should not dare for both my ears   930
Breathe one such syllable, smile one such smile,
Before my chaplain who reflects myself—
My shade's so much more potent than your flesh.
What's your reward, self-abnegating friend?
Stood you confessed of those exceptional
And privileged great natures that dwarf mine—
A zealot with a mad ideal in reach,
A poet just about to print his ode,
A statesman with a scheme to stop this war,
An artist whose religion is his art,   940
I should have nothing to object! such men
Carry the fire, all things grow warm to them,
Their drugget's worth my purple, they beat me.
But you,—you're just as little those as I—
You, Gigadibs, who, thirty years of age,
Write stately for Blackwood's Magazine,
Believe you see two points in Hamlet's soul
Unseized by the Germans yet—which view you'll print—
Meantime the best you have to show being still
That lively lightsome article we took   950

Almost for the true Dickens,—what's the name?
" The Slum and Cellar—or Whitechapel life
Limned after dark ! " it made me laugh, I know,
And pleased a month and brought you in ten pounds.
—Success I recognise and compliment,
And therefore give you, if you please, three words
(The card and pencil-scratch is quite enough)
Which whether here, in Dublin, or New York,
Will get you, prompt as at my eyebrow's wink,
Such terms as never you aspired to get   960
In all our own reviews and some not ours.
Go write your lively sketches—be the first
" Blougram, or The Eccentric Confidence "—
Or better simply say, " The Outward-bound."
Why, men as soon would throw it in my teeth
As copy and quote the infamy chalked broad
About me on the church-door opposite.
You will not wait for that experience though,
I fancy, howsoever you decide,
To discontinue—not detesting, not   970
Defaming, but at least—despising me!

　　Over his wine so smiled and talked his hour
Sylvester Blougram, styled *in partibus*
Episcopus, nec non—(the deuce knows what
It's changed to by our novel hierarchy)
With Gigadibs the literary man,
Who played with spoons, explored his plate's design,
And ranged the olive stones about its edge,
While the great bishop rolled him out his mind.

　　For Blougram, he believed, say, half he spoke.   980
The other portion, as he shaped it thus
For argumentatory purposes,
He felt his foe was foolish to dispute.
Some arbitrary accidental thoughts
That crossed his mind, amusing because new,
He chose to represent as fixtures there,
Invariable convictions (such they seemed
Beside his interlocutor's loose cards
Flung daily down, and not the same way twice)
While certain hell-deep instincts, man's weak tongue   990
Is never bold to utter in their truth
Because styled hell-deep ('tis an old mistake

To place hell at the bottom of the earth)
He ignored these,—not having in readiness
Their nomenclature and philosophy:
He said true things, but called them by wrong names.
" On the whole," he thought, " I justify myself
On every point where cavillers like this
Oppugn my life: he tries one kind of fence—
I close—he's worsted, that's enough for him;   *1000*
He's on the ground! if the ground should break away
I take my stand on, there's a firmer yet
Beneath it, both of us may sink and reach.
His ground was over mine and broke the first.
So let him sit with me this many a year!"

He did not sit five minutes. Just a week
Sufficed his sudden healthy vehemence.
(Something had struck him in the " Outward-bound "
Another way than Blougram's purpose was)
And having bought, not cabin-furniture   *1010*
But settler's-implements (enough for three)
And started for Australia—there, I hope,
By this time he has tested his first plough,
And studied his last chapter of St. John.

MEMORABILIA.

I. Ah, did you once see Shelley plain,
    And did he stop and speak to you?
And did you speak to him again?
    How strange it seems, and new!

II. But you were living before that,
    And you are living after,
And the memory I started at—
    My starting moves your laughter!

III. I crossed a moor with a name of its own
    And a use in the world no doubt,   *10*
Yet a hand's-breadth of it shines alone
    'Mid the blank miles round about—

IV. For there I picked up on the heather
    And there I put inside my breast
A moulted feather, an eagle-feather—
    Well, I forget the rest.

ANDREA DEL SARTO.

(CALLED THE " FAULTLESS PAINTER.")

But do not let us quarrel any more,
No, my Lucrezia; bear with me for once:
Sit down and all shall happen as you wish.
You turn your face, but does it bring your heart?
I'll work then for your friend's friend, never fear,
Treat his own subject after his own way,
Fix his own time, accept too his own price
And shut the money into this small hand
When next it takes mine.   Will it? tenderly?
Oh, I'll content him,—but to-morrow, Love!   *10*
I often am much wearier than you think,
This evening more than usual, and it seems
As if—forgive now—should you let me sit
Here by the window with your hand in mine
And look a half hour forth on Fiesole,
Both of one mind, as married people use,
Quietly, quietly, the evening through,
I might get up to-morrow to my work
Cheerful and fresh as ever.   Let us try.
To-morrow how you shall be glad for this!   *20*
Your soft hand is a woman of itself,
And mine the man's bared breast she curls inside.
Don't count the time lost, either; you must serve
For each of the five pictures we require—
It saves a model.   So! keep looking so—
My serpentining beauty, rounds on rounds!
—How could you ever prick those perfect ears,
Even to put the pearl there! oh, so sweet—
My face, my moon, my everybody's moon,
Which everybody looks on and calls his,   *30*
And, I suppose, is looked on by in turn,
While she looks—no one's: very dear, no less!
You smile? why, there's my picture ready made.
There's what we painters call our harmony!
A common greyness silvers everything,—
All in a twilight, you and I alike
—You, at the point of your first pride in me
(That's gone you know),—but I, at every point;

My youth, my hope, my art, being all toned down
To yonder sober pleasant Fiesole.   40
There's the bell clinking from the chapel-top;
That length of convent-wall across the way
Holds the trees safer, huddled more inside;
The last monk leaves the garden; days decrease
And autumn grows, autumn in everything.
Eh? the whole seems to fall into a shape
As if I saw alike my work and self
And all that I was born to be and do,
A twilight-piece. Love, we are in God's hand.
How strange now, looks the life he makes us lead!   50
So free we seem, so fettered fast we are:
I feel he laid the fetter: let it lie!
This chamber for example—turn your head—
All that's behind us! you don't understand
Nor care to understand about my art,
But you can hear at least when people speak;
And that cartoon, the second from the door
—It is the thing, Love! so such things should be—
Behold Madonna, I am bold to say.
I can do with my pencil what I know,   60
What I see, what at bottom of my heart
I wish for, if I ever wish so deep—
Do easily, too—when I say perfectly
I do not boast, perhaps: yourself are judge
Who listened to the Legate's talk last week,
And just as much they used to say in France.
At any rate, 'tis easy, all of it,
No sketches first, no studies, that's long past—
I do what many dream of all their lives
—Dream? strive to do, and agonise to do,   70
And fail in doing. I could count twenty such
On twice your fingers, and not leave this town,
Who strive—you don't know how the others strive
To paint a little thing like that you smeared
Carelessly passing with your robes afloat,
Yet do much less, so much less, some one says,
(I know his name, no matter) so much less!
Well, less is more, Lucrezia! I am judged.
There burns a truer light in them,
In their vexed, beating, stuffed and stopped-up brain,   80
Heart, or whate'er else, than goes on to prompt

This low-pulsed forthright craftsman's hand of mine.
Their works drop groundward, but themselves, I know,
Reach many a time a heaven that's shut to me,
Enter and take their place there sure enough,
Though they come back and cannot tell the world.
My works are nearer heaven, but I sit here.
The sudden blood of these men! at a word—
Praise them, it boils, or blame them, it boils too.
I, painting from myself and to myself,   **90**
Know what I do, am unmoved by men's blame
Or their praise either.   Somebody remarks
Morello's outline there is wrongly traced,
His hue mistaken—what of that? or else,
Rightly traced and well ordered—what of that?
Ah, but a man's reach should exceed his grasp,
Or what's a Heaven for? all is silver-grey
Placid and perfect with my art—the worse!
I know both what I want and what might gain—
And yet how profitless to know, to sigh   **100**
" Had I been two, another and myself,
Our head would have o'erlooked the world!"   No doubt.
Yonder's a work, now, of that famous youth
The Urbinate who died five years ago.
('Tis copied, George Vasari sent it me.)
Well, I can fancy how he did it all,
Pouring his soul, with kings and popes to see,
Reaching, that Heaven might so replenish him,
Above and through his art—for it gives way;
That arm is wrongly put—and there again—   **110**
A fault to pardon in the drawing's lines,
Its body, so to speak! its soul is right,
He means right—that, a child may understand.
Still, what an arm! and I could alter it.
But all the play, the insight and the stretch—
Out of me! out of me! And wherefore out?
Had you enjoined them on me, given me soul,
We might have risen to Rafael, I and you.
Nay, Love, you did give all I asked, I think—
More than I merit, yes, by many times.   **120**
But had you—oh, with the same perfect brow,
And perfect eyes, and more than perfect mouth,
And the low voice my soul hears, as a bird
The fowler's pipe, and follows to the snare—

Had you, with these the same, but brought a mind!
Some women do so.   Had the mouth there urged
" God and the glory! never care for gain.
The present by the future, what is that?
Live for fame, side by side with Angelo—
Rafael is waiting.   Up to God all three!"   *130*
I might have done it for you.   So it seems—
Perhaps not.   All is as God over-rules.
Beside, incentives come from the soul's self;
The rest avail not.   Why do I need you?
What wife had Rafael, or has Angelo?
In this world, who can do a thing, will not—
And who would do it, cannot, I perceive:
Yet the will's somewhat—somewhat, too, the power—
And thus we half-men struggle.   At the end,
God, I conclude, compensates, punishes.   *140*
'Tis safer for me, if the award be strict,
That I am something underrated here,
Poor this long while, despised, to speak the truth.
I dared not, do you know, leave home all day,
For fear of chancing on the Paris lords.
The best is when they pass and look aside;
But they speak sometimes; I must bear it all.
Well may they speak!   That Francis, that first time,
And that long festal year at Fontainebleau!
I surely then could sometimes leave the ground,   *150*
Put on the glory, Rafael's daily wear,
In that humane great monarch's golden look,—
One finger in his beard or twisted curl
Over his mouth's good mark that made the smile,
One arm about my shoulder, round my neck,
The jingle of his gold chain in my ear,
[I] painting proudly with his breath on me,
All his court round him, seeing with his eyes,
Such frank French eyes, and such a fire of souls
Profuse, my hand kept plying by those hearts,—   *160*
And, best of all, this, this, this face beyond,
This in the back-ground, waiting on my work,
To crown the issue with a last reward!
A good time, was it not, my kingly days?
And had you not grown restless—but I know—
'Tis done and past; 'twas right, my instinct said;
Too live the life grew, golden and not grey—

And I'm the weak-eyed bat no sun should tempt
Out of the grange whose four walls make his world.
How could it end in any other way? 170
You called me, and I came home to your heart.
The triumph was to have ended there—then if
I reached it ere the triumph, what is lost?
Let my hands frame your face in your hair's gold,
You beautiful Lucrezia that are mine!
"Rafael did this, Andrea painted that—
The Roman's is the better when you pray,
But still the other's Virgin was his wife—"
Men will excuse me. I am glad to judge
Both pictures in your presence; clearer grows 180
My better fortune, I resolve to think.
For, do you know, Lucrezia, as God lives,
Said one day Angelo, his very self,
To Rafael . . . I have known it all these years . . .
(When the young man was flaming out his thoughts
Upon a palace-wall for Rome to see,
Too lifted up in heart because of it)
"Friend, there's a certain sorry little scrub
Goes up and down our Florence, none cares how,
Who, were he set to plan and execute 190
As you are pricked on by your popes and kings,
Would bring the sweat into that brow of yours!"
To Rafael's!—And indeed the arm is wrong.
I hardly dare—yet, only you to see,
Give the chalk here—quick, thus the line should go!
Ay, but the soul! he's Rafael! rub it out!
Still, all I care for, if he spoke the truth,
(What he? why, who but Michael Angelo?
Do you forget already words like those?)
If really there was such a chance, so lost, 200
Is, whether you're—not grateful—but more pleased.
Well, let me think so. And you smile indeed!
This hour has been an hour! Another smile?
If you would sit thus by me every night
I should work better, do you comprehend?
I mean that I should earn more, give you more.
See, it is settled dusk now; there's a star;
Morello's gone, the watch-lights shew the wall,
The cue-owls speak the name we call them by.
Come from the window, Love,—come in, at last, 210

Inside the melancholy little house
We built to be so gay with.   God is just.
King Francis may forgive me.   Oft at nights
When I look up from painting, eyes tired out,
The walls become illumined, brick from brick
Distinct, instead of mortar fierce bright gold,
That gold of his I did cement them with!
Let us but love each other.   Must you go?
That Cousin here again? he waits outside?
Must see you—you, and not with me?   Those loans!   *220*
More gaming debts to pay? you smiled for that?
Well, let smiles buy me! have you more to spend?
While hand and eye and something of a heart
Are left me, work's my ware, and what's it worth?
I'll pay my fancy.   Only let me sit
The grey remainder of the evening out,
Idle, you call it, and muse perfectly
How I could paint were I but back in France,
One picture, just one more—the Virgin's face,
Not yours this time! I want you at my side   *230*
To hear them—that is, Michael Angelo—
Judge all I do and tell you of its worth.
Will you?   To-morrow, satisfy your friend.
I take the subjects for his corridor,
Finish the portrait out of hand—there, there,
And throw him in another thing or two
If he demurs; the whole should prove enough
To pay for this same Cousin's freak.   Beside,
What's better and what's all I care about,
Get you the thirteen scudi for the ruff.   *240*
Love, does that please you?   Ah, but what does he,
The Cousin! what does he to please you more?

   I am grown peaceful as old age to-night.
I regret little, I would change still less.
Since there my past life lies, why alter it?
The very wrong to Francis! it is true
I took his coin, was tempted and complied,
And built this house and sinned, and all is said.
My father and my mother died of want.
Well, had I riches of my own? you see   *250*
How one gets rich!   Let each one bear his lot.
They were born poor, lived poor, and poor they died:

And I have laboured somewhat in my time
And not been paid profusely.   Some good son
Paint my two hundred pictures—let him try!
No doubt, there's something strikes a balance.   Yes,
You loved me quite enough, it seems to-night.
This must suffice me here.   What would one have?
In heaven, perhaps, new chances, one more chance—
Four great walls in the New Jerusalem   *260*
Meted on each side by the angel's reed,
For Leonard, Rafael, Angelo and me
To cover—the three first without a wife,
While I have mine!   So—still they overcome
Because there's still Lucrezia,—as I choose.

Again the Cousin's whistle!   Go, my Love. .

BEFORE.

I.

Let them fight it out, friend! things have gone too far.
God must judge the couple! leave them as they are
—Whichever one's the guiltless, to his glory,
And whichever one the guilt's with, to my story.

II.

Why, you would not bid men, sunk in such a slough,
Strike no arm out further, stick and stink as now,
Leaving right and wrong to settle the embroilment,
Heaven with snaky Hell, in torture and entoilment?

III.

Which of them's the culprit, how must he conceive
God's the queen he caps to, laughing in his sleeve!   *10*
'Tis but decent to profess oneself beneath her.
Still, one must not be too much in earnest either.

IV.

Better sin the whole sin, sure that God observes,
Then go live his life out! life will try his nerves,
When the sky which noticed all, makes no disclosure,
And the earth keeps up her terrible composure.

v.

Let him pace at pleasure, past the walls of rose,
Pluck their fruits when grape-trees graze him as he goes.
For he 'gins to guess the purpose of the garden,
With the sly mute thing beside there for a warden.   *20*

vi.

What's the leopard-dog-thing, constant to his side,
A leer and lie in every eye on its obsequious hide?
When will come an end of all the mock obeisance,
And the price appear that pays for the misfeasance?

vii.

So much for the culprit. Who's the martyred man?
Let him bear one stroke more, for be sure he can.
He that strove thus evil's lump with good to leaven,
Let him give his blood at last and get his heaven.

viii.

All or nothing, stake it! trusts he God or no?
Thus far and no farther? farther? be it so.   *30*
Now, enough of your chicane of prudent pauses,
Sage provisos, sub-intents, and saving-clauses.

ix.

Ah, "forgive" you bid him? While God's champion lives,
Wrong shall be resisted: dead, why he forgives.
But you must not end my friend ere you begin him;
Evil stands not crowned on earth, while breath is in him.

x.

Once more—Will the wronger, at this last of all,
Dare to say "I did wrong," rising in his fall?
No?—Let go, then—both the fighters to their places—
While I count three, step you back as many paces.   *40*

AFTER.

TAKE the cloak from his face, and at first
    Let the corpse do its worst.
How he lies in his rights of a man!
    Death has done all death can.

And absorbed in the new life he leads,
  He recks not, he heeds
Nor his wrong nor my vengeance—both strike
  On his senses alike,
And are lost in the solemn and strange
  Surprise of the change.   *10*
Ha, what avails death to erase
  His offence, my disgrace?
I would we were boys as of old
  In the field, by the fold—
His outrage, God's patience, man's scorn
  Were so easily borne.

I stand here now, he lies in his place—
  Cover the face.

IN THREE DAYS.

I. So, I shall see her in three days
  And just one night, but nights are short,
  Then two long hours, and that is morn.
  See how I come, unchanged, unworn—
  Feel, where my life broke off from thine,
  How fresh the splinters keep and fine,—
  Only a touch and we combine!

II. Too long, this time of year, the days!
  But nights—at least the nights are short.
  As night shows where her one moon is,   *10*
  A hand's-breadth of pure light and bliss,
  So, life's night gives my lady birth
  And my eyes hold her! what is worth
  The rest of heaven, the rest of earth?

III. O loaded curls, release your store
  Of warmth and scent as once before
  The tingling hair did, lights and darks
  Out-breaking into fairy sparks
  When under curl and curl I pried
  After the warmth and scent inside   *20*
  Thro' lights and darks how manifold—
  The dark inspired, the light controlled!
  As early Art embrowned the gold.

iv. What great fear—should one say, " Three days
   That change the world, might change as well
   Your fortune; and if joy delays,
   Be happy that no worse befell."
   What small fear—if another says,
   " Three days and one short night beside
   May throw no shadow on your ways;   *30*
   But years must teem with change untried,
   With chance not easily defied,
   With an end somewhere undescried."
   No fear!—or if a fear be born
   This minute, it dies out in scorn.
   Fear? I shall see her in three days
   And one night, now the nights are short,
   Then just two hours, and that is morn.

IN A YEAR.

i. NEVER any more
    While I live,
  Need I hope to see his face
    As before.
  Once his love grown chill,
    Mine may strive—
  Bitterly we re-embrace,
    Single still.

ii. Was it something said,
    Something done,   *10*
  Vexed him? was it touch of hand,
    Turn of head?
  Strange! that very way
    Love begun.
  I as little understand
    Love's decay.

iii. When I sewed or drew,
    I recall
  How he looked as if I sang,
    —Sweetly too.   *20*
  If I spoke a word,
    First of all
  Up his cheek the colour sprang,
    Then he heard.

IV. Sitting by my side,
    At my feet,
So he breathed the air I breathed,
    Satisfied!
I, too, at love's brim
    Touched the sweet:
I would die if death bequeathed
    Sweet to him.   30

V. "Speak, I love thee best!"
    He exclaimed,
"Let my love thy own foretell,—"
    I confessed:
"Clasp my heart on thine
    Now unblamed,
Since upon thy soul as well
    Hangeth mine!"   40

VI. Was it wrong to own,
    Being truth?
Why should all the giving prove
    His alone?
I had wealth and ease,
    Beauty, youth—
Since my lover gave me love,
    I gave these.

VII. That was all I meant,
    —To be just.   50
And the passion I had raised
    To content.
Since he chose to change
    Gold for dust,
If I gave him what he praised
    Was it strange?

VIII. Would he love me yet,
    On and on,
While I found some way undreamed
    —Paid my debt!   60
Gave more life and more,
    Till, all gone,
He should smile "She never seemed
    Mine before.

IX. " What—she felt the while,
    Must I think?
Love's so different with us men,"
    He should smile.
" Dying for my sake—
    White and pink!
Can't we touch these bubbles then
    But they break?"   *70*

X. Dear, the pang is brief.
    Do thy part,
Have thy pleasure.   How perplext
    Grows belief!
Well, this cold clay clod
    Was man's heart.
Crumble it—and what comes next?
    Is it God?   *80*

OLD PICTURES IN FLORENCE.

I. THE morn when first it thunders in March,
    The eel in the pond gives a leap, they say.
As I leaned and looked over the aloed arch
    Of the villa-gate, this warm March day,
No flash snapt, no dumb thunder rolled
    In the valley beneath, where, white and wide,
Washed by the morning's water-gold,
    Florence lay out on the mountain-side.

II. River and bridge and street and square
    Lay mine, as much at my beck and call,   *10*
Through the live translucent bath of air,
    As the sights in a magic crystal ball.
And of all I saw and of all I praised,
    The most to praise and the best to see,
Was the startling bell-tower Giotto raised:
    But why did it more than startle me?

III. Giotto, how, with that soul of yours,
    Could you play me false who loved you so?
Some slights if a certain heart endures
    It feels, I would have your fellows know!   *20*

Faith—I perceive not why I should care
    To break a silence that suits them best,
But the thing grows somewhat hard to bear
    When I find a Giotto join the rest.

IV. On the arch where olives overhead
    Print the blue sky with twig and leaf,
    (That sharp-curled leaf they never shed)
    'Twixt the aloes I used to lean in chief,
And mark through the winter afternoons,
    By a gift God grants me now and then,   *30*
In the mild decline of those suns like moons,
    Who walked in Florence, besides her men.

V. They might chirp and chaffer, come and go
    For pleasure or profit, her men alive—
My business was hardly with them, I trow,
    But with empty cells of the human hive;
—With the chapter-room, the cloister-porch,
    The church's apsis, aisle or nave,
Its crypt, one fingers along with a torch—
    Its face, set full for the sun to shave.   *40*

VI. Wherever a fresco peels and drops,
    Wherever an outline weakens and wanes
Till the latest life in the painting stops,
    Stands One whom each fainter pulse-tick pains!
One, wishful each scrap should clutch its brick,
    Each tinge not wholly escape the plaster,
—A lion who dies of an ass's kick,
    The wronged great soul of an ancient Master.

VII. For oh, this world and the wrong it does!
    They are safe in heaven with their backs to it,   *50*
The Michaels and Rafaels, you hum and buzz
    Round the works of, you of the little wit!
Do their eyes contract to the earth's old scope,
    Now that they see God face to face,
And have all attained to be poets, I hope?
    'Tis their holiday now, in any case.

VIII. Much they reck of your praise and you!
    But the wronged great souls—can they be quit
Of a world where all their work is to do,
    Where you style them, you of the little wit,   *60*

Old Master this and Early the other,
    Not dreaming that Old and New are fellows,
That a younger succeeds to an elder brother,
    Da Vincis derive in good time from Dellos.

IX. And here where your praise would yield returns
    And a handsome word or two give help,
Here, after your kind, the mastiff girns
    And the puppy pack of poodles yelp.
What, not a word for Stefano there
    —Of brow once prominent and starry,   70
Called Nature's ape and the world's despair
    For his peerless painting (see Vasari)?

X. There he stands now.   Study, my friends,
    What a man's work comes to! so he plans it,
Performs it, perfects it, makes amends
    For the toiling and moiling, and there's its transit!
Happier the thrifty blind-folk labour,
    With upturned eye while the hand is busy,
Not sidling a glance at the coin of their neighbour!
    'Tis looking downward makes one dizzy.   80

XI. If you knew their work you would deal your dole.
    May I take upon me to instruct you?
When Greek Art ran and reached the goal,
    Thus much had the world to boast *in fructu*—
The truth of Man, as by God first spoken,
    Which the actual generations garble,
Was re-uttered,—and Soul (which Limbs betoken)
    And Limbs (Soul informs) were made new in marble.

XII. So you saw yourself as you wished you were,
    As you might have been, as you cannot be;   90
And bringing your own shortcomings there.
    You grew content in your poor degree
With your little power, by those statues' godhead,
    And your little scope, by their eyes' full sway,
And your little grace, by their grace embodied,
    And your little date, by their forms that stay.

XIII. You would fain be kinglier, say than I am?
    Even so, you would not sit like Theseus.
You'd fain be a model? the Son of Priam
    Has yet the advantage in arms' and knees' use.   100

You're wroth—can you slay your snake like Apollo?
    You're grieved—still Niobe's the grander!
You live—there's the Racer's frieze to follow—
    You die—there's the dying Alexander.

xiv. So, testing your weakness by their strength,
    Your meagre charms by their rounded beauty,
Measured by Art in your breadth and length,
    You learn—to submit is the worsted's duty.
—When I say " you " 'tis the common soul,
    The collective, I mean—the race of Man   *110*
That receives life in parts to live in a whole,
    And grow here according to God's own plan.

xv. Growth came when, looking your last on them all,
    You turned your eyes inwardly one fine day
And cried with a start—What if we so small
    Are greater, ay, greater the while than they!
Are they perfect of lineament, perfect of stature?
    In both, of such lower types are we
Precisely because of our wider nature;
    For time, theirs—ours, for eternity.   *120*

xvi. To-day's brief passion limits their range,
    It seethes with the morrow for us and more.
They are perfect—how else? they shall never change:
    We are faulty—why not? we have time in store.
The Artificer's hand is not arrested
    With us—we are rough-hewn, no-wise polished:
They stand for our copy, and, once invested
    With all they can teach, we shall see them abolished.

xvii. 'Tis a life-long toil till our lump be leaven—
    The better! what's come to perfection perishes.   *130*
Things learned on earth, we shall practise in heaven.
    Works done least rapidly, Art most cherishes.
Thyself shall afford the example, Giotto!
    Thy one work, not to decrease or diminish,
Done at a stroke, was just (was it not?) " O! "
    Thy great Campanile is still to finish.

xviii. Is it true, we are now, and shall be hereafter,
    And what—is depending on life's one minute?
Hails heavenly cheer or infernal laughter
    Our first step out of the gulf or in it?   *140*

And Man, this step within his endeavour,
　　His face, have no more play and action
Than joy which is crystallized for ever,
　　Or grief, an eternal petrifaction!

XIX. On which I conclude, that the early painters,
　　　To cries of " Greek Art and what more wish
　　　　you? "—
　　Replied, " Become now self-acquainters,
　　　And paint man, man,—whatever the issue!
　　Make the hopes shine through the flesh they fray,
　　　New fears aggrandise the rags and tatters.　　　　*150*
　　So bring the invisible full into play,
　　　Let the visible go to the dogs—what matters? "

XX. Give these, I say, full honour and glory
　　　For daring so much, before they well did it.
　　The first of the new, in our race's story,
　　　Beats the last of the old, 'tis no idle quiddit.
　　The worthies began a revolution
　　　Which if on the earth we intend to acknowledge
　　Honour them now—(ends my allocution)
　　　Nor confer our degree when the folks leave college.　*160*

XXI. There's a fancy some lean to and others hate—
　　　That, when this life is ended, begins
　　New work for the soul in another state,
　　　Where it strives and gets weary, loses and wins—
　　Where the strong and the weak, this world's
　　　　congeries,
　　　Repeat in large what they practised in small.
　　Through life after life in unlimited series;
　　　Only the scale's to be changed, that's all.

XXII. Yet I hardly know. When a soul has seen
　　　By the means of Evil that Good is best,　　　　　*170*
　　And through earth and its noise, what is heaven's
　　　　serene,—
　　　When its faith in the same has stood the test—
　　Why, the child grown man, you burn the rod,
　　　The uses of labour are surely done.
　　There remaineth a rest for the people of God,
　　　And I have had troubles enough for one.

XXIII. But at any rate I have loved the season
    Of Art's spring-birth so dim and dewy,
My sculptor is Nicolo the Pisan;
    My painter—who but Cimabue?   *180*
Nor ever was man of them all indeed,
    From these to Ghiberti and Ghirlandajo,
Could say that he missed my critic-meed.
    So now to my special grievance—heigh ho!

XXIV. Their ghosts now stand, as I said before,
    Watching each fresco flaked and rasped,
Blocked up, knocked out, or whitewashed o'er
    —No getting again what the church has grasped!
The works on the wall must take their chance,
    "Works never conceded to England's thick clime!" *190*
(I hope they prefer their inheritance
    Of a bucketful of Italian quick-lime.)

XXV. When they go at length, with such a shaking
    Of heads o'er the old delusions, sadly
Each master his way through the black streets taking,
    Where many a lost work breathes though badly—
Why don't they bethink them of who has merited?
    Why not reveal, while their pictures dree
Such doom, that a captive's to be out-ferreted?
    Why do they never remember me?   *200*

XXVI. Not that I expect the great Bigordi
    Nor Sandro to hear me, chivalric, bellicose;
Nor wronged Lippino—and not a word I
    Say of a scrap of Fra Angelico's.
But are you too fine, Taddeo Gaddi,
    To grant me a taste of your intonaco—
Some Jerome that seeks the heaven with a sad eye?
    No churlish saint, Lorenzo Monaco?

XXVII. Could not the ghost with the close red cap,
    My Pollajolo, the twice a craftsman,   *210*
Save me a sample, give me the hap
    Of a muscular Christ that shows the draughtsman?
No Virgin by him, the somewhat petty,
    Of finical touch and tempera crumbly—
Could not Alesso Baldovinetti
    Contribute so much, I ask him humbly?

XXVIII. Margheritone of Arezzo,
  With the grave-clothes garb and swaddling barret.
 (Why purse up mouth and beak in a pet so,
  You bald, saturnine, poll-clawed parrot?)   *220*
 No poor glimmering Crucifixion,
  Where in the foreground kneels the donor?
 If such remain, as in my conviction,
  The hoarding does you but little honour.

XXIX. They pass: for them the panels may thrill,
  The tempera grow alive and tinglish—
 Rot or are left to the mercies still
  Of dealers and stealers, Jews and the English!
 Seeing mere money's worth in their prize,
  Who sell it to some one calm as Zeno   *230*
 At naked Art, and in ecstacies
  Before some clay-cold, vile Carlino!

XXX. No matter for these! But Giotto, you,
  Have you allowed, as the town-tongues babble it,
 Never! it shall not be counted true—
  That a certain precious little tablet
 Which Buonarroti eyed like a lover,—
  Buried so long in oblivion's womb,
 Was left for another than I to discover,—
  Turns up at last, and to whom?—to whom?   *240*

XXXI. I, that have haunted the dim San Spirito,
  (Or was it rather the Ognissanti?)
 Stood on the altar-steps, patient and weary too!
  Nay, I shall have it yet, *detur amanti !*
 My Koh-i-noor—or (if that's a platitude)
  Jewel of Giamschid, the Persian Sofi's eye!
 So, in anticipative gratitude,
  What if I take up my hope and prophesy?

XXXII. When the hour is ripe, and a certain dotard
  Pitched, no parcel that needs invoicing,   *250*
 To the worse side of the Mont St. Gothard,
  Have, to begin by way of rejoicing,
 None of that shooting the sky (blank cartridge),
  No civic guards, all plumes and lacquer,
 Hunting Radetsky's soul like a partridge
  Over Morello with squib and cracker.

XXXIII. We'll shoot this time better game and bag 'em hot—
    No display at the stone of Dante,
But a kind of [sober] Witan-agemot
    ("Casa Guidi," quod videas ante)   260
To ponder Freedom restored to Florence,
    How Art may return that departed with her.
Go, hated house, go each trace of the Lorraine's!
    And bring us the days of Orgagna hither.

XXXIV. How we shall prologuise, how we shall perorate,
    Say fit things upon art and history—
Set truth at blood-heat and the false at a zero rate,
    Make of the want of the age no mystery!
Contrast the fructuous and sterile eras,
    Show, monarchy its uncouth cub licks   270
Out of the bear's shape to the chimæra's—
    Pure Art's birth being still the republic's!

XXXV. Then one shall propose (in a speech, curt Tuscan,
    Sober, expurgate, spare of an "*issimo*,")
Ending our half-told tale of Cambuscan,
    Turning the Bell-tower's alt altissimo.
And fine as the beak of a young beccaccia
    The Campanile, the Duomo's fit ally,
Soars up in gold its full fifty braccia,
    Completing Florence, as Florence, Italy.   280

XXXVI. Shall I be alive that morning the scaffold
    Is broken away, and the long-pent fire
Like the golden hope of the world unbaffled
    Springs from its sleep, and up goes the spire—
As, "God and the People" plain for its motto,
    Thence the new tricolor flaps at the sky?
Foreseeing the day that vindicates Giotto
    And Florence together, the first am I!

IN A BALCONY.

FIRST PART.

CONSTANCE *and* NORBERT.

NORBERT.

Now.

CONSTANCE.

Not now.

NORBERT.

          Give me them again, those hands—
Put them upon my forehead, how it throbs!
Press them before my eyes, the fire comes through.
You cruellest, you dearest in the world,
Let me! the Queen must grant whate'er I ask—
How can I gain you and not ask the Queen?
There she stays waiting for me, here stand you.
Some time or other this was to be asked,
Now is the one time—what I ask, I gain—
Let me ask now, Love!

CONSTANCE.

          Do, and ruin us.   *10*

NORBERT.

Let it be now, Love! All my soul breaks forth.
How I do love you! give my love its way!
A man can have but one life and one death,
One heaven, one hell. Let me fulfil my fate—
Grant me my heaven now. Let me know you mine,
Prove you mine, write my name upon your brow,
Hold you and have you, and then die away
If God please, with completion in my soul.

CONSTANCE.

I am not yours then? how content this man?
I am not his, who change into himself,   *20*
Have passed into his heart and beat its beats,
Who give my hands to him, my eyes, my hair,

Give all that was of me away to him
So well, that now, my spirit turned his own,
Takes part with him against the woman here,
Bids him not stumble at so mere a straw
As caring that the world be cognisant
How he loves her and how she worships him.
You have this woman, not as yet that world.
Go on, I bid, nor stop to care for me   *30*
By saving what I cease to care about,
The courtly name and pride of circumstance—
The name you'll pick up and be cumbered with
Just for the poor parade's sake, nothing more;
Just that the world may slip from under you—
Just that the world may cry " So much for him
The man predestined to the heap of crowns!
There goes his chance of winning one, at least."

NORBERT.

The world!

CONSTANCE.

   You love it. Love me quite as well,
And see if I shall pray for this in vain!   *40*
Why must you ponder what it knows or thinks?

NORBERT.

You pray for—what, in vain?

CONSTANCE.

     Oh my heart's heart.
How I do love you, Norbert!—that is right!
But listen, or I take my hands away.
You say, " let it be now "—you would go now
And tell the Queen, perhaps six steps from us,
You love me—so you do, thank God!

NORBERT.

     Thank God!
CONSTANCE.

Yes, Norbert,—but you fain would tell your love,
And, what succeeds the telling, ask of her
My hand. Now take this rose and look at it,   *50*
Listening to me. You are the minister,

The Queen's first favourite, nor without a cause.
To-night completes your wonderful year's-work
(This palace-feast is held to celebrate)
Made memorable by her life's success,
That junction of two crowns on her sole head
Her house had only dreamed of anciently.
That this mere dream is grown a stable truth
To-night's feast makes authentic.   Whose the praise?
Whose genius, patience, energy, achieved   60
What turned the many heads and broke the hearts?
You are the fate—your minute's in the heaven.
Next comes the Queen's turn.   Name your own reward!
With leave to clench the past, chain the to-come,
Put out an arm and touch and take the sun
And fix it ever full-faced on your earth,
Possess yourself supremely of her life,
You choose the single thing she will not grant—
The very declaration of which choice
Will turn the scale and neutralise your work.   70
At best she will forgive you, if she can.
You think I'll let you choose—her cousin's hand?

NORBERT.

Wait.   First, do you retain your old belief
The Queen is generous,—nay is just?

CONSTANCE.

                            There, there!
So men make women love them, while they know
No more of women's hearts than . . . look you here,
You that are just and generous beside,
Make it your own case.   For example now,
I'll say—I let you kiss me and hold my hands—
Why? do you know why? I'll instruct you, then—   80
The kiss, because you have a name at court,
This hand and this, that you may shut in each
A jewel, if you please to pick up such.
That's horrible!   Apply it to the Queen—
Suppose, I am the Queen to whom you speak.
" I was a nameless man: you needed me:
Why did I proffer you my aid? there stood
A certain pretty Cousin by your side.
Why did I make such common cause with you?

Access to her had not been easy else.   90
You give my labours here abundant praise:
'Faith, labour, while she overlooked, grew play,
How shall your gratitude discharge itself?
Give me her hand!"

NORBERT.

And still I urge the same.
Is the Queen just? just—generous or no!

CONSTANCE.

Yes, just.   You love a rose—no harm in that—
But was it for the rose's sake or mine
You put it in your bosom? mine, you said—
Then mine you still must say or else be false.
You told the Queen you served her for herself: 100
If so, to serve her was to serve yourself
She thinks, for all your unbelieving face!
I know her.   In the hall, six steps from us,
One sees the twenty pictures—there's a life
Better than life—and yet no life at all;
Conceive her born in such a magic dome,
Pictures all round her! why, she sees the world
Can recognise its given things and facts,
The fight of giants or the feast of gods,
Sages in senate, beauties at the bath,   110
Chaces and battles, the whole earth's display,
Landscape and sea-piece, down to flowers and fruit—
And who shall question that she knows them all
In better semblance than the things outside?
Yet bring into the silent gallery
Some live thing to contrast in breath and blood,
Some lion, with the painted lion there—
You think she'll understand composedly?
—Say, " that's his fellow in the hunting-piece
Yonder, I've turned to praise a hundred times?"   120
Not so.   Her knowledge of our actual earth,
Its hopes and fears, concerns and sympathies,
Must be too far, too mediate, too unreal.
The real exists for us outside, not her—
How should it, with that life in these four walls,
That father and that mother, first to last
No father and no mother—friends, a heap,

Lovers, no lack—a husband in due time,
And everyone of them alike a lie!
Things painted by a Rubens out of nought   *130*
Into what kindness, friendship, love should be;
All better, all more grandiose than life,
Only no life; mere cloth and surface-paint
You feel while you admire. How should she feel?
And now that she has stood thus fifty years
The sole spectator in that gallery,
You think to bring this warm real struggling love
In to her of a sudden, and suppose
She'll peep her state untroubled? Here's the truth—
She'll apprehend its value at a glance,   *140*
Prefer it to the pictured loyalty!
You only have to say " so men are made,
For this they act, the thing has many names
But this the right one—and now, Queen, be just!"
And life slips back—you lose her at the word—
You do not even for amends gain me.
He will not understand! oh, Norbert, Norbert,
Do you not understand?

NORBERT.

                         The Queen's the Queen,
I am myself—no picture, but alive
In every nerve and every muscle, here   *150*
At the palace-window or in the people's street,
As she in the gallery where the pictures glow.
The good of life is precious to us both.
She cannot love—what do I want with rule?
When first I saw your face a year ago
I knew my life's good—my soul heard one voice
" The woman yonder, there's no use of life
But just to obtain her! heap earth's woes in one
And bear them—make a pile of all earth's joys
And spurn them, as they help or help not here;   *160*
Only, obtain her!"—How was it to be?
I found she was the cousin of the Queen;
I must then serve the Queen to get to her—
No other way. Suppose there had been one,
And I by saying prayers to some white star
With promise of my body and my soul
Might gain you,—should I pray the star or no?

Instead, there was the Queen to serve! I served,
And did what other servants failed to do.
Neither she sought nor I declared my end.   170
Her good is hers, my recompense be mine,
And let me name you as that recompense.
She dreamed that such a thing could never be?
Let her wake now.   She thinks there was some cause—
The love of power, of fame, pure loyalty?
—Perhaps she fancies men wear out their lives
Chasing such shades.   Then I've a fancy too.
I worked because I want you with my soul—
I therefore ask your hand.   Let it be now.

CONSTANCE.

Had I not loved you from the very first,   180
Were I not yours, could we not steal out thus
So wickedly, so wildly, and so well,
You might be thus impatient.   What's conceived
Of us without here, by the folks within?
Where are you now? immersed in cares of state—
Where am I now?—intent on festal robes—
We two, embracing under death's spread hand!
What was this thought for, what this scruple of yours
Which broke the council up, to bring about
One minute's meeting in the corridor?   190
And then the sudden sleights, long secresies
The plots inscrutable, deep telegraphs,
Long-planned chance-meetings, hazards of a look,
" Does she know? does she not know? saved or lost? "
A year of this compression's ecstasy
All goes for nothing? you would give this up
For the old way, the open way, the world's,
His way who beats, and his who sells his wife?
What tempts you? their notorious happiness,
That you're ashamed of ours?   The best you'll get   200
Will be, the Queen grants all that you require,
Concedes the cousin, and gets rid of you
And her at once, and gives us ample leave
To live as our five hundred happy friends.
The world will show us with officious hand
Our chamber-entry and stand sentinel,
When we so oft have stolen across her traps!
Get the world's warrant, ring the falcon's foot,

And make it duty to be bold and swift,
When long ago 'twas nature. Have it so!　　　　　210
He never hawked by rights till flung from fist?
Oh, the man's thought!—no woman's such a fool.

NORBERT.

Yes, the man's thought and my thought, which is more—
One made to love you, let the world take note.
Have I done worthy work? be love's the praise,
Though hampered by restrictions, barred against
By set forms, blinded by forced secresies.
Set free my love, and see what love will do
Shown in my life—what work will spring from that!
The world is used to have its business done　　　　220
On other grounds, find great effects produced
For power's sake, fame's sake, motives you have named.
So good.　But let my low ground shame their high.
Truth is the strong thing.　Let man's life be true!
And love's the truth of mine.　Time prove the rest!
I choose to have you stamped all over me,
Your name upon my forehead and my breast,
You, from the sword's blade to the ribbon's edge,
That men may see, all over, you in me—
That pale loves may die out of their pretence　　　230
In face of mine, shames thrown on love fall off—
Permit this, Constance!　Love has been so long
Subdued in me, eating me through and through,
That now it's all of me and must have way.
Think of my work, that chaos of intrigues,
Those hopes and fears, surprises and delays,
That long endeavour, earnest, patient, slow,
Trembling at last to its assured result—
Then think of this revulsion.　I resume
Life, after death, (it is no less than life　　　　240
After such long unlovely labouring days)
And liberate to beauty life's great need
Of the beautiful, which, while it prompted work,
Supprest itself erewhile.　This eve's the time—
This eve intense with yon first trembling star
We seem to pant and reach; scarce ought between
The earth that rises and the heaven that bends—
All nature self-abandoned—every tree
Flung as it will, pursuing its own thoughts

And fixed so, every flower and every weed,   **250**
No pride, no shame, no victory, no defeat:
All under God, each measured by itself!
These statues round us, each abrupt, distinct,
The strong in strength, the weak in weakness fixed,
The Muse for ever wedded to her lyre,
The Nymph to her fawn, the Silence to her rose,
And God's approval on his universe!
Let us do so—aspire to live as these
In harmony with truth, ourselves being true.
Take the first way, and let the second come,   **260**
My first is to possess myself of you;
The music sets the march-step—forward then!
And there's the Queen, I go to claim you of,
The world to witness, wonder and applaud.
Our flower of life breaks open. No delay!

CONSTANCE.

And so shall we be ruined, both of us.
Norbert, I know her to the skin and bone—
You do not know her, were not born to it,
To feel what she can see or cannot see.
Love, she is generous,—ay, despite your Smile,   **270**
Generous as you are. For, in that thin frame
Pain-twisted, punctured through and through with cares,
There lived a lavish soul until it starved
Debarred all healthy food. Look to the soul—
Pity that, stoop to that, ere you begin
(The true man's way) on justice and your rights,
Exactions and acquittance of the past.
Begin so—see what justice she will deal!
We women hate a debt as men a gift.
Suppose her some poor keeper of a school   **280**
Whose business is to sit thro' summer-months
And dole out children's leave to go and play,
Herself superior to such lightness—she
In the arm-chair's state and pædagogic pomp,
To the life, the laughter, sun and youth outside—
We wonder such an one looks black on us?
I do not bid you wake her tenderness,
—That were vain truly—none is left to wake—
But, let her think her justice is engaged
To take the shape of tenderness, and mark   **290**

If she'll not coldly do its warmest deed!
Does she love me, I ask you? not a whit.
Yet, thinking that her justice was engaged
To help a kinswoman, she took me up—
Did more on that bare ground than other loves
Would do on greater argument.   For me,
I have no equivalent of that cold kind
To pay her with; my love alone to give
If I give anything.   I give her love.
I feel I ought to help her, and I will.   *300*
So for her sake, as yours, I tell you twice
That women hate a debt as men a gift.
If I were you, I could obtain this grace—
Would lay the whole I did to love's account,
Nor yet be very false as courtiers go—
Declare that my success was recompense;
It would be so, in fact: what were it else?
And then, once loosed her generosity
As you will mark it—then,—were I but you
To turn it, let it seem to move itself,   *310*
And make it give the thing I really take,
Accepting so, in the poor cousin's hand,
All value as the next thing to the queen—
Since none loves her directly, none dares that!
A shadow of a thing, a name's mere echo
Suffices those who miss the name and thing;
You pick up just a ribbon she has worn
To keep in proof how near her breath you came.
Say I'm so near I seem a piece of her—
Ask for me that way—(oh, you understand)   *320*
And find the same gift yielded with a grace,
Which if you make the least show to extort
—You'll see! and when you have ruined both of us,
Dis[s]ertate on the Queen's ingratitude!

NORBERT.

Then, if I turn it that way, you consent?
'Tis not my way; I have more hope in truth.
Still if you won't have truth—why, this indeed,
Is scarcely false, I'll so express the sense.
Will you remain here?

CONSTANCE.

O best heart of mine,
How I have loved you! then, you take my way?   *330*
Are mine as you have been her minister,
Work out my thought, give it effect for me,
Paint plain my poor conceit and make it serve?
I owe that withered woman everything—
Life, fortune, you, remember! Take my part—
Help me to pay her! Stand upon your rights?
You, with my rose, my hands, my heart on you?
Your rights are mine—you have no rights but mine.

NORBERT.

Remain here. How you know me!

CONSTANCE.

Ah, but still——

*[He breaks from her ; she remains. Dance-
music from within.*

SECOND PART.

Enter the QUEEN.

QUEEN.

Constance!—She is here as he said. Speak! quick!   *340*
Is it so? is it true—or false? One word!

CONSTANCE.

True.

QUEEN.

Mercifullest Mother, thanks to thee!

CONSTANCE.

Madam!

QUEEN.

I love you, Constance, from my soul.
Now say once more, with any words you will,
'Tis true—all true—as true as that I speak.

CONSTANCE.

Why should you doubt it?

QUEEN.

    Ah, why doubt? why doubt?
Dear, make me see it. Do you see it so?
None see themselves—another sees them best.
You say " why doubt it? "—you see him and me.
It is because the Mother has such grace   350
That if we had but faith—wherein we fail—
Whate'er we yearn for would be granted us;
Howbeit we let our whims prescribe despair,
Our very fancies thwart and cramp our will,
And so accepting life, abjure ourselves!
Constance, I had abjured the hope of love
And of being loved, as truly as yon palm
The hope of seeing Egypt from that turf.

CONSTANCE.

Heaven!

QUEEN.

   But it was so, Constance, it was so.
Men say—or do men say it? fancies say—   360
" Stop here, your life is set, you are grown old.
Too late—no love for you, too late for love—
Leave love to girls. Be queen—let Constance love! "
One takes the hint—half meets it like a child,
Ashamed at any feelings that oppose.
" Oh, love, true, never think of love again!
I am a queen—I rule, not love, indeed."
So it goes on; so a face grows like this,
Hair like this hair, poor arms as lean as these,
Till,—nay, it does not end so, I thank God!   370

CONSTANCE.

I cannot understand——

QUEEN.

     The happier you!
Constance, I know not how it is with men.
For women, (I am a woman now like you)
There is no good of life but love—but love!
What else looks good, is some shade flung from love—
Love gilds it, gives it worth. Be warned by me,
Never you cheat yourself one instant. Love,
Give love, ask only love, and leave the rest!
O Constance, how I love you!

CONSTANCE.

I love you.

QUEEN.

I do believe that all is come through you.   *380*
I took you to my heart to keep it warm
When the last chance of love seemed dead in me;
I thought your fresh youth warmed my withered heart.
Oh, I am very old now, am I not?
Not so! it is true and it shall be true!

CONSTANCE.

Tell it me! let me judge if true or false.

QUEEN.

Ah, but I fear you—you will look at me
And say " she's old, she's grown unlovely quite
Who ne'er was beauteous! men want beauty still."
Well, so I feared—the curse! so I felt sure.   *390*

CONSTANCE.

Be calm.   And now you feel not sure, you say?

QUEEN.

Constance, he came, the coming was not strange—
Do not I stand and see men come and go?
I turned a half look from my pedestal
Where I grow marble—" one young man the more!
He will love some one,—that is nought to me—
What would he with my marble stateliness? "
Yet this seemed somewhat worse than heretofore;
The man more gracious, youthful, like a god,
And I still older, with less flesh to change—   *400*
We two those dear extremes that long to touch.
It seemed still harder when he first began
Absorbed to labour at the state-affairs
The old way for the old end, interest.
Oh, to live with a thousand beating hearts
Around you, swift eyes, serviceable hands,
Professing they've no care but for your cause,
Thought but to help you, love but for yourself,

And you the marble statue all the time
They praise and point at as preferred to life,   *410*
Yet leave for the first breathing woman's cheek,
First dancer's, gypsy's, or street baladine's!
Why, how I have ground my teeth to hear men's speech
Stifled for fear it should alarm my ear,
Their gait subdued lest step should startle me,
Their eyes declined, such queendom to respect,
Their hands alert, such treasure to preserve,
While not a man of these broke rank and spoke,
Or wrote me a vulgar letter all of love,
Or caught my hand and pressed it like a hand.   *420*
There have been moments, if the sentinel
Lowering his halbert to salute the queen,
Had flung it brutally and clasped my knees,
I would have stooped and kissed him with my soul.

CONSTANCE.

Who could have comprehended!

QUEEN.
                              Ay, who—who?
Why, no one, Constance, but this one who did.
Not they, not you, not I. Even now perhaps
It comes too late—would you but tell the truth.

CONSTANCE.

I wait to tell it.

QUEEN.
                   Well, you see, he came,
Outfaced the others, did a work this year   *430*
Exceeds in value all was ever done
You know—it is not I who say it—all
Say it.   And so (a second pang and worse)
I grew aware not only of what he did,
But why so wondrously.   Oh, never work
Like his was done for work's ignoble sake—
It must have finer aims to spur it on!
I felt, I saw he loved—loved somebody.
And Constance, my dear Constance, do you know,
I did believe this while 'twas you he loved.   *440*

136

CONSTANCE.

Me, madam?

QUEEN.

It did seem to me your face
Met him where'er he looked: and whom but you
Was such a man to love? it seemed to me
You saw he loved you, and approved the love,
And that you both were in intelligence.
You could not loiter in the garden, step
Into this balcony, but I straight was stung
And forced to understand. It seemed so true,
So right, so beautiful, so like you both
That all this work should have been done by him   *450*
Not for the vulgar hope of recompense,
But that at last—suppose some night like this—
Borne on to claim his due reward of me
He might say, " Give her hand and pay me so."
And I (O Constance, you shall love me now)
I thought, surmounting all the bitterness,
—" And he shall have it. I will make her blest,
My flower of youth, my woman's self that was,
My happiest woman's self that might have been!
These two shall have their joy and leave me here."   *460*
Yes—yes—

CONSTANCE.

Thanks!

QUEEN.

And the word was on my lips
When he burst in upon me. I looked to hear
A mere calm statement of his just desire
In payment of his labour. When, O Heaven,
How can I tell you? cloud was on my eyes
And thunder in my ears at that first word
Which told 'twas love of me, of me, did all—
He loved me—from the first step to the last,
Loved me!

CONSTANCE.

You did not hear . . . you thought he spoke
Of love? what if you should mistake?

QUEEN.

No, no— . 470

No mistake! Ha, there shall be no mistake!
He had not dared to hint the love he felt—
You were my reflex—how I understood!
He said you were the ribbon I had worn,
He kissed my hand, he looked into my eyes,
And love, love was the end of every phrase.
Love is begun—this much is come to pass,
The rest is easy.   Constance, I am yours—
I will learn, I will place my life on you,
But teach me how to keep what I have won. 480
Am I so old? this hair was early grey;
But joy ere now has brought hair brown again,
And joy will bring the cheek's red back, I feel.
I could sing once too; that was in my youth.
Still, when men paint me, they declare me . . . yes,
Beautiful—for the last French Painter did!
I know they flatter somewhat; you are frank—
I trust you.   How I loved you from the first!
Some queens would hardly seek a cousin out
And set her by their side to take the eye: 490
I must have felt that good would come from you.
I am not generous—like him—like you!
But he is not your lover after all—
It was not you he looked at.   Saw you him?
You have not been mistaking words or looks?
He said you were the reflex of myself—
And yet he is not such a paragon
To you, to younger women who may choose
Among a thousand Norberts.   Speak the truth!
You know you never named his name to me— 500
You know, I cannot give him up—ah God,
Not up now, even to you!

CONSTANCE.

Then calm yourself.

QUEEN.

See, I am old—look here, you happy girl,
I will not play the fool, deceive myself;
'Tis all gone—put your cheek beside my cheek—
Ah, what a contrast does the moon behold!

But then I set my life upon one chance,
The last chance and the best—am *I* not left,
My soul, myself?   All women love great men
If young or old—it is in all the tales—   *510*
Young beauties love old poets who can love—
Why should not he the poems in my soul,
The love, the passionate faith, the sacrifice,
The constancy?   I throw them at his feet.
Who cares to see the fountain's very shape
And whether it be a Triton's or a Nymph's
That pours the foam, makes rainbows all around?
You could not praise indeed the empty conch;
But I'll pour floods of love and hide myself.
How I will love him! cannot men love love?   *520*
Who was a queen and loved a poet once
Humpbacked, a dwarf? ah, women can do that!
Well, but men too! at least, they tell you so.
They love so many women in their youth,
And even in age they all love whom they please;
And yet the best of them confide to friends
That 'tis not beauty makes the lasting love—
They spend a day with such and tire the next;
They like soul,—well then, they like phantasy,
Novelty even.   Let us confess the truth   *530*
Horrible though it be—that prejudice,
Prescription . . . Curses! they will love a queen.
They will—they do.   And will not, does not—he?

CONSTANCE.

How can he?   You are wedded—'tis a name
We know, but still a bond.   Your rank remains,
His rank remains.   How can he, nobly souled
As you believe and I incline to think,
Aspire to be your favourite, shame and all?

QUEEN.

Hear her! there, there now—could she love like me?
What did I say of smooth-cheeked youth and grace?   *540*
See all it does or could do! so, youth loves!
Oh, tell him, Constance, you could never do
What I will—you, it was not born in! I
Will drive these difficulties far and fast
As yonder mists curdling before the moon.

I'll use my light too, gloriously retrieve
My youth from its enforced calamity,
Dissolve that hateful marriage, and be his,
His own in the eyes alike of God and man.

CONSTANCE.

You will do—dare do—Pause on what you say!   *550*

QUEEN.

Hear her! I thank you, Sweet, for that surprise.
You have the fair face: for the soul, see mine!
I have the strong soul: let me teach you, here.
I think I have borne enough and long enough,
And patiently enough, the world remarks,
To have my own way now, unblamed by all.
It does so happen, I rejoice for it,
This most unhoped-for issue cuts the knot.
There's not a better way of settling claims
Than this; God sends the accident express;   *560*
And were it for my subjects' good, no more,
'Twere best thus ordered. I am thankful now,
Mute, passive, acquiescent. I receive,
And bless God simply, or should almost fear
To walk so smoothly to my ends at last.
Why, how I baffle obstacles, spurn fate!
How strong I am! could Norbert see me now!

CONSTANCE.

Let me consider. It is all too strange.

QUEEN.

You, Constance, learn of me; do you, like me.
You are young, beautiful: my own, best girl,   *570*
You will have many lovers, and love one—
Light hair, not hair like Norbert's, to suit yours,
And taller than he is, for you are tall.
Love him like me! give all away to him;
Think never of yourself; throw by your pride,
Hope, fear,—your own good as you saw it once,
And love him simply for his very self.
Remember, I (and what am I to you?)
Would give up all for one, leave throne, lose life,
Do all but just unlove him! he loves me.   *580*

CONSTANCE.

He shall.

QUEEN.

You, step inside my inmost heart.
Give me your own heart—let us have one heart—
I'll come to you for counsel; " This he says,
This he does, what should this amount to, pray?
Beseech you, change it into current coin.
Is that worth kisses? shall I please him there? "
And then we'll speak in turn of you—what else?
Your love (according to your beauty's worth)
For you shall have some noble love, all gold—
Whom choose you? we will get him at your choice.   *590*
—Constance, I leave you. Just a minute since
I felt as I must die or be alone
Breathing my soul into an ear like yours.
Now, I would face the world with my new life,
With my new crown. I'll walk around the rooms,
And then come back and tell you how it feels.
How soon a smile of God can change the world!
How we are all made for happiness—how work
Grows play, adversity a winning fight!
True, I have lost so many years. What then?   *600*
Many remain—God has been very good.
You, stay here. 'Tis as different from dreams,—
From the mind's cold calm estimate of bliss,
As these stone statues from the flesh and blood.
The comfort thou hast caused mankind, God's moon!
    [*She goes out. Dance-music from within.*

PART THIRD.

NORBERT *enters*.

NORBERT.

Well! we have but one minute and one word—

CONSTANCE.

I am yours, Norbert!

NORBERT.

Yes, mine.

CONSTANCE.
                              Not till now!
You were mine.   Now I give myself to you.

NORBERT.

Constance!

CONSTANCE.

              Your own!   I know the thriftier way
Of giving—haply, 'tis the wiser way.   *610*
Meaning to give a treasure, I might dole
Coin after coin out (each, as that were all,
With a new largess still at each despair)
And force you keep in sight the deed, reserve
Exhaustless till the end my part and yours,
My giving and your taking, both our joys
Dying together.   Is it the wiser way?
I choose the simpler; I give all at once.
Know what you have to trust to, trade upon.
Use it, abuse it,—anything but say   *620*
Hereafter, "Had I known she loved me so,
And what my means, I might have thriven with it."
This is your means.   I give you all myself.

NORBERT.

I take you and thank God.

CONSTANCE.

                    Look on through years!
We cannot kiss a second day like this,
Else were this earth, no earth.

NORBERT.

                        With this day's heat
We shall go on through years of cold.

CONSTANCE.

                              So best.
I try to see those years—I think I see.
You walk quick and new warmth comes; you look back
And lay all to the first glow—not sit down   *630*
For ever brooding on a day like this
While seeing the embers whiten and love die.

Yes, love lives best in its effect; and mine,
Full in its own life, yearns to live in yours.

NORBERT.

Just so.   I take and know you all at once.
Your soul is disengaged so easily,
Your face is there, I know you; give me time,
Let me be proud and think you shall know me.
My soul is slower; in a life I roll
The minute out in which you condense yours—   *640*
The whole slow circle round you I must move,
To be just you.   I look to a long life
To decompose this minute, prove its worth.
'Tis the sparks' long succession one by one
Shall show you in the end what fire was crammed
In that mere stone you struck: you could not know,
If it lay ever unproved in your sight,
As now my heart lies? your own warmth would hide
Its coldness, were it cold.

CONSTANCE.

But how prove, how?

NORBERT.

Prove in my life, you ask?

CONSTANCE.

Quick, Norbert—how?   *650*

NORBERT.

That's easy told.   I count life just a stuff
To try the soul's strength on, educe the man.
Who keeps one end in view makes all things serve.
As with the body—he who hurls a lance
Or heaps up stone on stone, shows strength alike,
So I will seize and use all means to prove
And show this soul of mine you crown as yours,
And justify us both.

CONSTANCE.

Could you write books,
Paint pictures! one sits down in poverty
And writes or paints, with pity for the rich.   *660*

NORBERT.

And loves one's painting and one's writing too,
And not one's mistress! All is best, believe,
And we best as no other than we are.
We live, and they experiment on life
Those poets, painters, all who stand aloof
To overlook the farther. Let us be
The thing they look at! I might take that face
And write of it and paint it—to what end?
For whom? what pale dictatress in the air
Feeds, smiling sadly, her fine ghost-like form   670
With earth's real blood and breath, the beauteous life
She makes despised for ever? You are mine,
Made for me, not for others in the world,
Nor yet for that which I should call my art,
That cold calm power to see how fair you look.
I come to you—I leave you not, to write
Or paint. You are, I am. Let Rubens there
Paint us.

CONSTANCE.

So best!

NORBERT.

I understand your soul.
You live, and rightly sympathise with life,
With action, power, success: this way is straight.   680
And days were short beside, to let me change
The craft my childhood learnt; my craft shall serve.
Men set me here to subjugate, enclose,
Manure their barren lives and force the fruit
First for themselves, and afterward for me
In the due tithe; the task of some one man,
By ways of work appointed by themselves.
I am not bid create, they see no star
Transfiguring my brow to warrant that—
But bind in one and carry out their wills.   690
So I began: to-night sees how I end.
What if it see, too, my first outbreak here
Amid the warmth, surprise and sympathy,
The instincts of the heart that teach the head?
What if the people have discerned in me
The dawn of the next nature, the new man
Whose will they venture in the place of theirs,

And whom they trust to find them out new ways
To the new heights which yet he only sees?
I felt it when you kissed me. See this Queen,   *700*
This people—in our phrase, this mass of men—
See how the mass lies passive to my hand
And how my hand is plastic, and you by
To make the muscles iron! Oh, an end
Shall crown this issue as this crowns the first.
My will be on this people! then, the strain,
The grappling of the potter with his clay,
The long uncertain struggle,—the success
In that uprising of the spirit-work,
The vase shaped to the curl of the god's lip,   *710*
While rounded fair for lower men to see
The Graces in a dance they recognise
With turbulent applause and laughs of heart!
So triumph ever shall renew itself;
Ever to end in efforts higher yet,
Ever begun——

CONSTANCE.

I ever helping?

NORBERT.
Thus!
[*As he embraces her, enter the* QUEEN.

CONSTANCE.

Hist, madam,—so I have performed my part.
You see your gratitude's true decency,
Norbert? a little slow in seeing it!
Begun to end the sooner. What's a kiss?   *720*

NORBERT.
Constance!

CONSTANCE.
Why, must I teach it you again?
You want a witness to your dullness, sir?
What was I saying these ten minutes long?
Then I repeat—when some young handsome man
Like you has acted out a part like yours,
Is pleased to fall in love with one beyond,
So very far beyond him, as he says—
So hopelessly in love, that but to speak

Would prove him mad, he thinks judiciously,
And makes some insignificant good soul   730
Like me, his friend, adviser, confidant
And very stalking-horse to cover him
In following after what he dares not face—
When his end's gained—(sir, do you understand?)
When she, he dares not face, has loved him first,
—May I not say so, madam?—tops his hope,
And overpasses so his wildest dream,
With glad consent of all, and most of her
The confidant who brought the same about—
Why, in the moment when such joy explodes,   740
I do say that the merest gentleman
Will not start rudely from the stalking-horse,
Dismiss it with a " There, enough of you! "
Forget it, show his back unmannerly;
But like a liberal heart will rather turn
And say, " A tingling time of hope was ours—
Betwixt the fears and falterings—we two lived
A chanceful time in waiting for the prize.
The confidant, the Constance, served not ill;
And though I shall forget her in due time,   750
Her use being answered now, as reason bids,
Nay as herself bids from her heart of hearts,
Still, she has rights, the first thanks go to her,
The first good praise goes to the prosperous tool,
And the first—which is the last—thankful kiss."

NORBERT.

—Constance? it is a dream—ah see you smile!

CONSTANCE.

So, now his part being properly performed,
Madam, I turn to you and finish mine
As duly—I do justice in my turn.
Yes, madam, he has loved you—long and well—   760
He could not hope to tell you so—'twas I
Who served to prove your soul accessible.
I led his thoughts on, drew them to their place,
When oft they had wandered out into despair,
And kept love constant toward its natural aim.
Enough—my part is played; you stoop half-way
And meet us royally and spare our fears—

'Tis like yourself—he thanks you, so do I.
Take him—with my full heart! my work is praised
By what comes of it.   Be you happy, both!   *770*
Yourself—the only one on earth who can—
Do all for him, much more than a mere heart
Which though warm is not useful in its warmth
As the silk vesture of a queen! fold that
Around him gently, tenderly.   For him—
For him,—he knows his own part.

NORBERT.

               Have you done?
I take the jest at last.   Should I speak now?
Was yours the wager, Constance, foolish child,
Or did you but accept it?   Well—at least,
You lose by it.

CONSTANCE.

           Now madam, 'tis your turn.   *780*
Restrain him still from speech a little more
And make him happier and more confident!
Pity him, madam, he is timid yet.
Mark, Norbert! do not shrink now!   Here I yield
My whole right in you to the Queen, observe!
With her go put in practice the great schemes
You teem with, follow the career else closed—
Be all you cannot be except by her!
Behold her.—Madam, say for pity's sake
Anything—frankly say you love him.   Else   *790*
He'll not believe it: there's more earnest in
His fear than you conceive—I know the man.

NORBERT.

I know the woman somewhat, and confess
I thought she had jested better—she begins
To overcharge her part.   I gravely wait
Your pleasure, madam: where is my reward?

QUEEN.

Norbert, this wild girl (whom I recognise
Scarce more than you do, in her fancy-fit,
Eccentric speech and variable mirth,
Not very wise perhaps and somewhat bold   *800*

Yet suitable, the whole night's work being strange)
—May still be right: I may do well to speak
And make authentic what appears a dream
To even myself. For, what she says, is true—
Yes, Norbert—what you spoke but now of love,
Devotion, stirred no novel sense in me,
But justified a warmth felt long before.
Yes, from the first—I loved you, I shall say,—
Strange! but I do grow stronger, now 'tis said,
Your courage helps mine: you did well to speak   *810*
To-night, the night that crowns your twelvemonths' toil—
But still I had not waited to discern
Your heart so long, believe me! From the first
The source of so much zeal was almost plain,
In absence even of your own words just now
Which opened out the truth. 'Tis very strange,
But takes a happy ending—in your love
Which mine meets: be it so—as you choose me,
So I choose you.

NORBERT.

                    And worthily you choose!
I will not be unworthy your esteem,   *820*
No, madam. I do love you; I will meet
Your nature, now I know it; this was well,
I see,—you dare and you are justified:
But none had ventured such experiment,
Less versed than you in nobleness of heart,
Less confident of finding it in me.
I like that thus you test me ere you grant
The dearest, richest, beauteousest and best
Of women to my arms! 'tis like yourself!
So—back again into my part's set words—   *830*
Devotion to the uttermost is yours,
But no, you cannot, madam, even you,
Create in me the love our Constance does.
Or—something truer to the tragic phrase—
Not yon magnolia-bell superb with scent
Invites a certain insect—that's myself—
But the small eye-flower nearer to the ground:
I take this lady!

CONSTANCE.

                Stay—not hers, the trap—
Stay, Norbert—that mistake were worst of all.

148

(He is too cunning, madam!) it was I, 840
I, Norbert, who . . .

NORBERT.

       You, was it, Constance?   Then,
But for the grace of this divinest hour
Which gives me you, I should not pardon here.
I am the Queen's: she only knows my brain—
She may experiment therefore on my heart
And I instruct her too by the result;
But you, sweet, you who know me, who so long
Have told my heart-beats over, held my life
In those white hands of yours,—it is not well!

CONSTANCE.

Tush! I have said it, did I not say it all? 850
The life, for her—the heart-beats, for her sake!

NORBERT.

Enough! my cheek grows red, I think.   Your test!
There's not the meanest woman in the world,
Not she I least could love in all the world,
Whom, did she love me, did love prove itself,
I dared insult as you insult me now.
Constance, I could say, if it must be said,
" Take back the soul you offer—I keep mine "
But—" Take the soul still quivering on your hand,
The soul so offered, which I cannot use, 860
And, please you, give it to some friend of mine,
For—what's the trifle he requites me with? "
I, tempt a woman, to amuse a man,
That two may mock her heart if it succumb?
No! fearing God and standing 'neath his heaven,
I would not dare insult a woman so,
Were she the meanest woman in the world,
And he, I cared to please, ten emperors!

CONSTANCE.

Norbert!

NORBERT.

    I love once as I live but once.
What case is this to think or talk about? 870
I love you.   Would it mend the case at all

Should such a step as this kill love in me?
Your part were done: account to God for it.
But mine—could murdered love get up again,
And kneel to whom you pleased to designate
And make you mirth? It is too horrible.
You did not know this, Constance? now you know
That body and soul have each one life, but one:
And here's my love, here, living, at your feet.

CONSTANCE.

See the Queen! Norbert—this one more last word—   880
If thus you have taken jest for earnest—thus
Loved me in earnest . . .

NORBERT.

          Ah, no jest holds here!
Where is the laughter in which jests break up?
And what this horror that grows palpable?
Madam—why grasp you thus the balcony?
Have I done ill? Have I not spoken the truth?
How could I other? Was it not your test,
To try me, and what my love for Constance meant?
Madam, your royal soul itself approves,
The first, that I should choose thus! so one takes   890
A beggar—asks him what would buy his child,
And then approves the expected laugh of scorn
Returned as something noble from the rags.
Speak, Constance, I'm the beggar! Ha, what's this?
You two glare each at each like panthers now.
Constance—the world fades; only you stand there!
You did not in to-night's wild whirl of things
Sell me—your soul of souls for any price?
No—no—'tis easy to believe in you.
Was it your love's mad trial to o'ertop   900
Mine by this vain self-sacrifice? well, still—
Though I should curse, I love you. I am love
And cannot change! love's self is at your feet.

                      [QUEEN *goes out.*

CONSTANCE.

Feel my heart; let it die against your own.

NORBERT.

Against my own! explain not; let this be.
This is life's height.

CONSTANCE
Yours! Yours! Yours!

NORBERT.
You and I—
Why care by what meanders we are here
In the centre of the labyrinth? men have died
Trying to find this place out, which we have found.

CONSTANCE.
Found, found!

NORBERT.
Sweet, never fear what she can do—   *910*
We are past harm now.

CONSTANCE.
On the breast of God.
I thought of men—as if you were a man.
Tempting him with a crown!

NORBERT.
This must end here—
It is too perfect!

CONSTANCE.
There's the music stopped.
What measured heavy tread? it is one blaze
About me and within me.

NORBERT.
Oh, some death
Will run its sudden finger round this spark,
And sever us from the rest—

CONSTANCE.
And so do well.
Now the doors open—

NORBERT.
'Tis the guard comes.

CONSTANCE.
Kiss!

SAUL.

I.

SAID Abner, "At last thou are come! Ere I tell, ere thou
    speak,
Kiss my cheek, wish me well!" Then I wished it, and did
    kiss his cheek.
And he, "Since the King, O my friend, for thy countenance
    sent,
Neither drunken nor eaten have we; nor until from his tent
Thou return with the joyful assurance the King liveth yet,
Shall our lip with the honey be bright, with the water be wet.
For out of the black mid-tent's silence, a space of three days,
Not a sound hath escaped to thy servants, of prayer or of
    praise
To betoken that Saul and the Spirit have ended their strife,
And that, faint in his triumph, the monarch sinks back upon
    life.   *10*

II.

Yet now my heart leaps, O beloved! God's child, with his
    dew
On thy gracious gold hair, and those lilies still living and blue
Just broken to twine round thy harp-strings, as if no wild
    heat
Were now raging to torture the desert!"

III.

                          Then I, as was meet,
Knelt down to the God of my fathers, and rose on my feet,
And ran o'er the sand burnt to powder. The tent was
    unlooped;
I pulled up the spear that obstructed, and under I stooped;
Hands and knees on the slippery grass-patch, all withered
    and gone,
That extends to the second enclosure, I groped my way on
Till I felt where the foldskirts fly open. Then once more I
    prayed,   *20*
And opened the foldskirts and entered, and was not afraid,
But spoke, "Here is David, thy servant!" And no voice
    replied.

At the first I saw nought but the blackness; but soon I
    descried
A something more black than the blackness—the vast the
    upright
Main prop which sustains the pavilion: and slow into sight
Grew a figure against it, gigantic and blackest of all;—
Then a sunbeam, that burst thro' the tent-roof,—showed
    Saul.

IV.

He stood as erect as that tent-prop; both arms stretched
    out wide
On the great cross-support in the centre, that goes to each
    side:
He relaxed not a muscle, but hung there,—as, caught in his
    pangs   *30*
And waiting his change the king-serpent all heavily hangs,
Far away from his kind, in the pine, till deliverance come
With the spring-time,—so agonized Saul, drear and stark,
    blind and dumb.

V.

Then I tuned my harp,—took off the lilies we twine round its
    chords
Lest they snap 'neath the stress of the noontide—those sun-
    beams like swords!
And I first played the tune all our sheep know, as, one after
    one,
So docile they come to the pen-door, till folding be done.
They are white and untorn by the bushes, for lo, they have
    fed
Where the long grasses stifle the water within the stream's
    bed:
And now one after one seeks its lodging, as star follows star *40*
Into eve and the blue far above us,—so blue and so far!

VI.

—Then the tune, for which quails on the cornland will each
    leave his mate
To fly after the player; then, what makes the crickets elate,
Till for boldness they fight one another; and then, what has
    weight
To set the quick jerboa a-musing outside his sand house—

There are none such as he for a wonder, half bird and half
    mouse!—
God made all the creatures and gave them our love and our
    fear,
To give sign, we and they are his children, one family here.

VII.

Then I played the help-tune of our reapers, their wine-song,
    when hand
Grasps at hand, eye lights eye in good friendship, and great
    hearts expand   50
And grow one in the sense of this world's life.—And then, the
    last song
When the dead man is praised on his journey—" Bear, bear
    him along
With his few faults shut up like dead flowerets! are balm-
    seeds not here
To console us? The land has none left, such as he on the
    bier.
Oh, would we might keep thee, my brother!"—And then,
    the glad chaunt
Of the marriage,—first go the young maidens, next, she
    whom we vaunt
As the beauty, the pride of our dwelling.—And then, the
    great march
Wherein man runs to man to assist him and buttress an arch
Nought can break; who shall harm them, our friends?—
    Then, the chorus intoned
As the Levites go up to the altar in glory enthroned . . .   60
But I stopped here—for here in the darkness, Saul groaned.

VIII.

And I paused, held my breath in such silence, and listened
    apart;
And the tent shook, for mighty Saul shuddered,—and
    sparkles 'gan dart
From the jewels that woke in his turban at once with a start—
All its lordly male-sapphires, and rubies courageous at heart.
So the head—but the body still moved not, still hung there
    erect.
And I bent once again to my playing, pursued it unchecked,
As I sang,—

IX.

"Oh, our manhood's prime vigour! **no**
  spirit feels waste,
Not a muscle is stopped in its playing, nor sinew unbraced.
Oh, the wild joys of living! the leaping from rock up to rock— *70*
The strong rending of boughs from the fir-tree,—the cool
  silver shock
Of the plunge in a pool's living water,—the hunt of the bear,
And the sultriness showing the lion is couched in his lair.
And the meal—the rich dates—yellowed over with gold dust
  divine,
And the locust's-flesh steeped in the pitcher; the full draught
  of wine,
And the sleep in the dried river-channel where bulrushes tell
That the water was wont to go warbling so softly and well.
How good is man's life, the mere living! how fit to employ
All the heart and the soul and the senses, for ever in joy!
Hast thou loved the white locks of thy father, whose sword
  thou didst guard   *80*
When he trusted thee forth with the armies, for glorious
  reward?
Didst thou see the thin hands of thy mother, held up as men
  sung
The low song of the nearly-departed, and heard her faint
  tongue
Joining in while it could to the witness, 'Let one more
  attest,
I have lived, seen God's hand thro' a lifetime, and all was
  for best . . .'
Then they sung thro' their tears in strong triumph, not much,
  —but the rest.
And thy brothers, the help and the contest, the working
  whence grew
Such result as from seething grape-bundles, the spirit strained
  true!
And the friends of thy boyhood—that boyhood of wonder
  and hope,
Present promise, and wealth of the future beyond the eye's
  scope,—   *90*
Till lo, thou art grown to a monarch; a people is thine;
And all gifts which the world offers singly, on one head
  combine!

155

On one head, all the beauty and strength, love and rage,
    like the throe
That, a-work in the rock, helps its labour, and lets the gold
    go:
High ambition and deeds which surpass it, fame crowning
    it,—all
Brought to blaze on the head of one creature—King Saul!"

x.

And lo, with that leap of my spirit, heart, hand, harp and
    voice,
Each lifting Saul's name out of sorrow, each bidding rejoice
Saul's fame in the light it was made for—as when, dare I say,
The Lord's army in rapture of service, strains through its
    array,   *100*
And upsoareth the cherubim-chariot—" Saul!" cried I, and
    stopped,
And waited the thing that should follow.   Then Saul, who
    hung propt
By the tent's cross-support in the centre, was struck by his
    name.
Have ye seen when Spring's arrowy summons goes right to
    the aim,
And some mountain, the last to withstand her, that held, (he
    alone,
While the vale laughed in freedom and flowers) on a broad
    bust of stone
A year's snow bound about for a breastplate,—leaves grasp
    of the sheet?
Fold on fold all at once it crowds thunderously down to his
    feet,
And there fronts you, stark, black but alive yet, your moun-
    tain of old,
With his rents, the successive bequeathings of ages untold— *110*
Yea, each harm got in fighting your battles, each furrow and
    scar
Of his head thrust 'twixt you and the tempest—all hail, there
    they are!
Now again to be softened with verdure, again hold the nest
Of the dove, tempt the goat and its young to the green on
    its crest
For their food in the ardours of summer!   One long shudder
    thrilled

All the tent till the very air tingled, then sank and was
  stilled,
At the King's self left standing before me, released and
  aware.
What was gone, what remained? all to traverse 'twixt hope
  and despair—
Death was past, life not come—so he waited. Awhile his
  right hand
Held the brow, helped the eyes left too vacant forthwith to
  remand   *120*
To their place what new object should enter: 'twas Saul as
  before.
I looked up and dared gaze at those eyes, nor was hurt any
  more
Than by slow pallid sunsets in autumn, ye watch from the
  shore
At their sad level gaze o'er the ocean—a sun's slow decline
Over hills which, resolved in stern silence, o'erlap and en-
  twine
Base with base to knit strength more intense: so, arm folded
  in arm
O'er the chest whose slow heavings subsided.

XI.

                      What spell or what charm,
(For, awhile there was trouble within me) what next should
  I urge
To sustain him where song had restored him?—Song filled
  to the verge
His cup with the wine of this life, pressing all that it yields *130*
Of mere fruitage, the strength and the beauty! Beyond, on
  what fields,
Glean a vintage more potent and perfect to brighten the eye
And bring blood to the lip, and commend them the cup they
  put by?
He saith, " It is good; " still he drinks not—he lets me praise
  life,
Gives assent, yet would die for his own part.

XII.

                      Then fancies grew rife
Which had come long ago on the pastures, when round me
  the sheep

Fed in silence—above, the one eagle wheeled slow as in sleep,
And I lay in my hollow, and mused on the world that might
    lie
'Neath his ken, though I saw but the strip 'twixt the hill and
    the sky:
And I laughed—" Since my days are ordained to be passed
    with my flocks,   *140*
Let me people at least with my fancies, the plains and the
    rocks,
Dream the life I am never to mix with, and image the show
Of mankind as they live in those fashions I hardly shall know!
Schemes of life, its best rules and right uses, the courage
    that gains,
And the prudence that keeps what men strive for." And
    now these old trains
Of vague thought came again; I grew surer; so once more
    the string
Of my harp made response to my spirit, as thus—

XIII.

                   " Yea, my king,"
I began—" thou dost well in rejecting mere comforts that
    spring
From the mere mortal life held in common by man and by
    brute:
In our flesh grows the branch of this life, in our soul it bears
    fruit.   *150*
Thou hast marked the slow rise of the tree,—how its stem
    trembled first
Till it passed the kid's lip, the stag's antler; then safely
    outburst
The fan-branches all round; and thou mindest when these
    too, in turn
Broke a-bloom and the palm-tree seemed perfect; yet more
    was to learn
Ev'n the good that comes in with the palm-fruit. Our
    dates shall we slight,
When their juice brings a cure for all sorrow? or care for the
    plight
Of the palm's self whose slow growth produced them? Not
    so! stem and branch
Shall decay, nor be known in their place, while the palm-
    wine shall staunch

Every wound of man's spirit in winter. I pour thee such
 wine.
Leave the flesh to the fate it was fit for: the spirit be
 thine!   *160*
By the spirit, when age shall o'ercome thee, thou still shalt
 enjoy
More indeed, than at first when inconscious, the life of a boy.
Crush that life, and behold its wine running! each deed thou
 hast done
Dies, revives, goes to work in the world; until e'en as
 the sun
Looking down on the earth, though clouds spoil him, though
 tempests efface,
Can find nothing his own deed produced not, must every
 where trace
The results of his past summer-prime,—so, each ray of thy
 will,
Every flash of thy passion and prowess, long over, shall thrill
Thy whole people the countless, with ardour, till they too
 give forth
A like cheer to their sons, who in turn, fill the south and the
 north   *170*
With the radiance thy deed was the germ of. Carouse in the
 past.
But the license of age has its limit; thou diest at last.
As the lion when age dims his eye-ball, the rose at her
 height,
So with man—so his power and his beauty for ever take
 flight.
No! again a long draught of my soul-wine! look forth o'er
 the years—
Thou hast done now with eyes for the actual; begin with the
 seer's!
Is Saul dead? in the depth of the vale make his tomb—bid
 arise
A grey mountain of marble heaped four-square, till built to
 the skies.
Let it mark where the great First King slumbers—whose
 fame would ye know?
Up above see the rock's naked face, where the record shall go *180*
In great characters cut by the scribe,—Such was Saul, so he
 did,
With the sages directing the work, by the populace chid,—

For not half, they'll affirm, is comprised there! Which fault
 to amend,
In the grove with his kind grows the cedar, whereon they
 shall spend
(See, in tablets 'tis level before them) their praise, and record
With the gold of the graver, Saul's story,—the statesman's
 great word
Side by side with the poet's sweet comment. The river's
 a-wave
With smooth paper-reeds grazing each other when prophet
 winds rave:
So the pen gives unborn generations their due and their part
In thy being! Then, first of the mighty, thank God that
 thou art."   *190*

XIV.

And behold while I sang . . . But O Thou who didst grant
 me that day,
And before it not seldom hast granted, thy help to essay
Carry on and complete an adventure,—my Shield and my
 Sword
In that act where my soul was thy servant, thy word was my
 word,—
Still be with me, who then at the summit of human endeavour
And scaling the highest man's thought could, gazed hopeless
 as ever
On the new stretch of Heaven above me—till, Mighty to save,
Just one lift of thy hand cleared that distance—God's throne
 from man's grave!
Let me tell out my tale to its ending—my voice to my heart,
Which can scarce dare believe in what marvels that night I
 took part,   *200*
As this morning I gather the fragments, alone with my sheep,
And still fear lest the terrible glory evanish like sleep!
For I wake in the grey dewy covert, while Hebron upheaves
The dawn struggling with night on his shoulder, and Kidron
 retrieves
Slow the damage of yesterday's sunshine.

XV.

I say then,—my song
While I sang thus, assuring the monarch, and ever more
 strong

Made a proffer of good to console him—he slowly resumed
His old motions and habitudes kingly. The right hand replumed
His black locks to their wonted composure, adjusted the swathes
Of his turban, and see—the huge sweat that his countenance bathes,   *210*
He wipes off with the robe; and he girds now his loins as of yore,
And feels slow for the armlets of price, with the clasp set before.
He is Saul, ye remember in glory,—ere error had bent
The broad brow from the daily communion; and still, though much spent
Be the life and the bearing that front you, the same God did choose,
To receive what a man may waste, desecrate, never quite lose.
So sank he along by the tent-prop, till, stayed by the pile
Of his armour and war-cloak and garments, he leaned there awhile,
And so sat out my singing,—one arm round the tent-prop, to raise
His bent head, and the other hung slack—till I touched on the praise   *220*
I foresaw from all men in all times, to the man patient there,
And thus ended, the harp falling forward. Then first I was
   'ware
That he sat, as I say, with my head just above his vast knees
Which were thrust out on each side around me, like oak-roots which please
To encircle a lamb when it slumbers. I looked up to know
If the best I could do had brought solace: he spoke not, but slow
Lifted up the hand slack at his side, till he laid it with care
Soft and grave, but in mild settled will, on my brow: thro' my hair
The large fingers were pushed, and he bent back my head, with kind power—
All my face back, intent to peruse it, as men do a flower.   *230*
Thus held he me there with his great eyes that scrutinised mine—
And oh, all my heart how it loved him! but where was the sign?

I yearned—" Could I help thee, my father, inventing a bliss,
I would add to that life of the past, both the future and this,
I would give thee new life altogether, as good, ages hence,
As this moment,—had love but the warrant, love's heart to
    dispense! "

XVI.

Then the truth came upon me. No harp more—no song
    more! out-broke—

XVII.

" I have gone the whole round of Creation: I saw and I spoke!
I, a work of God's hand for that purpose, received in my
    brain
And pronounced on the rest of his handwork—returned him
    again   *240*
His creation's approval or censure: I spoke as I saw.
I report, as a man may of God's work—all's love, yet all's law!
Now I lay down the judgeship he lent me. Each faculty
    tasked
To perceive him, has gained an abyss, where a dewdrop was
    asked.
Have I knowledge? confounded it shrivels at wisdom laid
    bare.
Have I forethought? how purblind, how blank, to the
    Infinite care!
Do I task any faculty highest, to image success?
I but open my eyes,—and perfection, no more and no less,
In the kind I imagined, full-fronts me, and God is seen God
In the star, in the stone, in the flesh, in the soul and the clod. *250*
And thus looking within and around me, I ever renew
(With that stoop of the soul which in bending upraises it too)
The submission of Man's nothing-perfect to God's All-
    Complete,
As by each new obeisance in spirit, I climb to his feet!
Yet with all this abounding experience, this Deity known,
I shall dare to discover some province, some gift of my own.
There's one faculty pleasant to exercise, hard to hoodwink,
I am fain to keep still in abeyance, (I laugh as I think)
Lest, insisting to claim and parade in it, wot ye, I worst
E'en the Giver in one gift. Behold! I could love if I durst! *260*
But I sink the pretension as fearing a man may o'ertake
God's own speed in the one way of love: I abstain, for love's
    sake!

—What, my soul? see thus far and no farther? when door
    great and small,
Nine-and-ninety flew ope at our touch, should the hundredth
    appal?
In the least things, have faith, yet distrust in the greatest
    of all?
Do I find love so full in my nature, God's ultimate gift,
That I doubt his own love can compete with it? here, the
    parts shift?
Here, the creature surpass the Creator, the end, what Began?—
Would I fain in my impotent yearning do all for this man,
And dare doubt He alone shall not help him, who yet alone
    can?   *270*
Would it ever have entered my mind, the bare will, much less
    power,
To bestow on this Saul what I sang of, the marvellous dower
Of the life he was gifted and filled with? to make such a soul,
Such a body, and then such an earth for insphering the whole?
And doth it not enter my mind (as my warm tears attest)
These good things being given, to go on, and give one more,
    the best?
Ay, to save and redeem and restore him, maintain at the
    height
This perfection,—succeed with life's dayspring, death's
    minute of night?
Interpose at the difficult minute, snatch Saul, the mistake,
Saul, the failure, the ruin he seems now,—and bid him awake *280*
From the dream, the probation, the prelude, to find himself
    set
Clear and safe in new light and new life,—a new harmony yet
To be run, and continued, and ended—who knows?—or
    endure!
The man taught enough by life's dream, of the rest to make
    sure.
By the pain-throb, triumphantly winning intensified bliss,
And the next world's reward and repose, by the struggle in
    this.

XVIII.

" I believe it! 'tis Thou, God, that givest, 'tis I who receive:
In the first is the last, in thy will is my power to believe.
All's one gift: thou canst grant it moreover, as prompt to
    my prayer

As I breathe out this breath, as I open these arms to the air. *290*
From thy will, stream the worlds, life and nature, thy dread
    Sabaoth:
I will?—the mere atoms despise me! and why am I loth
To look that, even that in the face too? why is it I dare
Think but lightly of such impuissance? what stops my
    despair?
This:—'tis not what man Does which exalts him, but what
    man Would do!
See the king—I would help him but cannot, the wishes fall
    through.
Could I wrestle to raise him from sorrow, grow poor to enrich,
To fill up his life, starve my own out, I would—knowing
    which,
I know that my service is perfect.—Oh, speak through me
    now!
Would I suffer for him that I love? So wilt Thou—so wilt
    Thou! *300*
So shall crown thee the topmost, ineffablest, uttermost
    Crown—
And thy love fill infinitude wholly, nor leave up nor down
One spot for the creature to stand in! It is by no breath,
Turn of eye, wave of hand, that Salvation joins issue with
    death!
As thy Love is discovered almighty, almighty be proved
Thy power, that exists with and for it, of Being beloved!
He who did most, shall bear most; the strongest shall stand
    the most weak.
'Tis the weakness in strength that I cry for! my flesh, that
    I seek
In the Godhead! I seek and I find it. O Saul, it shall be
A Face like my face that receives thee: a Man like to me, *310*
Thou shalt love and be loved by, for ever! a Hand like this
    hand
Shall throw open the gates of new life to thee! See the
    Christ stand!"

XIX.

I know not too well how I found my way home in the night.
There were witnesses, cohorts about me, to left and to right,
Angels, powers, the unuttered, unseen, the alive—the aware—
I repressed, I got through them as hardly, as strugglingly
    there,

As a runner beset by the populace famished for news—
Life or death. The whole earth was awakened, hell loosed
    with her crews;
And the stars of night beat with emotion, and tingled and
    shot
Out in fire the strong pain of pent knowledge: but I fainted
    not.   *320*
For the Hand still impelled me at once and supported—
    suppressed
All the tumult, and quenched it with quiet, and holy behest,
Till the ràpture was shut in itself, and the earth sank to rest.
Anon at the dawn, all that trouble had withered from earth—
Not so much, but I saw it die out in the day's tender birth;
In the gathered intensity brought to the grey of the hills;
In the shuddering forests' new awe; in the sudden wind-
    thrills;
In the startled wild beasts that bore off, each with eye
    sidling still
Tho' averted, in wonder and dread; and the birds stiff and
    chill
That rose heavily, as I approached them, made stupid with
    awe!   *330*
E'en the serpent that slid away silent,—he felt the new Law.
The same stared in the white humid faces upturned by the
    flowers;
The same worked in the heart of the cedar, and moved the
    vine-bowers.
And the little brooks witnessing murmured, persistent and
    low,
With their obstinate, all but hushed voices—E'en so! it is so.

"DE GUSTIBUS—"

1. YOUR ghost will walk, you lover of trees,
    (If loves remain)
      In an English lane,
  By a cornfield-side a-flutter with poppies.
  Hark, those two in the hazel coppice—
  A boy and a girl, if the good fates please,
    Making love, say,—
      The happier they!

Draw yourself up from the light of the moon,
And let them pass, as they will too soon,   *10*
    With the beanflowers' boon,
    And the blackbird's tune,
    And May, and June!

II. What I love best in all the world,
Is, a castle, precipice-encurled,
In a gash of the wind-grieved Apennine.
Or look for me, old fellow of mine,
(If I get my head from out the mouth
O' the grave, and loose my spirit's bands,
And come again to the land of lands)—   *20*
In a sea-side house to the farther south,
Where the baked cicalas die of drouth,
And one sharp tree ('tis a cypress) stands,
By the many hundred years red-rusted,
Rough iron-spiked, ripe fruit-o'ercrusted,
My sentinel to guard the sands
To the water's edge.   For, what expands
Without the house, but the great opaque
Blue breadth of sea, and not a break?
While, in the house, for ever crumbles   *30*
Some fragment of the frescoed walls,
From blisters where a scorpion sprawls.
A girl bare-footed brings and tumbles
Down on the pavement, green-flesh melons,
And says there's news to-day—the king
Was shot at, touched in the liver-wing,
Goes with his Bourbon arm in a sling.
—She hopes they have not caught the felons.
    Italy, my Italy!
Queen Mary's saying serves for me—   *40*
    (When fortune's malice
    Lost her, Calais.)
Open my heart and you will see
Graved inside of it, " Italy."
Such lovers old are I and she;
So it always was, so it still shall be!

WOMEN AND ROSES.

I. I DREAM of a red-rose tree.
   And which of its roses three
   Is the dearest rose to me?

II. Round and round, like a dance of snow
In a dazzling drift, as its guardians, go
Floating the women faded for ages,
Sculptured in stone, on the poet's pages.
Then follow the women fresh and gay,
Living and loving and loved to-day.
Last, in the rear, flee the multitude of maidens,   *10*
Beauties unborn.   And all, to one cadence,
They circle their rose on my rose tree.

III. Dear rose, thy turn is reached,
   Thy leaf hangs loose and bleached:
   Bees pass it unimpeached.

IV. Stay then, stoop, since I cannot climb,
You, great shapes of the antique time!
How shall I fix you, fire you, freeze you,
Break my heart at your feet to please you?
Oh! to possess, and be possessed!   *20*
Hearts that beat 'neath each pallid breast!
But once of love, the poesy, the passion,
Drink once and die!—In vain, the same fashion,
They circle their rose on my rose tree.

V. Dear rose, thy joy's undimmed;
   Thy cup is ruby-rimmed,
   Thy cup's heart nectar-brimmed.

VI. Deep as drops from a statue's plinth
The bee sucked in by the hyacinth,
So will I bury me while burning,   *30*
Quench like him at a plunge my yearning,
Eyes in your eyes, lips on your lips!
Fold me fast where the cincture slips,
Prison all my soul in eternities of pleasure!
Girdle me once! But no—in their old measure
They circle their rose on my rose tree.

VII. Dear rose without a thorn,
  Thy bud's the babe unborn:
  First streak of a new morn.

VIII. Wings, lend wings for the cold, the clear!   *40*
  What's far conquers what is near.
  Roses will bloom nor want beholders,
  Sprung from the dust where our own flesh moulders.
  What shall arrive with the cycle's change?
  A novel grace and a beauty strange.
  I will make an Eve, be the artist that began her,
  Shaped her to his mind!—Alas! in like manner
  They circle their rose on my rose tree.

PROTUS

AMONG these latter busts we count by scores,
Half-emperors and quarter-emperors,
Each with his bay-leaf fillet, loose-thonged vest,
Loric and low-browed Gorgon on the breast
One loves a baby face, with violets there,
Violets instead of laurel in the hair,
As those were all the little locks could bear.

Now read here. "Protus ends a period
Of empery beginning with a god:
Born in the porphyry chamber at Byzant;   *10*
Queens by his cradle, proud and ministrant.
And if he quickened breath there, 'twould like fire
Pantingly through the dim vast realm transpire.
A fame that he was missing, spread afar—
The world, from its four corners, rose in war,
Till he was borne out on a balcony
To pacify the world when it should see.
The captains ranged before him, one, his hand
Made baby points at, gained the chief command.
And day by day more beautiful he grew   *20*
In shape, all said, in feature and in hue,
While young Greek sculptors gazing on the child
Were, so, with old Greek sculpture, reconciled.
Already sages laboured to condense

In easy tomes a life's experience:
And artists took grave counsel to impart
In one breath and one hand-sweep, all their art—
To make his graces prompt as blossoming
Of plentifully-watered palms in spring:
Since well beseems it, whoso mounts the throne,⁣   *30*
For beauty, knowledge, strength, should stand alone,
And mortals love the letters of his name."

—Stop! have you turned two pages?   Still the same.
New reign, same date.   The scribe goes on to say
How that same year, on such a month and day,
" John the Pannonian, groundedly believed
A blacksmith's bastard, whose hard hand reprieved
The Empire from its fate the year before,—
Came, had a mind to take the crown, and wore
The same for six years, (during which the Huns⁣   *40*
Kept off their fingers from us) till his sons
Put something in his liquor "—and so forth.
Then a new reign.   Stay—" Take at its just worth "
(Subjoins an annotator) " what I give
As hearsay.   Some think John let Protus live
And slip away.   'Tis said, he reached man's age
At some blind northern court; made first a page,
Then, tutor to the children—last, of use
About the hunting-stables.   I deduce
He wrote the little tract ' On worming dogs,'⁣   *50*
Whereof the name in sundry catalogues
Is extant yet.   A Protus of the Race
Is rumoured to have died a monk in Thrace,—
And if the same, he reached senility."

Here's John the Smith's rough-hammered head.   Great eye,
Gross jaw and griped lips do what granite can
To give you the crown-grasper.   What a man!

HOLY-CROSS DAY

ON WHICH THE JEWS WERE FORCED TO ATTEND AN ANNUAL
CHRISTIAN SERMON IN ROME

['Now was come about Holy-Cross day, and now must my lord
preach his first sermon to the Jews: as it was of old cared for in the
merciful bowels of the Church, that, so to speak, a crumb at least
from her conspicuous table here in Rome, should be, though but once
yearly, cast to the famishing dogs, under-trampled and bespitten-
upon beneath the feet of the guests. And a moving sight in truth, this,
of so many of the besotted, blind, restive and ready-to-perish
Hebrews! now paternally brought—nay, (for He saith, "Compel
them to come in") haled, as it were, by the head and hair, and
against their obstinate hearts, to partake of the heavenly grace. What
awakening, what striving with tears, what working of a yeasty
conscience! Nor was my lord wanting to himself on so apt an occa-
sion; witness the abundance of conversions which did incontinently
reward him: though not to my lord be altogether the glory.'—*Diary
by the Bishop's Secretary*, 1600.]

Though what the Jews really said, on thus being driven to church,
was rather to this effect:

I. FEE, faw, fum! bubble and squeak!
    Blessedest Thursday's the fat of the week.
    Rumble and tumble, sleek and rough,
    Stinking and savoury, smug and gruff,
    Take the church-road, for the bell's due chime
    Gives us the summons—'tis sermon-time.

II. Boh, here's Barnabas! Job, that's you?
    Up stumps Solomon—bustling too?
    Shame, man! greedy beyond your years
    To handsel the bishop's shaving-shears?   *10*
    Fair play's a jewel! leave friends in the lurch?
    Stand on a line ere you start for the church.

III. Higgledy piggledy, packed we lie,
     Rats in a hamper, swine in a sty,
     Wasps in a bottle, frogs in a sieve,
     Worms in a carcase, fleas in a sleeve.
     Hist! square shoulders, settle your thumbs
     And buzz for the bishop—here he comes.

IV. Bow, wow, wow—a bone for the dog!
    I liken his Grace to an acorned hog.   *20*
    What, a boy at his side, with the bloom of a lass,
    To help and handle my lord's hour-glass!
    Didst ever behold so lithe a chine?
    His cheek hath laps like a fresh-singed swine.

v. Aaron's asleep—shove hip to haunch,
  Or somebody deal him a dig in the paunch!
  Look at the purse with the tassel and knob,
  And the gown with the angel and thingumbob.
  What's he at, quotha? reading his text!
  Now you've his curtsey—and what comes next?   30

vi. See to our converts—you doomed black dozen—
  No stealing away—nor cog nor cozen!
  You five that were thieves, deserve it fairly;
  You seven that were beggars, will live less sparely
  You took your turn and dipped in the hat,
  Got fortune—and fortune gets you; mind that!

vii. Give your first groan—compunction's at work;
  And soft! from a Jew you mount to a Turk.
  Lo, Micah,—the self-same beard on chin
  He was four times already converted in!   40
  Here's a knife, clip quick—it's a sign of grace—
  Or he ruins us all with his hanging-face.

viii. Whom now is the bishop a-leering at?
  I know a point where his text falls pat.
  I'll tell him to-morrow, a word just now
  Went to my heart and made me vow
  I meddle no more with the worst of trades—
  Let somebody else pay his serenades.

ix. Groan all together now, whee—hee—hee!
  It's a-work, it's a-work, ah, woe is me!   50
  It began, when a herd of us, picked and placed,
  Were spurred through the Corso, stripped to the waist;
  Jew-brutes, with sweat and blood well spent
  To usher in worthily Christian Lent.

x. It grew, when the hangman entered our bounds,
  Yelled, pricked us out to this church like hounds.
  It got to a pitch, when the hand indeed
  Which gutted my purse, would throttle my creed.
  And it overflows, when, to even the odd,
  Men I helped to their sins, help me to their God.   60

xi. But now, while the scapegoats leave our flock,
  And the rest sit silent and count the clock,
  Since forced to muse the appointed time

On these precious facts and truths sublime,—
Let us fitly employ it, under our breath,
In saying Ben Ezra's Song of Death.

XII. For Rabbi Ben Ezra, the night he died,
Called sons and sons' sons to his side,
And spoke, " This world has been harsh and strange,
Something is wrong, there needeth a change.   70
But what, or where? at the last, or first?
In one point only we sinned, at worst.

XIII. " The Lord will have mercy on Jacob yet,
And again in his border see Israel set.
When Judah beholds Jerusalem,
The stranger-seed shall be joined to them:
To Jacob's House shall the Gentiles cleave.
So the prophet saith and his sons believe.

XIV. " Ay, the children of the chosen race
Shall carry and bring them to their place;   80
In the land of the Lord shall lead the same,
Bondsmen and handmaids.   Who shall blame,
When the slaves enslave, the oppressed ones o'er
The oppressor triumph for evermore?

XV. " God spoke, and gave us the word to keep:
Bade never fold the hands nor sleep
'Mid a faithless world,—at watch and ward,
Till the Christ at the end relieve our guard.
By his servant Moses the watch was set:
Though near upon cock-crow—we keep it yet.   90

XVI. " Thou! if thou wast He, who at mid-watch came,
By the starlight naming a dubious Name!
And if we were too heavy with sleep—too rash
With fear—O thou, if that martyr-gash
Fell on thee coming to take thine own,
And we gave the Cross, when we owed the Throne—

XVII. " Thou art the Judge.   We are bruised thus.
But, the judgment over, join sides with us!
Thine too is the cause! and not more thine
Than ours, is the work of these dogs and swine,   100
Whose life laughs through and spits at their creed,
Who maintain thee in word, and defy thee in deed!

XVIII. " We withstood Christ then? be mindful how
At least we withstand Barabbas now!
Was our outrage sore? but the worst we spared,
To have called these—Christians,—had we dared!
Let defiance to them, pay mistrust of thee,
And Rome make amends for Calvary!

XIX. " By the torture, prolonged from age to age,
By the infamy, Israel's heritage,   *110*
By the Ghetto's plague, by the garb's disgrace,
By the badge of shame, by the felon's place,
By the branding-tool, the bloody whip,
And the summons to Christian fellowship,

XX. " We boast our proofs, that at least the Jew
Would wrest Christ's name from the Devil's crew.
Thy face took never so deep a shade
But we fought them in it, God our aid!
A trophy to bear, as we march, a band
South, east, and on to the Pleasant Land! "   *120*

THE GUARDIAN-ANGEL:

A PICTURE AT FANO.

I. DEAR and great Angel, wouldst thou only leave
That child, when thou hast done with him, for me!
Let me sit all the day here, that when eve
Shall find performed thy special ministry
And time come for departure, thou, suspending
Thy flight, mayst see another child for tending,
Another still, to quiet and retrieve.

II. Then I shall feel thee step one step, no more,
From where thou standest now, to where I gaze,
And suddenly my head be covered o'er   *10*
With those wings, white above the child who prays
Now on that tomb—and I shall feel thee guarding
Me, out of all the world! for me, discarding
Yon heaven thy home, that waits and opes its door!

III. I would not look up thither past thy head
Because the door opes, like that child, I know,
For I should have thy gracious face instead,

Thou bird of God!   And wilt thou bend me low
Like him, and lay, like his, my hands together,
And lift them up to pray, and gently tether   20
   Me, as thy lamb there, with thy garment's spread?

IV. If this was ever granted, I would rest
   My head beneath thine, while thy healing hands
Close-covered both my eyes beside thy breast,
   Pressing the brain, which too much thought expands
Back to its proper size again, and smoothing
Distortion down till every nerve had soothing,
   And all lay quiet, happy and supprest.

V. How soon all worldly wrong would be repaired!
   I think how I should view the earth and skies   30
And sea, when once again my brow was bared
   After thy healing, with such different eyes.
O, world, as God has made it! all is beauty:
And knowing this, is love, and love is duty.
   What further may be sought for or declared?

VI. Guercino drew this angel I saw teach
   (Alfred, dear friend)—that little child to pray,
Holding the little hands up, each to each
   Pressed gently,—with his own head turned away
Over the earth where so much lay before him   40
Of work to do, though heaven was opening o'er him,
   And he was left at Fano by the beach.

VII. We were at Fano, and three times we went
   To sit and see him in his chapel there,
And drink his beauty to our soul's content
   —My angel with me too: and since I care
For dear Guercino's fame, (to which in power
And glory comes this picture for a dower,
   Fraught with a pathos so magnificent)

VIII. And since he did not work so earnestly   50
   At all times, and has else endured some wrong,—
I took one thought his picture struck from me,
   And spread it out, translating it to song.
My love is here.   Where are you, dear old friend?
How rolls the Wairoa at your world's far end?
   This is Ancona, yonder is the sea.

CLEON.

" As certain also of your own poets have said."—

CLEON the poet, (from the sprinkled isles,
Lily on lily, that o'erlace the sea,
And laugh their pride when the light wave lisps " Greece ")—
To Protos in his Tyranny: much health!

   They give thy letter to me, even now:
I read and seem as if I heard thee speak.
The master of thy galley still unlades
Gift after gift; they block my court at last
And pile themselves along its portico
Royal with sunset, like a thought of thee: *10*
And one white she-slave from the group dispersed
Of black and white slaves, (like the chequer-work
Pavement, at once my nation's work and gift,
Now covered with this settle-down of doves)
One lyric woman, in her crocus vest
Woven of sea-wools, with her two white hands
Commends to me the strainer and the cup
Thy lip hath bettered ere it blesses mine.

   Well-counselled, king, in thy munificence!
For so shall men remark, in such an act   *20*
Of love for him whose song gives life its joy,
Thy recognition of the use of life;
Nor call thy spirit barely adequate
To help on life in straight ways, broad enough
For vulgar souls, by ruling and the rest.
Thou, in the daily building of thy tower,
Whether in fierce and sudden spasms of toil,
Or through dim lulls of unapparent growth,
Or when the general work 'mid good acclaim
Climbed with the eye to cheer the architect,   *30*
Didst ne'er engage in work for mere work's sake—
Hadst ever in thy heart the luring hope
Of some eventual rest a-top of it,
Whence, all the tumult of the building hushed,
Thou first of men mightst look out to the east.
The vulgar saw thy tower; thou sawest the sun.
For this, I promise on thy festival

To pour libation, looking o'er the sea,
Making this slave narrate thy fortunes, speak
Thy great words, and describe thy royal face— 40
Wishing thee wholly where Zeus lives the most
Within the eventual element of calm.

   Thy letter's first requirement meets me here.
It is as thou hast heard: in one short life
I, Cleon, have effected all those things
Thou wonderingly dost enumerate.
That epos on thy hundred plates of gold
Is mine,—and also mine the little chant,
So sure to rise from every fishing-bark
When, lights at prow, the seamen haul their nets. 50
The image of the sun-god on the phare
Men turn from the sun's self to see, is mine;
The Pœcile, o'er-storied its whole length,
As thou didst hear, with painting, is mine too.
I know the true proportions of a man
And woman also, not observed before;
And I have written three books on the soul,
Proving absurd all written hitherto,
And putting us to ignorance again.
For music,—why, I have combined the moods,
Inventing one. In brief, all arts are mine; 60
Thus much the people know and recognise,
Throughout our seventeen islands. Marvel not.
We of these latter days, with greater mind
Than our forerunners, since more composite,
Look not so great (beside their simple way)
To a judge who only sees one way at once,
One mind-point, and no other at a time,—
Compares the small part of a man of us
With some whole man of the heroic age,
Great in his way,—not ours, nor meant for ours, 70
And ours is greater, had we skill to know.
Yet, what we call this life of men on earth,
This sequence of the soul's achievements here,
Being, as I find much reason to conceive,
Intended to be viewed eventually
As a great wnole, not analysed to parts,
But each part having reference to all,—
How shall a certain part, pronounced complete,

Endure effacement by another part?
Was the thing done?—Then what's to do again? *80*
See, in the chequered pavement opposite,
Suppose the artist made a perfect rhomb,
And next a lozenge, then a trapezoid—
He did not overlay them, superimpose
The new upon the old and blot it out,
But laid them on a level in his work,
Making at last a picture; there it lies.
So, first the perfect separate forms were made,
The portions of mankind—and after, so,
Occurred the combination of the same. *90*
Or where had been a progress, or otherwise?
Mankind, made up of all the single men,—
In such a synthesis the labour ends.
Now, mark me—those divine men of old time
Have reached, thou sayest well, each at one point
The outside verge that rounds our faculty;
And where they reached, who can do more than reach?
It takes but little water just to touch
At some one point the inside of a sphere,
And, as we turn the sphere, touch all the rest *100*
In due succession; but the finer air
Which not so palpably nor obviously,
Though no less universally, can touch
The whole circumference of that emptied sphere,
Fills it more fully than the water did;
Holds thrice the weight of water in itself
Resolved into a subtler element.
And yet the vulgar call the sphere first full
Up to the visible height—and after, void;
Not knowing air's more hidden properties. *110*
And thus our soul, misknown, cries out to Zeus
To vindicate his purpose in its life—
Why stay we on the earth unless to grow?
Long since, I imaged, wrote the fiction out,
That he or other God, descended here
And, once for all, showed simultaneously
What, in its nature, never can be shown
Piecemeal or in succession;—showed, I say,
The worth both absolute and relative
Of all his children from the birth of time, *120*
His instruments for all appointed work.

I now go on to image,—might we hear
The judgment which should give the due to each,
Show where the labour lay and where the ease,
And prove Zeus' self, the latent, everywhere!
This is a dream.   But no dream, let us hope,
That years and days, the summers and the springs
Follow each other with unwaning powers—
The grapes which dye thy wine, are richer far
Through culture, than the wild wealth of the rock;   *130*
The suave plum than the savage-tasted drupe;
The pastured honey-bee drops choicer sweet!
The flowers turn double, and the leaves turn flowers;
That young and tender crescent-moon, thy slave,
Sleeping upon her robe as if on clouds,
Refines upon the women of my youth.
What, and the soul alone deteriorates?
I have not chanted verse like Homer's, no—
Nor swept string like Terpander, no—nor carved
And painted men like Phidias and his friend: *140*
I am not great as they are, point by point:
But I have entered into sympathy
With these four, running these into one soul,
Who, separate, ignored each others' arts.
Say, is it nothing that I know them all?
The wild flower was the larger—I have dashed
Rose-blood upon its petals, pricked its cup's
Honey with wine, and driven its seed to fruit,
And show a better flower if not so large.
I stand, myself.   Refer this to the gods   *150*
Whose gift alone it is! which, shall I dare
(All pride apart) upon the absurd pretext
That such a gift by chance lay in my hand,
Discourse of lightly or depreciate?
It might have fallen to another's hand—what then?
I pass too surely—let at least truth stay!

And next, of what thou followest on to ask.
This being with me as I declare, O king,
My works, in all these varicoloured kinds,
So done by me, accepted so by men—   *160*
Thou askest if (my soul thus in men's hearts)
I must not be accounted to attain
The very crown and proper end of life.

Inquiring thence how, now life closeth up,
I face death with success in my right hand:
Whether I fear death less than dost thyself
The fortunate of men. " For " (writest thou)
" Thou leavest much behind, while I leave nought:
Thy life stays in the poems men shall sing,
The pictures men shall study; while my life, *170*
Complete and whole now in its power and joy,
Dies altogether with my brain and arm,
Is lost indeed; since,—what survives myself?
The brazen statue that o'erlooks my grave,
Set on the promontory which I named.
And that—some supple courtier of my heir
Shall use its robed and sceptred arm, perhaps,
To fix the rope to, which best drags it down.
I go, then: triumph thou, who dost not go! "

 Nay, thou art worthy of hearing my whole mind. *180*
Is this apparent, when thou turn'st to muse
Upon the scheme of earth and man in chief,
That admiration grows as knowledge grows?
That imperfection means perfection hid,
Reserved in part, to grace the after-time?
If, in the morning of philosophy,
Ere ought had been recorded, ought perceived,
Thou, with the light now in thee, could'st have looked
On all earth's tenantry, from worm to bird,
Ere man had yet appeared upon the stage— *190*
Thou wouldst have seen them perfect, and deduced
The perfectness of others yet unseen.
Conceding which,—had Zeus then questioned thee
" Wilt thou go on a step, improve on this,
Do more for visible creatures than is done? "
Thou wouldst have answered, " Ay, by making each
Grow conscious in himself—by that alone.
All's perfect else: the shell sucks fast the rock,
The fish strikes through the sea, the snake both swims
And slides; the birds take flight, forth range the beasts, *200*
Till life s mechanics can no further go—
And all this joy in natural life, is put,
Like fire from off Thy finger into each,
So exquisitely perfect is the same.
But 'tis pure fire—and they mere matter are;

It has them, not they it: and so I choose,
For man, Thy last premeditated work
(If I might add a glory to this scheme)
That a third thing should stand apart from both,
A quality arise within the soul,   *210*
Which, intro-active, made to supervise
And feel the force it has, may view itself,
And so be happy." Man might live at first
The animal life: but is there nothing more?
In due time, let him critically learn
How he lives; and, the more he gets to know
Of his own life's adaptabilities,
The more joy-giving will his life become.
The man who hath this quality, is best.

But thou, king, hadst more reasonably said: *220*
" Let progress end at once,—man make no step
Beyond the natural man, the better beast,
Using his senses, not the sense of sense."
In man there's failure, only since he left
The lower and inconscious forms of life.
We called it an advance, the rendering plain
A spirit might grow conscious of that life,
And, by new lore so added to the old,
Take each step higher over the brute's head.
This grew the only life, the pleasure-house,   *230*
Watch-tower and treasure-fortress of the soul,
Which whole surrounding flats of natural life
Seemed only fit to yield subsistence to;
A tower that crowns a country. But alas!
The soul now climbs it just to perish there,
For thence we have discovered ('tis no dream—
We know this, which we had not else perceived)
That there's a world of capability
For joy, spread round about us, meant for us,
Inviting us; and still the soul craves all,   *240*
And still the flesh replies, " Take no jot more
Than ere you climbed the tower to look abroad!
Nay, so much less, as that fatigue has brought
Deduction to it." We struggle—fain to enlarge
Our bounded physical recipiency,
Increase our power, supply fresh oil to life,
Repair the waste of age and sickness. No,

It skills not: life's inadequate to joy,
As the soul sees joy, tempting life to take.
They praise a fountain in my garden here   250
Wherein a Naiad sends the water-spurt
Thin from her tube; she smiles to see it rise.
What if I told her, it is just a thread
From that great river which the hills shut up,
And mock her with my leave to take the same?
The artificer has given her one small tube
Past power to widen or exchange—what boots
To know she might spout oceans if she could?
She cannot lift beyond her first straight thread.
And so a man can use but a man's joy   260
While he sees God's. Is it, for Zeus to boast
" See, man, how happy I live, and despair—
That I may be still happier—for thy use!"
If this were so, we could not thank our Lord,
As hearts beat on to doing: 'tis not so—
Malice it is not. Is it carelessness?
Still, no. If care—where is the sign, I ask—
And get no answer: and agree in sum,
O king, with thy profound discouragement,
Who seest the wider but to sigh the more.   270
Most progress is most failure! thou sayest well.

    The last point now:—thou dost except a case—
Holding joy not impossible to one
With artist-gifts—to such a man as I—
Who leave behind me living works indeed;
For, such a poem, such a painting lives.
What? dost thou verily trip upon a word,
Confound the accurate view of what joy is
(Caught somewhat clearer by my eyes than thine)
With feeling joy? confound the knowing how   280
And showing how to live (my faculty)
With actually living?—Otherwise
Where is the artist's vantage o'er the king?
Because in my great epos I display
How divers men young, strong, fair, wise, can act—
Is this as though I acted? if I paint,
Carve the young Phœbus, am I therefore young?
Methinks I'm older that I bowed myself
The many years of pain that taught me art!

Indeed, to know is something, and to prove   *290*
How all this beauty might be enjoyed, is more:
But, knowing nought, to enjoy is something too.
Yon rower with the moulded muscles there
Lowering the sail, is nearer it than I.
I can write love-odes—thy fair slave's an ode.
I get to sing of love, when grown too grey
For being beloved: she turns to that young man
The muscles all a-ripple on his back.
I know the joy of kingship: well—thou art king!

" But," sayest thou—(and I marvel, I repeat,   *300*
To find thee tripping on a mere word) " what
Thou writest, paintest, stays: that does not die:
Sappho survives, because we sing her songs,
And Æschylus, because we read his plays!"
Why, if they live still, let them come and take
Thy slave in my despite—drink from thy cup—
Speak in my place. Thou diest while I survive?
Say rather that my fate is deadlier still,—
In this, that every day my sense of joy
Grows more acute, my soul (intensified   *310*
In power and insight) more enlarged, more keen;
While every day my hairs fall more and more,
My hand shakes, and the heavy years increase—
The horror quickening still from year to year,
The consummation coming past escape
When I shall know most, and yet least enjoy—
When all my works wherein I prove my worth,
Being present still to mock me in men's mouths,
Alive still, in the phrase of such as thou,
I, I, the feeling, thinking, acting man,   *320*
The man who loved his life so over much,
Shall sleep in my urn. It is so horrible,
I dare at times imagine to my need
Some future state revealed to us by Zeus,
Unlimited in capability
For joy, as this is in desire for joy,
To seek which, the joy-hunger forces us.
That, stung by straitness of our life, made strait
On purpose to make sweet the life at large—
Freed by the throbbing impulse we call death   *330*
We burst there as the worm into the fly,

Who, while a worm still, wants his wings.   But, no!
Zeus has not yet revealed it; and, alas!
He must have done so—were it possible!

Live long and happy, and in that thought die,
Glad for what was.   Farewell.   And for the rest,
I cannot tell thy messenger aright
Where to deliver what he bears of thine
To one called Paulus—we have heard his fame
Indeed, if Christus be not one with him—   340
I know not, nor am troubled much to know,
Thou canst not think a mere barbarian Jew,
As Paulus proves to be, one circumcised,
Hath access to a secret shut from us?
Thou wrongest our philosophy, O king,
In stooping to inquire of such an one,
As if his answer could impose at all.
He writeth, doth he? well, and he may write.
Oh, the Jew findeth scholars! certain slaves
Who touched on this same isle, preached him and Christ;   350
And (as I gathered from a bystander)
Their doctrines could be held by no sane man

THE TWINS.

" Give " and " It-shall-be-given-unto-you."

I. GRAND rough old Martin Luther
      Bloomed fables—flowers on furze,
   The better the uncouther:
      Do roses stick like burrs?

II. A beggar asked an alms
      One day at an abbey-door,
   Said Luther; but, seized with qualms,
      The Abbot replied, " We're poor! "

III. " Poor, who had plenty once,
      " When gifts fell thick as rain: 10
   " But they give us nought, for the nonce,
      " And how should we give again? "

IV. Then the beggar, " See your sins!
      " Of old, unless I err,
   " Ye had brothers for inmates, twins,
      " Date and Dabitur."

v. " While Date was in good case
   " Dabitur flourished too:
" For Dabitur's lenten face,
   " No wonder if Date rue."   **20**

vi. " Would ye retrieve the one?
   " Try and make plump the other!
" When Date's penance is done,
   " Dabitur helps his brother."

vii. " Only, beware relapse! "
   The abbot hung his head.
This beggar might be, perhaps,
   An angel, Luther said.

POPULARITY.

i. STAND still, true poet that you are,
   I know you; let me try and draw you.
Some night you'll fail us. When afar
   You rise, remember one man saw you,
Knew you, and named a star.

ii. My star, God's glow-worm! Why extend
   That loving hand of His which leads you,
Yet locks you safe from end to end
   Of this dark world, unless He needs you—
Just saves your light to spend?   **10**

iii. His clenched Hand shall unclose at last
   I know, and let out all the beauty.
My poet holds the future fast,
   Accepts the coming ages' duty,
Their present for this past.

iv. That day, the earth's feast-master's brow
   Shall clear, to God the chalice raising;
" Others give best at first, but Thou
   For ever set'st our table praising,—
Keep'st the good wine till now."   **20**

v. Meantime, I'll draw you as you stand,
   With few or none to watch and wonder.
I'll say—a fisher (on the sand
   By Tyre the Old) his ocean-plunder,
A netful, brought to land.

VI. Who has not heard how Tyrian shells
    Enclosed the blue, that dye of dyes
Whereof one drop worked miracles,
    And coloured like Astarte's eyes
Raw silk the merchant sells?   *30*

VII. And each bystander of them all
    Could criticise, and quote tradition
How depths of blue sublimed some pall,
    To get which, pricked a king's ambition;
Worth sceptre, crown and ball.

VIII. Yet there's the dye,—in that rough mesh,
    The sea has only just o'er-whispered!
Live whelks, the lip's-beard dripping fresh,
    As if they still the water's lisp heard
Through foam the rock-weeds thresh.   *40*

IX. Enough to furnish Solomon
    Such hangings for his cedar-house,
That when gold-robed he took the throne
    In that abyss of blue, the Spouse
Might swear his presence shone

X. Most like the centre-spike of gold
    Which burns deep in the blue-bell's womb,
What time, with ardours manifold,
    The bee goes singing to her groom,
Drunken and overbold.   *50*

XI. Mere conchs! not fit for warp or woof!
    Till art comes,—comes to pound and squeeze
And clarify,—refines to proof
    The liquor filtered by degrees,
While the world stands aloof.

XII. And there's the extract, flasked and fine,
    And priced, and saleable at last!
And Hobbs, Nobbs, Stokes and Nokes combine
    To paint the future from the past,
Put blue into their line.   *60*

XIII. Hobbs hints blue,—straight he turtle eats.
    Nobbs prints blue,—claret crowns his cup.
Nokes outdares Stokes in azure feats,—
    Both gorge. Who fished the murex up?
What porridge had John Keats?

Men and Women

THE HERETIC'S TRAGEDY

A MIDDLE-AGE INTERLUDE

(*In the original*) ROSA MUNDI; SEU, FULCITE ME FLORIBUS. A CONCEIT OF MASTER GYSBRECHT, CANON-REGULAR OF SAINT JODOCUS-BY-THE-BAR, YPRES CITY. CANTUQUE, *Virgilius*. AND HATH OFTEN BEEN SUNG AT HOCK-TIDE AND FESTIVALS. GAVISUS ERAM, *Jessides*.

(It would seem to be a glimpse from the burning of Jacques du Bourg-Molay, at Paris, A.D. 1314; as distorted by the refraction from Flemish brain to brain, during the course of a couple of centuries.—R.B.)

I.

PREADMONISHETH THE ABBOT DEODAET.

THE Lord, we look to once for all,
    Is the Lord we should look at, all at once:
He knows not to vary, saith St. Paul,
    Nor the shadow of turning, for the nonce.
See him no other than as he is;
    Give both the Infinites their due—
Infinite mercy, but, I wis,
        As infinite a justice too. [*Organ : plagal-cadence.*
        As infinite a justice too. 10

II.

ONE SINGETH.

John, Master of the Temple of God,
    Falling to sin the Unknown Sin,
What he bought of Emperor Aldabrod,
    He sold it to Sultan Saladin—
Till, caught by Pope Clement, a-buzzing there,
    Hornet-prince of the mad wasps' hive,
And clipt of his wings in Paris square,
    They bring him now to be burned alive.

    [*And wanteth there grace of lute or clavicithern, ye* 20
        shall say to confirm him who singeth—

We bring John now to be burned alive.

III.

In the midst is a goodly gallows built;
    'Twixt fork and fork a stake is stuck;
But first they set divers tumbrils a-tilt,
    Make a trench all round with the city muck,

186

Inside they pile log upon log, good store;
 Faggots not few, blocks great and small,
Reached a man's mid-thigh, no less, no more,—
 For they mean he should roast in the sight of all.   *30*

CHORUS.

We mean he should roast in the sight of all.

IV.

Good sappy bavins that kindle forthwith;
 Billets that blaze substantial and slow;
Pine-stump split deftly, dry as pith;
 Larch-heart that chars to a chalk-white glow:
Then up they hoist me John in a chafe,
 Sling him fast like a hog to scorch,
Spit in his face, then leap back safe,
 Sing " Laudes " and bid clap-to the torch.

CHORUS.

Laus Deo—who bids clap-to the torch.   *40*

V.

John of the Temple, whose fame so bragged,
 Is burning alive in Paris square!
How can he curse, if his mouth is gagged?
 Or wriggle his neck, with a collar there?
Or heave his chest, while a band goes round?
 Or threat with his fist, since his arms are spliced?
Or kick with his feet, now his legs are bound?
 —Thinks John—I will call upon Jesus Christ.
                [Here one crosseth himself.

VI.

Jesus Christ—John had bought and sold,   *50*
 Jesus Christ—John had eaten and drunk;
To him, the Flesh meant silver and gold.
 (*Salvâ reverentiâ.*)
Now it was, " Saviour, bountiful lamb,
 I have roasted thee Turks, though men roast me.
See thy servant, the plight wherein I am!
 Art thou a Saviour? Save thou me! "

CHORUS.

'Tis John the mocker cries, Save thou me!

VII.

Who maketh God's menace an idle word?
  —Saith, it no more means what it proclaims,   *60*
Than a damsel's threat to her wanton bird?—
  For she too prattles of ugly names.
—Saith, he knoweth but one thing,—what he knows?
  That God is good and the rest is breath;
Why else is the same styled, Sharon's rose?
  Once a rose, ever a rose, he saith.

CHORUS.

O, John shall yet find a rose, he saith!

VIII.

Alack, there be roses and roses, John!
  Some honied of taste like your leman's tongue.
Some, bitter—for why? (roast gaily on!)   *70*
  Their tree struck root in devil's dung!
When Paul once reasoned of righteousness
  And of temperance and of judgment to come,
Good Felix trembled, he could no less—
  John, snickering, crook'd his wicked thumb.

CHORUS.

What cometh to John of the wicked thumb?

IX.

Ha ha, John plucks now at his rose
  To rid himself of a sorrow at heart!
Lo,—petal on petal, fierce rays unclose;
  Anther on anther, sharp spikes outstart;   *80*
And with blood for dew, the bosom boils;
  And a gust of sulphur is all its smell;
And lo, he is horribly in the toils
  Of a coal-black giant flower of Hell!

CHORUS.

What maketh Heaven, that maketh Hell.

X.

So, as John called now, through the fire amain,
  On the Name, he had cursed with, all his life—
To the Person, he bought and sold again—
  For the Face, with his daily buffets rife—
Feature by feature It took its place!   *90*
  And his voice like a mad dog's choking bark
At the steady Whole of the Judge's Face—
  Died. Forth John's soul flared into the dark.

SUBJOINETH THE ABBOT DEODAET.

God help all poor souls lost in the dark!

TWO IN THE CAMPAGNA.

I. I WONDER do you feel to-day
    As I have felt, since, hand in hand,
  We sat down on the grass, to stray
    In spirit better through the land,
  This morn of Rome and May?

II. For me, I touched a thought, I know,
    Has tantalised me many times,
  (Like turns of thread the spiders throw
    Mocking across our path) for rhymes
  To catch at and let go.   *10*

III. Help me to hold it: first it left
    The yellowing fennel, run to seed
  There, branching from the brickwork's cleft,
    Some old tomb's ruin: yonder weed
  Took up the floating weft,

IV. Where one small orange cup amassed
    Five beetles,—blind and green they grope
  Among the honey-meal,—and last
    Everywhere on the grassy slope
  I traced it. Hold it fast!   *20*

V. The champaign with its endless fleece
    Of feathery grasses everywhere!
  Silence and passion, joy and peace,
    An everlasting wash of air—
  Rome's ghost since her decease.

VI. Such life there, through such lengths of hours,
    Such miracles performed in play,
  Such primal naked forms of flowers,
    Such letting Nature have her way
While Heaven looks from its towers.   30

VII. How say you? Let us, O my dove,
    Let us be unashamed of soul,
  As earth lies bare to heaven above.
    How is it under our control
To love or not to love?

VIII. I would that you were all to me,
    You that are just so much, no more—
  Nor yours, nor mine,—nor slave nor free!
    Where does the fault lie? what the core
Of the wound, since wound must be?   40

IX. I would I could adopt your will,
    See with your eyes, and set my heart
Beating by yours, and drink my fill
    At your soul's springs,—your part, my part
In life, for good and ill.

X. No. I yearn upward—touch you close,
    Then stand away. I kiss your cheek,
Catch your soul's warmth,—I pluck the rose
    And love it more than tongue can speak—
Then the good minute goes.   50

XI. Already how am I so far
    Out of that minute? Must I go
Still like the thistle-ball, no bar,
    Onward, whenever light winds blow,
Fixed by no friendly star?

XII. Just when I seemed about to learn!
    Where is the thread now? Off again!
The old trick! Only I discern—
    Infinite passion and the pain
Of finite hearts that yearn.   60

A GRAMMARIAN'S FUNERAL.

LET us begin and carry up this corpse,
    Singing together.
Leave we the common crofts, the vulgar thorpes,
    Each in its tether
Sleeping safe on the bosom of the plain,
    Cared-for till cock-crow.
Look out if yonder's not the day again
    Rimming the rock-row!
That's the appropriate country—there, man's thought,
    Rarer, intenser,   10
Self-gathered for an outbreak, as it ought,
    Chafes in the censer!
Leave we the unlettered plain its herd and crop;
    Seek we sepulture
On a tall mountain, cited to the top,
    Crowded with culture!
All the peaks soar, but one the rest excels;
    Clouds overcome it;
No, yonder sparkle is the citadel's
    Circling its summit!   20
Thither our path lies—wind we up the heights—
    Wait ye the warning?
Our low life was the level's and the night's;
    He's for the morning!
Step to a tune, square chests, erect the head,
    'Ware the beholders!
This is our master, famous, calm, and dead,
    Borne on our shoulders.
Sleep, crop and herd! sleep, darkling thorpe and croft,
    Safe from the weather!   30
He, whom we convey to his grave aloft,
    Singing together,
He was a man born with thy face and throat,
    Lyric Apollo!
Long he lived nameless: how should spring take note
    Winter would follow?
Till lo, the little touch, and youth was gone!
    Cramped and diminished,

Moaned he, " New measures, other feet anon!
    My dance is finished? "   **40**
No, that's the world's way! (keep the mountain-side,
    Make for the city.)
He knew the signal, and stepped on with pride
    Over men's pity;
Left play for work, and grappled with the world
    Bent on escaping:
" What's in the scroll," quoth he, " thou keepest furled?
    Show me their shaping,
Theirs, who most studied man, the bard and sage,—
    Give! "—So he gowned him,   **50**
Straight got by heart that book to its last page:
    Learned, we found him!
Yea, but we found him bald too—eyes like lead,
    Accents uncertain:
" Time to taste life," another would have said,
    " Up with the curtain! "
This man said rather, " Actual life comes next?
    Patience a moment!
Grant I have mastered learning's crabbed text,
    Still, there's the comment.   **60**
Let me know all.   Prate not of most or least,
    Painful or easy:
Even to the crumbs I'd fain eat up the feast,
    Ay, nor feel queasy! "
Oh, such a life as he resolved to live,
    When he had learned it,
When he had gathered all books had to give;
    Sooner, he spurned it!
Image the whole, then execute the parts—
    Fancy the fabric   **70**
Quite, ere you build, ere steel strike fire from quartz,
    Ere mortar dab brick!

(Here's the town-gate reached: there's the market-place
    Gaping before us.)
Yea, this in him was the peculiar grace
    (Hearten our chorus)
Still before living he'd learn how to live—
    No end to learning.
Earn the means first—God surely will contrive
    Use for our earning.   **80**

Others mistrust and say—" But time escapes,—
    Live now or never! "
He said, " What's Time? leave Now for dogs and apes!
    Man has For ever."
Back to his book then: deeper drooped his head;
    Calculus racked him:
Leaden before, his eyes grew dross of lead;
    Tussis attacked him.
" Now, Master, take a little rest! "—not he!
    (Caution redoubled!   *90*
Step two a-breast, the way winds narrowly.)
    Not a whit troubled,
Back to his studies, fresher than at first,
    Fierce as a dragon
He, (soul-hydroptic with a sacred thirst)
    Sucked at the flagon.
Oh, if we draw a circle premature,
    Heedless of far gain,
Greedy for quick returns of profit, sure,
    Bad is our bargain!   *100*
Was it not great? did not he throw on God,
    (He loves the burthen)—
God's task to make the heavenly period
    Perfect the earthen?
Did not he magnify the mind, shew clear
    Just what it all meant?
He would not discount life, as fools do here,
    Paid by instalment!
He ventured neck or nothing—heaven's success
    Found, or earth's failure: *110*
" Wilt thou trust death or not? " he answered " Yes.
    Hence with life's pale lure! "
That low man seeks a little thing to do,
    Sees it and does it:
This high man, with a great thing to pursue,
    Dies ere he knows it.
That low man goes on adding one to one,
    His hundred's soon hit:
This high man, aiming at a million,
    Misses an unit.   *120*
That, has the world here—should he need the next,
    Let the world mind him!
This, throws himself on God, and unperplext

Seeking shall find Him.
So, with the throttling hands of Death at strife,
    Ground he at grammar;
Still, thro' the rattle, parts of speech were rife.
    While he could stammer
He settled *Hoti*'s business—let it be!—
    Properly based *Oun*—   *130*
Gave us the doctrine of the enclitic *De*,
    Dead from the waist down.
Well, here's the platform, here's the proper place.
    Hail to your purlieus
All ye highfliers of the feathered race,
    Swallows and curlews!
Here's the top-peak! the multitude below
    Live, for they can there.
This man decided not to Live but Know—
    Bury this man there?   *140*
Here—here's his place, where meteors shoot, clouds form,
    Lightnings are loosened,
Stars come and go! let joy break with the storm—
    Peace let the dew send!
Lofty designs must close in like effects:
    Loftily lying,
Leave him—still loftier than the world suspects,
    Living and dying.

ONE WAY OF LOVE.

I. ALL June I bound the rose in sheaves.
   Now, rose by rose, I strip the leaves,
   And strew them where Pauline may pass.
   She will not turn aside? Alas!
   Let them lie. Suppose they die?
   The chance was they might take her eye.

II. How many a month I strove to suit
   These stubborn fingers to the lute!
   To-day I venture all I know.
   She will not hear my music? So!   *10*
   Break the string—fold music's wing.
   Suppose Pauline had bade me sing!

III. My whole life long I learned to love.
This hour my utmost art I prove
And speak my passion.—Heaven or hell?
She will not give me heaven? 'Tis well!
Lose who may—I still can say,
Those who win heaven, blest are they.

ANOTHER WAY OF LOVE.

I. JUNE was not over,
Though past the full,
And the best of her roses
Had yet to blow,
When a man I know
(But shall not discover,
Since ears are dull,
And time discloses)
Turned him and said with a man's true air,
Half sighing a smile in a yawn, as 'twere,—   *10*
" If I tire of your June, will she greatly care? "

II. Well, Dear, in-doors with you!
True, serene deadness
Tries a man's temper.
What's in the blossom
June wears on her bosom?
Can it clear scores with you?
Sweetness and redness,
Eadem semper !
Go, let me care for it greatly or slightly!   *20*
If June mends her bowers now, your hand left unsightly
By plucking their roses,—my June will do rightly.

III. And after, for pastime,
If June be refulgent
With flowers in completeness,
All petals, no prickles,
Delicious as trickles
Of wine poured at mass-time,—
And choose One indulgent
To redness and sweetness: *30*
Or if, with experience of man and of spider,
She use my June-lightning, the strong insect-ridder,
To stop the fresh spinning,—why, June will consider.

195

"TRANSCENDENTALISM:"

A POEM IN TWELVE BOOKS.

STOP playing, poet! may a brother speak?
'Tis you speak, that's your error.   Song's our art:
Whereas you please to speak these naked thoughts
Instead of draping them in sights and sounds.
—True thoughts, good thoughts, thoughts fit to treasure up!
But why such long prolusion and display,
Such turning and adjustment of the harp,
And taking it upon your breast at length,
Only to speak dry words across its strings?
Stark-naked thought is in request enough—   10
Speak prose and holloa it till Europe hears!
The six-foot Swiss tube, braced about with bark,
Which helps the hunter's voice from Alp to Alp—
Exchange our harp for that,—who hinders you?

　　But here's your fault; grown men want thought, you think;
Thought's what they mean by verse, and seek in verse:
Boys seek for images and melody,
Men must have reason—so you aim at men.
Quite otherwise!   Objects throng our youth, 'tis true,
We see and hear and do not wonder much.   20
If you could tell us what they mean, indeed!
As Swedish Bœhme never cared for plants
Until it happed, a-walking in the fields,
He noticed all at once that plants could speak,
Nay, turned with loosened tongue to talk with him.
That day the daisy had an eye indeed—
Colloquised with the cowslip on such themes!
We find them extant yet in Jacob's prose.
But by the time youth slips a stage or two
While reading prose in that tough book he wrote,   30
(Collating, and amendating the same
And settling on the sense most to our mind)
We shut the clasps and find life's summer past.
Then, who helps more, pray, to repair our loss—
Another Bœhme with a tougher book
And subtler meanings of what roses say,—

Or some stout Mage like him of Halberstadt,
John, who made things Bœhme wrote thoughts about?
He with a " look you! " vents a brace of rhymes,
And in there breaks the sudden rose herself,   *40*
Over us, under, round us every side,
Nay, in and out the tables and the chairs
And musty volumes, Bœhme's book and all,—
Buries us with a glory, young once more,
Pouring heaven into this shut house of life.

   So come, the harp back to your heart again!
You are a poem, though your poem's naught.
The best of all you did before, believe,
Was your own boy's face o'er the finer chords
Bent, following the cherub at the top   *50*
That points to God with his paired half-moon wings.

MISCONCEPTIONS.

I. THIS is a spray the Bird clung to,
   Making it blossom with pleasure,
Ere the high tree-top she sprung to,
   Fit for her nest and her treasure.
   Oh, what a hope beyond measure
Was the poor spray's, which the flying feet hung to,—
So to be singled out, built in, and sung to!

II. This is a heart the Queen leant on,
   Thrilled in a minute erratic,
Ere the true bosom she bent on,   *10*
   Meet for love's regal dalmatic.
   Oh, what a fancy ecstatic
Was the poor heart's, ere the wanderer went on—
Love to be saved for it, proffered to, spent on!

ONE WORD MORE.

TO E. B. B.

I. THERE they are, my fifty men and women
 Naming me the fifty poems finished!
 Take them, Love, the book and me together.
 Where the heart lies, let the brain lie also.

II. Rafael made a century of sonnets,
 Made and wrote them in a certain volume
 Dinted with the silver-pointed pencil
 Else he only used to draw Madonnas:
 These, the world might view—but One, the volume.
 Who that one, you ask?   Your heart instructs you. *10*
 Did she live and love it all her life-time?
 Did she drop, his lady of the sonnets,
 Die, and let it drop beside her pillow
 Where it lay in place of Rafael's glory,
 Rafael's cheek so duteous and so loving—
 Cheek, the world was wont to hail a painter's,
 Rafael's cheek, her love had turned a poet's?

III. You and I would rather read that volume,
 (Take to his beating bosom by it)
 Lean and list the bosom-beats of Rafael, *20*
 Would we not? than wonder at Madonnas—
 Her, San Sisto names, and Her, Foligno,
 Her, that visits Florence in a vision,
 Her, that's left with lilies in the Louvre—
 Seen by us and all the world in circle.

IV. You and I will never read that volume.
 Guido Reni, like his own eye's apple
 Guarded long the treasure-book and loved it.
 Guido Reni dying, all Bologna
 Cried, and the world with it, " Ours—the treasure! " *30*
 Suddenly, as rare things will, it vanished.

V. Dante once prepared to paint an angel:
 Whom to please?   You whisper " Beatrice."
 While he mused and traced it and retraced it,
 (Peradventure with a pen corroded

Still by drops of that hot ink he dipped for,
When, his left hand i' the hair o' the wicked,
Back he held the brow and pricked its stigma,
Bit into the live man's flesh for parchment,
Loosed him, laughed to see the writing rankle, 40
Let the wretch go festering thro' Florence)—
Dante, who loved well because he hated,
Hated wickedness that hinders loving,
Dante standing, studying his angel,—
In there broke the folk of his Inferno.
Says he—" Certain people of importance "
(Such he gave his daily, dreadful line to)
Entered and would seize, forsooth, the poet.
Says the poet—" Then I stopped my painting."

VI. You and I would rather see that angel, 50
Painted by the tenderness of Dante,
Would we not?—than read a fresh Inferno.

VII. You and I will never see that picture.
While he mused on love and Beatrice,
While he softened o'er his outlined angel,
In they broke, those " people of importance: "
We and Bice bear the loss forever.

VIII. What of Rafael's sonnets, Dante's picture?

IX. This: no artist lives and loves that longs not
Once, and only once, and for One only,
(Ah, the prize!) to find his love a language 60
Fit and fair and simple and sufficient—
Using nature that's an art to others,
Not, this one time, art that's turned his nature.
Ay, of all the artists living, loving,
None but would forego his proper dowry,—
Does he paint? he fain would write a poem,—
Does he write? he fain would paint a picture,
Put to proof art alien to the artist's,
Once, and only once, and for One only, 70
So to be the man and leave the artist,
Save the man's joy, miss the artist's sorrow.

X. Wherefore? Heaven's gift takes earth's abatement!
He who smites the rock and spreads the water,
Bidding drink and live a crowd beneath him,

Even he, the minute makes immortal,
Proves, perchance, his mortal in the minute,
Desecrates, belike, the deed in doing.
While he smites, how can he but remember,
So he smote before, in such a peril,   *80*
When they stood and mocked—" Shall smiting help
    us? "
When they drank and sneered—" A stroke is easy! "
When they wiped their mouths and went their journey,
Throwing him for thanks—" But drought was pleas-
    ant."
Thus old memories mar the actual triumph;
Thus the doing savours of disrelish;
Thus achievement lacks a gracious somewhat;
O'er importuned brows becloud the mandate,
Carelessness or consciousness, the gesture.
For he bears an ancient wrong about him,   *90*
Sees and knows again those phalanxed faces,
Hears, yet one time more, the 'customed prelude—
" How should'st thou, of all men, smite, and save
    us? "
Guesses what is like to prove the sequel—
" Egypt's flesh-pots—nay, the drought was better."

  xi. Oh, the crowd must have emphatic warrant!
Theirs, the Sinai-forehead's cloven brilliance,
Right-arm's rod-sweep, tongue's imperial fiat.
Never dares the man put off the prophet.

  xii. Did he love one face from out the thousands,   *100*
(Were she Jethro's daughter, white and wifely,
Were she but the Æthiopian bondslave,)
He would envy yon dumb patient camel,
Keeping a reserve of scanty water
Meant to save his own life in the desert;
Ready in the desert to deliver
(Kneeling down to let his breast be opened)
Hoard and life together for his mistress.

  xiii. I shall never, in the years remaining,
Paint you pictures, no, nor carve you statues,   *110*
Make you music that should all-express me;
So it seems: I stand on my attainment.

This of verse alone, one life allows me;
Verse and nothing else have I to give you.
Other heights in other lives, God willing—
All the gifts from all the heights, your own, Love!

XIV. Yet a semblance of resource avails us—
Shade so finely touched, love's sense must seize it.
Take these lines, look lovingly and nearly,
Lines I write the first time and the last time.   *120*
He who works in fresco, steals a hair-brush.
Curbs the liberal hand, subservient proudly,
Cramps his spirit, crowds its all in little,
Makes a strange art of an art familiar,
Fills his lady's missal-marge with flowerets.
He who blows thro' bronze, may breathe thro' silver
Fitly serenade a slumbrous princess.
He who writes, may write for once, as I do.

XV. Love, you saw me gather men and women,
Live or dead or fashioned by my fancy,   *130*
Enter each and all, and use their service,
Speak from every mouth,—the speech, a poem.
Hardly shall I tell my joys and sorrows,
Hopes and fears, belief and disbelieving:
I am mine and yours—the rest be all men's,
Karshish, Cleon, Norbert and the fifty.
Let me speak this once in my true person,
Not as Lippo, Roland or Andrea,
Though the fruit of speech be just this sentence—
Pray you, look on these my men and women,   *140*
Take and keep my fifty poems finished;
Where my heart lies, let my brain lie also!
Poor the speech; be how I speak, for all things.

XVI. Not but that you know me! Lo, the moon's self!
Here in London, yonder late in Florence,
Still we find her face, the thrice-transfigured.
Curving on a sky imbrued with colour,
Drifted over Fiesole by twilight,
Came she, our new crescent of a hair's-breadth.
Full she flared it, lamping Samminiato,   *150*
Rounder 'twixt the cypresses and rounder,
Perfect till the nightingales applauded.

Now, a piece of her old self, impoverished,
Hard to greet, she traverses the houseroofs,
Hurries with unhandsome thrift of silver,
Goes dispiritedly,—glad to finish.

XVII. What, there's nothing in the moon note-worthy?
Nay—for if that moon could love a mortal,
Use, to charm him (so to fit a fancy)
All her magic ('tis the old sweet mythos)   *160*
She would turn a new side to her mortal,
Side unseen of herdsman, huntsman, steersman—
Blank to Zoroaster on his terrace,
Blind to Galileo on his turret,
Dumb to Homer, dumb to Keats—him, even!
Think, the wonder of the moonstruck mortal—
When she turns round, comes again in heaven,
Opens out anew for worse or better?
Proves she like some portent of an ice-berg
Swimming full upon the ship it founders,   *170*
Hungry with huge teeth of splintered chrystals?
Proves she as the paved-work of a sapphire
Seen by Moses when he climbed the mountain?
Moses, Aaron, Nadab and Abihu
Climbed and saw the very God, the Highest,
Stand upon the paved-work of a sapphire.
Like the bodied heaven in his clearness
Shone the stone, the sapphire of that paved-work,
When they ate and drank and saw God also!

XVIII. What were seen? None knows, none ever shall
know.   *180*
Only this is sure—the sight were other,
Not the moon's same side, born late in Florence,
Dying now impoverished here in London.
God be thanked, the meanest of his creatures
Boasts two soul-sides, one to face the world with,
One to show a woman when he loves her.

XIX. This I say of me, but think of you, Love!
This to you—yourself my moon of poets!
Ah, but that's the world's side—there's the wonder—
Thus they see you, praise you, think they know you.   *190*
There, in turn I stand with them and praise you,

202

Out of my own self, I dare to phrase it.
But the best is when I glide from out them,
Cross a step or two of dubious twilight,
Come out on the other side, the novel
Silent silver lights and darks undreamed of,
Where I hush and bless myself with silence.

xx. Oh, their Rafael of the dear Madonnas,
Oh, their Dante of the dread Inferno,
Wrote one song—and in my brain I sing it,   *200*
Drew one angel—borne, see, on my bosom!

EARLIER POEMS

I.—MADHOUSE CELL.

JOHANNES AGRICOLA IN MEDITATION.

THERE's Heaven above, and night by night,
   I look right through its gorgeous roof:
No sun and moons though e'er so bright
   Avail to stop me; splendour-proof
I keep the broods of stars aloof:
For I intend to get to God,
   For 'tis to God I speed so fast,
For in God's breast, my own abode,
   Those shoals of dazzling glory past,
I lay my spirit down at last.   10
I lie where I have always lain,
   God smiles as he has always smiled;
Ere suns and moons could wax and wane,
   Ere stars were thundergirt, or piled
The Heavens, God thought on me his child;
Ordained a life for me, arrayed
   Its circumstances, every one
To the minutest; ay, God said
   This head this hand should rest upon
Thus, ere he fashioned star or sun.   20
And having thus created me,
   Thus rooted me, he bade me grow,
Guiltless for ever, like a tree
   That buds and blooms, nor seeks to know
The law by which it prospers so:
But sure that thought and word and deed
   All go to swell his love for me,
Me, made because that love had need
   Of something irrevocably
Pledged solely its content to be.   30
Yes, yes, a tree which must ascend,—
   No poison-gourd foredoomed to stoop!
I have God's warrant, could I blend
   All hideous sins, as in a cup,
To drink the mingled venoms up,

Secure my nature will convert
  The draught to blossoming gladness **fast,**
While sweet dews turn to the gourd's hurt,
  And bloat, and while they bloat it, **blast,**
As from the first its lot was cast.   *40*
For as I lie, smiled on, full fed
  By unexhausted power to bless,
I gaze below on Hell's fierce bed,
  And those its waves of flame oppress,
Swarming in ghastly wretchedness;
Whose life on earth aspired to be
  One altar-smoke, so pure!—to win
If not love like God's love to me,
  At least to keep his anger in,
And all their striving turned to sin!   *50*
  Priest, doctor, hermit, monk grown **white**
With prayer, the broken-hearted nun,
  The martyr, the wan acolyte,
The incense-swinging child,—undone
Before God fashioned star or sun!
God, whom I praise; how could I praise,
  If such as I might understand,
Make out, and reckon on, his ways,
  And bargain for his love, and stand,
Paying a price, at his right hand?   *60*

II.—MADHOUSE CELL.

PORPHYRIA'S LOVER.

THE rain set early in to-night
  The sullen wind was soon awake,
It tore the elm-tops down for spite,
  And did its worst to vex the lake,
I listened with heart fit to break;
When glided in Porphyria: straight
  She shut the cold out and the storm,
And kneeled and made the cheerless grate
  Blaze up, and all the cottage warm;
Which done, she rose, and from her form   *10*
Withdrew the dripping cloak and shawl,
  And laid her soiled gloves by, untied
Her hat and let the damp hair fall,

And last, she sate down by my side
And called me.   When no voice replied,
She put my arm about her waist,
    And made her smooth white shoulder bare,
And all her yellow hair displaced,
    And, stooping, made my cheek lie there,
And spread o'er all her yellow hair,   20
Murmuring how she loved me; she
    Too weak, for all her heart's endeavour,
To set its struggling passion free
    From pride, and vainer ties dissever,
And give herself to me for ever:
But passion sometimes would prevail,
    Nor could to-night's gay feast restrain
A sudden thought of one so pale
    For love of her, and all in vain;
So, she was come through wind and rain.   30
Be sure I looked up at her eyes
    Proud, very proud; at last I knew
Porphyria worshipped me; surprise
    Made my heart swell, and still it grew
While I debated what to do.
That moment she was mine, mine, fair,
    Perfectly pure and good: I found
A thing to do, and all her hair
    In one long yellow string I wound
Three times her little throat around,   40
And strangled her.   No pain felt she;
    I am quite sure she felt no pain.
As a shut bud that holds a bee
    I warily oped her lids; again
Laughed the blue eyes without a stain.
And I untightened next the tress
    About her neck; her cheek once more
Blushed bright beneath my burning kiss:
    I propped her head up as before,
Only, this time *my* shoulder bore   50
Her head, which droops upon it still:
    The smiling rosy little head,
So glad it has its utmost will,
    That all it scorned at once is fled,
And I, its love, am gained instead!
Porphyria's love: she guessed not how

Her darling one wish would be heard.
And thus we sit together now,
 And all night long we have not stirred,
And yet God has not said a word!   *60*

MY LAST DUCHESS.

FERRARA.

THAT'S my last Duchess painted on the wall,
Looking as if she were alive; I call
That piece a wonder, now: Frà Pandolf's hands
Worked busily a day, and there she stands.
Will't please you sit and look at her? I said
" Frà Pandolf " by design, for never read
Strangers like you that pictured countenance,
The depth and passion of its earnest glance,
But to myself they turned (since none puts by
The curtain I have drawn for you, but I)   *10*
And seemed as they would ask me, if they durst,
How such a glance came there; so, not the first
Are you to turn and ask thus. Sir, 'twas not
Her husband's presence only, called that spot
Of joy into the Duchess' cheek: perhaps
Frà Pandolf chanced to say " Her mantle laps
" Over my Lady's wrist too much," or " Paint
" Must never hope to reproduce the faint
" Half-flush that dies along her throat; " such stuff
Was courtesy, she thought, and cause enough *20*
For calling up that spot of joy. She had
A heart . . . how shall I say? . . . too soon made glad,
Too easily impressed; she liked whate'er
She looked on, and her looks went everywhere.
Sir, 'twas all one! My favour at her breast,
The drooping of the daylight in the West,
The bough of cherries some officious fool
Broke in the orchard for her, the white mule
She rode with round the terrace—all and each
Would draw from her alike the approving speech, *30*

Or blush, at least. She thanked men,—good; but thanked
Somehow . . . I know not how . . . as if she ranked
My gift of a nine hundred years old name
With anybody's gift. Who'd stoop to blame
This sort of trifling? Even had you skill
In speech—(which I have not)—to make your will
Quite clear to such an one, and say " Just this
" Or that in you disgusts me; here you miss,
" Or there exceed the mark "—and if she let
Herself be lessoned so, nor plainly set   40
Her wits to yours, forsooth, and made excuse,
—E'en then would be some stooping, and I chuse
Never to stoop. Oh, Sir, she smiled, no doubt,
Whene'er I passed her; but who passed without
Much the same smile? This grew; I gave commands;
    Then all smiles stopped together. There she stands
As if alive. Will't please you rise? We'll meet
The company below, then. I repeat,
The Count your Master's known munificence
Is ample warrant that no just pretence   50
Of mine for dowry will be disallowed;
Though his fair daughter's self, as I avowed
At starting, is my object. Nay, we'll go
Together down, Sir! Notice Neptune, tho',
Taming a sea-horse, thought a rarity,
Which Claus of Innsbruck cast in bronze for me.

PICTOR IGNOTUS.

[FLORENCE, 15—.]

I COULD have painted pictures like that youth's
  Ye praise so. How my soul springs up! No bar
Stayed me—ah, thought which saddens while it soothes!—
  Never did fate forbid me, star by star,
To outburst on your night with all my gift
  Of fires from God: nor would my flesh have shrunk
From seconding my soul, with eyes uplift
  And wide to Heaven, or, straight like thunder, sunk
To the centre, of an instant; or around
  Turned calmly and inquisitive, to scan   *10*
The licence and the limit, space and bound,
  Allowed to Truth made visible in Man.
And, like that youth ye praise so, all I saw,
  Over the canvas could my hand have flung,
Each face obedient to its passion's law,
  Each passion clear proclaimed without a tongue;
Whether Hope rose at once in all the blood,
  A tip-toe for the blessing of embrace,
Or Rapture drooped the eyes, as when her brood
  Pull down the nesting dove's heart to its place,   *20*
Or Confidence lit swift the forehead up,
  And locked the mouth fast, like a castle braved,—
O Human faces, hath it spilt, my cup?
  What did ye give me that I have not saved?
Nor will I say I have not dreamed (how well!)
  Of going—I, in each new picture,—forth,
As, making new hearts beat and bosoms swell,
  To Pope or Kaiser, East, West, South or North,
Bound for the calmly satisfied great State,
  Or glad aspiring little burgh, it went,   *30*
Flowers cast upon the car which bore the freight,
  Through old streets named afresh from its event,
Till it reached home, where learned Age should greet
  My face, and Youth, the star not yet distinct
Above his hair, lie learning at my feet!—
  Oh, thus to live, I and my picture, linked
With love about, and praise, till life should end,
  And then not go to Heaven, but linger here,

Here on my earth, earth's every man my friend,—
   The thought grew frightful, 'twas so wildly dear!   *40*
But a voice changed it! Glimpses of such sights
   Have scared me, like the revels thro' a door
Of some strange House of Idols at its rites;
   This world seemed not the world it was before!
Mixed with my loving trusting ones there trooped
   . . . Who summoned those cold faces that begun
To press on me and judge me? Tho' I stooped
   Shrinking, as from the soldiery a nun,
They drew me forth, and spite of me . . . enough!
   These buy and sell our pictures, take and give,   *50*
Count them for garniture and household-stuff,
   And where they live our pictures needs must live,
And see their faces, listen to their prate,
   Partakers of their daily pettiness,
Discussed of,—" This I love, or this I hate,
   " This likes me more, and this affects me less!"
Wherefore I chose my portion. If at whiles
   My heart sinks, as monotonous I paint
These endless cloisters and eternal aisles
   With the same series, Virgin, Babe, and Saint,   *60*
With the same cold, calm, beautiful regard,
   At least no merchant traffics in my heart;
The sanctuary's gloom at least shall ward
   Vain tongues from where my pictures stand apart,
Only prayer breaks the silence of the shrine
   While, blackening in the daily candle-smoke,
They moulder on the damp wall's travertine,
   'Mid echoes the light footstep never woke.
So die, my pictures; surely, gently die!
   Oh, youth, men praise so,—holds their praise its worth?   *70*
Blown harshly, keeps the trump its golden cry?
   Tastes sweet the water with such specks of earth?

THE BISHOP ORDERS HIS TOMB AT ST. PRAXED'S CHURCH.

[ROME, 15—.]

VANITY, saith the preacher, vanity!
Draw round my bed: is Anselm keeping back?
Nephews—sons mine . . . ah God, I know not! Well—
She, men would have to be your mother once,
Old Gandolf envied me, so fair she was!
What's done is done, and she is dead beside,
Dead long ago, and I am bishop since,
And as she died so must we die ourselves,
And thence ye may perceive the world's a dream.
Life, how and what is it? As here I lie   *10*
In this state-chamber, dying by degrees,
Hours and long hours in the dead night, I ask
" Do I live, am I dead? " Peace, peace seems all.
St. Praxed's ever was the church for peace;
And so, about this tomb of mine. I fought
With tooth and nail to save my niche, ye know:
—Old Gandolf cozened me, despite my care;
Shrewd was that snatch from out the corner South
He graced his carrion with, God curse the same!
Yet still my niche is not so cramped but thence   *20*
One sees the pulpit o' the epistle-side,
And somewhat of the choir, those silent seats,
And up into the aery dome where live
The angels, and a sunbeam's sure to lurk:
And I shall fill my slab of basalt there,
And 'neath my tabernacle take my rest,
With those nine columns round me, two and two,
The odd one at my feet where Anselm stands:
Peach-blossom marble all, the rare, the ripe
As fresh-poured red wine of a mighty pulse   *30*
—Old Gandolf with his paltry onion-stone,
Put me where I may look at him! True peach,
Rosy and flawless: how I earned the prize!
Draw close: that conflagration of my church
—What then? So much was saved if aught were missed!
My sons, ye would not be my death? Go dig
The white-grape vineyard where the oil-press stood,
Drop water gently till the surface sinks,

And if ye find . . . Ah, God I know not, I ! . . .
Bedded in store of rotton figleaves soft,   40
And corded up in a tight olive-frail,
Some lump, ah God, of *lapis lazuli*,
Big as a Jew's head cut off at the nape,
Blue as a vein o'er the Madonna's breast . . .
Sons, all have I bequeathed you, villas, all,
That brave Frascati villa with its bath,
So, let the blue lump poise between my knees,
Like God the Father's globe on both his hands
Ye worship in the Jesu Church so gay,
For Gandolf shall not choose but see and burst!   50
Swift as a weaver's shuttle fleet our years:
Man goeth to the grave, and where is he?
Did I say basalt for my slab, sons?   Black—
'Twas ever antique-black I meant!   How else
Shall ye contrast my frieze to come beneath?
The bas-relief in bronze ye promised me,
Those Pans and Nymphs ye wot of, and perchance
Some tripod, thyrsus, with a vase or so,
The Saviour at his sermon on the mount,
St. Praxed in a glory, and one Pan   60
Ready to twitch the Nymph's last garment off,
And Moses with the tables . . . but I know
Ye mark me not!   What do they whisper thee,
Child of my bowels, Anselm?   Ah, ye hope
To revel down my villas while I gasp
Bricked o'er with beggar's mouldy travertine
Which Gandolf from his tomb-top chuckles at!
Nay, boys, ye love me—all of jasper, then!
'Tis jasper ye stand pledged to, lest I grieve
My bath must needs be left behind, alas!   70
One block, pure green as a pistachio-nut,
There's plenty jasper somewhere in the world—
And have I not St. Praxed's ear to pray
Horses for ye, and brown Greek manuscripts,
And mistresses with great smooth marbly limbs?
—That's if ye carve my epitaph aright,
Choice Latin, picked phrase, Tully's every word,
No gaudy ware like Gandolf's second line—
Tully, my masters?   Ulpian serves his need!
And then how I shall lie through centuries,   80
And hear the blessed mutter of the mass,

And see God made and eaten all day long,
And feel the steady candle-flame, and taste
Good strong thick stupifying incense-smoke!
For as I lie here, hours of the dead night,
Dying in state and by such slow degrees,
I fold my arms as if they clasped a crook,
And stretch my feet forth straight as stone can point,
And let the bedclothes for a mortcloth drop
Into great laps and folds of sculptor's-work: 90
And as yon tapers dwindle, and strange thoughts
Grow, with a certain humming in my ears,
About the life before I lived this life,
And this life too, Popes, Cardinals and Priests,
St. Praxed at his sermon on the mount,
Your tall pale mother with her talking eyes,
And new-found agate urns as fresh as day,
And marble's language, Latin pure, discreet,
—Aha, ELUCESCEBAT quoth our friend?
No Tully, said I, Ulpian at the best!   100
Evil and brief hath been my pilgrimage.
All *lapis*, all, sons!   Else I give the Pope
My villas: will ye ever eat my heart?
Ever your eyes were as a lizard's quick,
They glitter like your mother's for my soul,
Or ye would heighten my impoverished frieze,
Piece out its starved design, and fill my vase
With grapes, and add a vizor and a Term,
And to the tripod ye would tie a lynx
That in his struggle throws the thyrsus down,   110
To comfort me on my entablature
Whereon I am to lie till I must ask
" Do I live, am I dead? "   There, leave me, there!
For ye have stabbed me with ingratitude
To death—ye wish it—God, ye wish it!   Stone—
Gritstone, a-crumble!   Clammy squares which sweat
As if the corpse they keep were oozing through—
And no more *lapis* to delight the world!
Well, go!   I bless ye.   Fewer tapers there,
But in a row: and, going, turn your backs   120
—Ay, like departing altar-ministrants,
And leave me in my church, the church for peace,
That I may watch at leisure if he leers—
Old Gandolf, at me, from his onion-stone,
As still he envied me, so fair she was!

MEETING AT NIGHT.

I. THE grey sea and the long black land;
  And the yellow half-moon large and low;
  And the startled little waves that leap
  In fiery ringlets from their sleep,
  As I gain the cove with pushing prow,
  And quench its speed in the slushy sand.

II. Then a mile of warm sea-scented beach;
  Three fields to cross till a farm appears;
  A tap at the pane, the quick sharp scratch
  And blue spurt of a lighted match, 10
  And a voice less loud, thro' its joys and fears,
  Than the two hearts beating each to each!

PARTING AT MORNING.

ROUND the cape of a sudden came the sea,
And the sun looked over the mountain's rim—
And straight was a path of gold for him,
And the need of a world of men for me.

LATER POEMS

CALIBAN UPON SETEBOS; OR, NATURAL
THEOLOGY IN THE ISLAND.

" Thou thoughtest that I was altogether such a one as thyself."

['WILL sprawl, now that the heat of day is best,
Flat on his belly in the pit's much mire,
With elbows wide, fists clenched to prop his chin.
And, while he kicks both feet in the cool slush,
And feels about his spine small eft-things course,
Run in and out each arm, and make him laugh:
And while above his head a pompion-plant,
Coating the cave-top as a brow its eye,
Creeps down to touch and tickle hair and beard,
And now a flower drops with a bee inside,   *10*
And now a fruit to snap at, catch and crunch,—
He looks out o'er yon sea which sunbeams cross
And recross till they weave a spider-web
(Meshes of fire, some great fish breaks at times)
And talks to his own self, howe'er he please,
Touching that other, whom his dam called God.
Because to talk about Him, vexes—ha,
Could He but know! and time to vex is now,
When talk is safer than in winter-time.
Moreover Prosper and Miranda sleep   *20*
In confidence he drudges at their task,
And it is good to cheat the pair, and gibe,
Letting the rank tongue blossom into speech.]
Setebos, Setebos, and Setebos!
'Thinketh, He dwelleth i' the cold o' the moon.

'Thinketh He made it, with the sun to match,
But not the stars; the stars came otherwise;
Only made clouds, winds, meteors, such as that:
Also this isle, what lives and grows thereon,
And snaky sea which rounds and ends the same.   *30*

'Thinketh, it came of being ill at ease:
He hated that He cannot change His cold,
Nor cure its ache.   'Hath spied an icy fish
That longed to 'scape the rock-stream where she lived,
And thaw herself within the lukewarm brine

215

O' the lazy sea her stream thrusts far amid,
A crystal spike 'twixt two warm walls of wave;
Only, she ever sickened, found repulse
At the other kind of water, not her life,
(Green-dense and dim-delicious, bred o' the sun)   *40*
Flounced back from bliss she was not born to breathe,
And in her old bounds buried her despair,
Hating and loving warmth alike: so He.

'Thinketh, He made thereat the sun, this isle,
Trees and the fowls here, beast and creeping thing.
Yon otter, sleek-wet, black, lithe as a leech;
Yon auk, one fire-eye in a ball of foam,
That floats and feeds; a certain badger brown
He hath watched hunt with that slant white-wedge eye
By moonlight; and the pie with the long tongue   *50*
That pricks deep into oakwarts for a worm,
And says a plain word when she finds her prize,
But will not eat the ants; the ants themselves
That build a wall of seeds and settled stalks
About their hole—He made all these and more,
Made all we see, and us, in spite: how else?
He could not, Himself, make a second self
To be His mate: as well have made Himself:
He would not make what he mislikes or slights,
An eyesore to Him, or not worth His pains: *60*
But did, in envy, listlessness or sport,
Make what Himself would fain, in a manner, be—
Weaker in most points, stronger in a few,
Worthy, and yet mere playthings all the while,
Things He admires and mocks too,—that is it.
Because, so brave, so better though they be,
It nothing skills if He begin to plague.
Look now, I melt a gourd-fruit into mash,
Add honeycomb and pods, I have perceived,
Which bite like finches when they bill and kiss,—   *70*
Then, when froth rises bladdery, drink up all,
Quick, quick, till maggots scamper through my brain;
Last, throw me on my back i' the seeded thyme,
And wanton, wishing I were born a bird.
Put case, unable to be what I wish,
I yet could make a live bird out of clay:
Would not I take clay, pinch my Caliban

Able to fly?—for, there, see, he hath wings,
And great comb like the hoopoe's to admire,
And there, a sting to do his foes offence,   *80*
There, and I will that he begin to live,
Fly to yon rock-top, nip me off the horns
Of grigs high up that make the merry din,
Saucy through their veined wings, and mind me not.
In which feat, if his leg snapped, brittle clay,
And he lay stupid-like,—why, I should laugh;
And if he, spying me, should fall to weep,
Beseech me to be good, repair his wrong,
Bid his poor leg smart less or grow again,—
Well, as the chance were, this might take or else *90*
Not take my fancy: I might hear his cry,
And give the mankin three sound legs for one,
Or pluck the other off, leave him like an egg,
And lessoned he was mine and merely clay.
Were this no pleasure, lying in the thyme,
Drinking the mash, with brain become alive,
Making and marring clay at will? So He.

'Thinketh, such shows nor right nor wrong in Him,
Nor kind, nor cruel: He is strong and Lord.
'Am strong myself compared to yonder crabs *100*
That march now from the mountain to the sea;
'Let twenty pass, and stone the twenty-first,
Loving not, hating not, just choosing so.
'Say, the first straggler that boasts purple spots
Shall join the file, one pincer twisted off;
'Say, this bruised fellow shall receive a worm,
And two worms he whose nippers end in red;
As it likes me each time, I do: so He.

Well then, 'supposeth He is good i' the main,
Placable if His mind and ways were guessed, *110*
But rougher than His handiwork, be sure!
Oh, He hath made things worthier than Himself,
And envieth that, so helped, such things do more
Than He who made them! What consoles but this?
That they, unless through Him, do nought at all,
And must submit: what other use in things?
'Hath cut a pipe of pithless elder joint
That, blown through, gives exact the scream o' the jay

When from her wing you twitch the feathers blue:
Sound this, and little birds that hate the jay   *120*
Flock within stone's throw, glad their foe is hurt:
Put case such pipe could prattle and boast forsooth
" I catch the birds, I am the crafty thing,
" I make the cry my maker cannot make
" With his great round mouth; he must blow through mine! "
Would not I smash it with my foot?   So He.

But wherefore rough, why cold and ill at ease?
Aha, that is a question!   Ask, for that,
What knows,—the something over Setebos
That made Him, or He, may be, found and fought,   *130*
Worsted, drove off and did to nothing, perchance.
There may be something quiet o'er His head,
Out of His reach, that feels nor joy nor grief,
Since both derive from weakness in some way.
I joy because the quails come; would not joy
Could I bring quails here when I have a mind:
This Quiet, all it hath a mind to, doth.
'Esteemeth stars the outposts of its couch,
But never spends much thought nor care that way.
It may look up, work up,—the worse for those   *140*
It works on!   'Careth but for Setebos
The many-handed as a cuttle-fish,
Who, making Himself feared through what He does,
Looks up, first, and perceives he cannot soar
To what is quiet and hath happy life;
Next looks down here, and out of very spite
Makes this a bauble-world to ape yon real,
These good things to match those as hips do grapes.
'Tis solace making baubles, ay, and sport.
Himself peeped late, eyed Prosper at his books   *150*
Careless and lofty, lord now of the isle:
Vexed, 'stitched a book of broad leaves, arrow-shaped,
Wrote thereon, he knows what, prodigious words;
Has peeled a wand and called it by a name;
Weareth at whiles for an enchanter's robe
The eyed skin of a supple oncelot;
And hath an ounce sleeker than youngling mole,
A four-legged serpent he makes cower and couch,
Now snarl, now hold its breath and mind his eye,
And saith she is Miranda and my wife: *160*

'Keeps for his Ariel a tall pouch-bill crane
He bids go wade for fish and straight disgorge;
Also a sea-beast, lumpish, which he snared,
Blinded the eyes of, and brought somewhat tame,
And split its toe-webs, and now pens the drudge
In a hole o' the rock and calls him Caliban;
A bitter heart that bides its time and bites.
'Plays thus at being Prosper in a way,
Taketh his mirth with make-believes: so He.

His dam held that the Quiet made all things   *170*
Which Setebos vexed only: 'holds not so.
Who made them weak, meant weakness He might vex.
Had He meant other, while His hand was in,
Why ..ot make horny eyes no thorn could prick,
Or plate my scalp with bone against the snow,
Or overscale my flesh 'neath joint and joint,
Like an orc's armour? Ay,—so spoil His sport!
He is the One now: only He doth all.

'Saith, He may like, perchance, what profits Him.
Ay, himself loves what does him good; but why?   *180*
'Gets good no otherwise. This blinded beast
Loves whoso places flesh-meat on his nose,
But, had he eyes, would want no help, but hate
Or love, just as it liked him: He hath eyes.
Also it pleaseth Setebos to work,
Use all His hands, and exercise much craft,
By no means for the love of what is worked.
'Tasteth, himself, no finer good i' the world
When all goes right, in this safe summer-time,
And he wants little, hungers, aches not much,   *190*
Than trying what to do with wit and strength.
'Falls to make something: 'piled yon pile of turfs,
And squared and stuck there squares of soft white chalk,
And, with a fish-tooth, scratched a moon on each,
And set up endwise certain spikes of tree,
And crowned the whole with a sloth's skull a-top,
Found dead i' the woods, too hard for one to kill.
No use at all i' the work, for work's sole sake;
'Shall some day knock it down again: so He.

'Saith He is terrible: watch His feats in proof!   *200*
One hurricane will spoil six good months' hope.
He hath a spite against me, that I know,
Just as He favours Prosper, who knows why?
So it is, all the same, as well I find.
'Wove wattles half the winter, fenced them firm
With stone and stake to stop she-tortoises
Crawling to lay their eggs here: well, one wave,
Feeling the foot of Him upon its neck,
Gaped as a snake does, lolled out its large tongue,
And licked the whole labour flat: so much for spite.   *210*
'Saw a ball flame down late (yonder it lies)
Where, half an hour before, I slept i' the shade:
Often they scatter sparkles: there is force!
'Dug up a newt He may have envied once
And turned to stone, shut up inside a stone.
Please Him and hinder this?—What Prosper does?
Aha, if He would tell me how! Not He!
There is the sport: discover how or die!
All need not die, for of the things o' the isle
Some flee afar, some dive, some run up trees;   *220*
Those at His mercy,—why, they please Him most
When . . . when . . . well, never try the same way twice!
Repeat what act has pleased, He may grow wroth.
You must not know His ways, and play Him off,
Sure of the issue. 'Doth the like himself:
'Spareth a squirrel that it nothing fears
But steals the nut from underneath my thumb,
And when I threat, bites stoutly in defence:
'Spareth an urchin that contrariwise,
Curls up into a ball, pretending death   *230*
For fright at my approach: the two ways please.
But what would move my choler more than this,
That either creature counted on its life
To-morrow and next day and all days to come,
Saying, forsooth, in the inmost of its heart,
" Because he did so yesterday with me,
" And otherwise with such another brute,
" So must he do henceforth and always."—Ay?
Would teach the reasoning couple what " must " means!
'Doth as he likes, or wherefore Lord? So He.   *240*

'Conceiveth all things will continue thus,

And we shall have to live in fear of Him
So long as He lives, keeps His strength: no change,
If He have done His best, make no new world
To please Him more, so leave off watching this,—
If He surprise not even the Quiet's self
Some strange day,—or, suppose, grow into it
As grubs grow butterflies: else, here are we,
And there is He, and nowhere help at all.

'Believeth with the life, the pain shall stop.   *250*
His dam held different, that after death
He both plagued enemies and feasted friends:
Idly! He doth His worst in this our life,
Giving just respite lest we die through pain,
Saving last pain for worst,—with which, an end.
Meanwhile, the best way to escape His ire
Is, not to seem too happy. 'Sees, himself,
Yonder two flies, with purple films and pink,
Bask on the pompion-bell above; kills both.
'Sees two black painful beetles roll their ball   *260*
On head and tail as if to save their lives:
Moves them the stick away they strive to clear.

Even so, 'would have Him misconceive, suppose
This Caliban strives hard and ails no less,
And always, above all else, envies Him;
Wherefore he mainly dances on dark nights,
Moans in the sun, gets under holes to laugh,
And never speaks his mind save housed as now:
Outside, 'groans, curses. If He caught me here,
O'erheard this speech, and asked " What chucklest at?"   *270*
'Would, to appease Him, cut a finger off,
Or of my three kid yearlings burn the best,
Or let the toothsome apples rot on tree,
Or push my tame beast for the orc to taste:
While myself lit a fire, and made a song
And sung it, " *What I hate, be consecrate*
" *To celebrate Thee and Thy state, no mate*
" *For Thee ; what see for envy in poor me ?* "
Hoping the while, since evils sometimes mend,
Warts rub away and sores are cured with slime,   *280*
That some strange day, will either the Quiet catch
And conquer Setebos, or likelier He
Decrepit may doze, doze, as good as die.

[What, what?   A curtain o'er the world at once!
Crickets stop hissing; not a bird—or, yes,
There scuds His raven that has told Him all!
It was fool's play, this prattling!   Ha!   The wind
Shoulders the pillared dust, death's house o' the move,
And fast invading fires begin!   White blaze—
A tree's head snaps—and there, there, there, there, there,   *290*
His thunder follows!   Fool to gibe at Him!
Lo!   'Lieth flat and loveth Setebos!
'Maketh his teeth meet through his upper lip,
Will let those quails fly, will not eat this month
One little mess of whelks, so he may 'scape!]

CONFESSIONS.

I. WHAT is he buzzing in my ears?
      " Now that I come to die,
   " Do I view the world as a vale of tears? "
      Ah, reverend sir, not I!

II. What I viewed there once, what I view again
      Where the physic bottles stand
   On the table's edge,—is a suburb lane,
      With a wall to my bedside hand.

III. That lane sloped, much as the bottles do,
      From a house you could descry   *10*
   O'er the garden-wall: is the curtain blue
      Or green to a healthy eye?

IV. To mine, it serves for the old June weather
      Blue above lane and wall;
   And that farthest bottle labelled " Ether"
      Is the house o'ertopping all.

V. At a terrace, somewhere near the stopper,
      There watched for me, one June,
   A girl: I know, sir, it's improper,
      My poor mind's out of tune.   *20*

VI. Only, there was a way . . . you crept
    Close by the side, to dodge
Eyes in the house, two eyes except;
    They styled their house " The Lodge."

VII. What right had a lounger up their lane?
    But, by creeping very close,
With the good wall's help,—their eyes might strain
    And stretch themselves to Oes.

VIII. Yet never catch her and me together,
    As she left the attic, there,   *30*
By the rim of the bottle labelled " Ether,"
    And stole from stair to stair,

IX. And stood by the rose-wreathed gate.   Alas,
    We loved, sir—used to meet:
How sad and bad and mad it was—
    But then, how it was sweet!

APPARENT FAILURE.

" We shall soon lose a celebrated building."—*Paris Newspaper*.

I. No, for I'll save it! Seven years since,
        I passed through Paris, stopped a day
    To see the baptism of your Prince;
        Saw, made my bow, and went my way:
    Walking the heat and headache off,
        I took the Seine-side, you surmise,
    Thought of the Congress, Gortschakoff,
        Cavour's appeal and Buol's replies,
    So sauntered till—what met my eyes?

II. Only the Doric little Morgue!   10
        The dead-house where you show your drowned:
    Petrarch's Vaucluse makes proud the Sorgue,
        Your Morgue has made the Seine renowned.
    One pays one's debt in such a case;
        I plucked up heart and entered,—stalked,
    Keeping a tolerable face
        Compared with some whose cheeks were chalked:
    Let them! No Briton's to be baulked!

III. First came the silent gazers; next,
        A screen of glass, we're thankful for;   20
    Last, the sight's self, the sermon's text,
        The three men who did most abhor
    Their life in Paris yesterday,
        So killed themselves: and now, enthroned
    Each on his copper couch, they lay
        Fronting me, waiting to be owned.
    I thought, and think, their sin's atoned.

IV. Poor men, God made, and all for that!
        The reverence struck me; o'er each head
    Religiously was hung its hat,   30
        Each coat dripped by the owner's bed,
    Sacred from touch: each had his berth,
        His bounds, his proper place of rest,
    Who last night tenanted on earth
        Some arch, where twelve such slept abreast,—
    Unless the plain asphalte seemed best.

v. How did it happen, my poor boy?
   You wanted to be Buonaparte
And have the Tuileries for toy,
   And could not, so it broke your heart?   *40*
You, old one by his side, I judge,
   Were, red as blood, a socialist,
A leveller! Does the Empire grudge
   You've gained what no Republic missed?
Be quiet, and unclench your fist!

vi. And this—why, he was red in vain,
   Or black,—poor fellow that is blue!
What fancy was it turned your brain?
   Oh, women were the prize for you!
Money gets women, cards and dice   *50*
   Get money, and ill-luck gets just
The copper couch and one clear nice
   Cool squirt of water o'er your bust,
The right thing to extinguish lust!

vii. It's wiser being good than bad;
   It's safer being meek than fierce:
It's fitter being sane than mad.
   My own hope is, a sun will pierce
The thickest cloud earth ever stretched;
   That, after Last, returns the First,   *60*
Though a wide compass round be fetched;
   That what began best, can't end worst,
Nor what God blessed once, prove accurst.

NUMPHOLEPTOS

STILL you stand, still you listen, still you smile!
Still melts your moonbeam through me, white awhile,
Softening, sweetening, till sweet and soft
Increase so round this heart of mine, that oft
I could believe your moonbeam-smile has past
The pallid limit, lies, transformed at last
To sunlight and salvation—warms the soul
It sweetens, softens!   Would you pass that goal,
Gain love's birth at the limit's happier verge,
And, where an iridescence lurks, but urge   10
The hesitating pallor on to prime
Of dawn!—true blood-streaked, sun-warmth, action-time,
By heart-pulse ripened to a ruddy glow
Of gold above my clay—I scarce should know
From gold's self, thus suffused!   For gold means love.
What means the sad slow silver smile above
My clay but pity, pardon?—at the best,
But acquiescence that I take my rest,
Contented to be clay, while in your heaven
The sun reserves love for the Spirit-Seven   20
Companioning God's throne they lamp before,
—Leaves earth a mute waste only wandered o'er
By that pale soft sweet disempassioned moon
Which smiles me slow forgiveness!   Such the boon
I beg?   Nay, dear, submit to this—just this
Supreme endeavour!   As my lips now kiss
Your feet, my arms convulse your shrouding robe,
My eyes, acquainted with the dust, dare probe
Your eyes above for—what, if born, would blind
Mine with redundant bliss, as flash may find   30
The inert nerve, sting awake the palsied limb,
Bid with life's ecstasy sense overbrim
And suck back death in the resurging joy—
Love, the love whole and sole without alloy!

Vainly!   The promise withers!   I employ
Lips, arms, eyes, pray the prayer which finds the word,
Make the appeal which must be felt, not heard,

And none the more is changed your calm regard:
Rather, its sweet and soft grow harsh and hard—
Forbearance, then repulsion, then disdain.   **40**
Avert the rest!   I rise, see!—make, again
Once more, the old departure for some track
Untried yet through a world which brings me back
Ever thus fruitlessly to find your feet,
To fix your eyes, to pray the soft and sweet
Which smile there—take from his new pilgrimage
Your outcast, once your inmate, and assuage
With love—not placid pardon now—his thirst
For a mere drop from out the ocean erst
He drank at!   Well, the quest shall be renewed.   **50**
Fear nothing!   Though I linger, unembued
With any drop, my lips thus close.   I go!
So did I leave you, I have found you so,
And doubtlessly, if fated to return,
So shall my pleading persevere and earn
Pardon—not love—in that same smile, I learn,
And lose the meaning of, to learn once more.
Vainly!

          What fairy track do I explore?
What magic hall return to, like the gem
Centuply-angled o'er a diadem?   **60**
You dwell there, hearted; from your midmost home
Rays forth—through that fantastic world I roam
Ever—from centre to circumference,
Shaft upon coloured shaft: this crimsons thence,
That purples out its precinct through the waste.
Surely I had your sanction when I faced,
Fared forth upon that untried yellow ray
Whence I retrack my steps?   They end to-day
Where they began—before your feet, beneath
Your eyes, your smile: the blade is shut in sheath,   **70**
Fire quenched in flint; irradiation, late
Triumphant through the distance, finds its fate,
Merged in your blank pure soul, alike the source
And tomb of that prismatic glow: divorce
Absolute, all-conclusive!   Forth I fared,
Treading the lambent flamelet: little cared
If now its flickering took the topaz tint,
If now my dull-caked path gave sulphury hint

Of subterranean rage—no stay nor stint
To yellow, since you sanctioned that I bathe,　　　　　*80*
Burnish me, soul and body, swim and swathe
In yellow license.　Here I reek suffused
With crocus, saffron, orange, as I used
With scarlet, purple, every dye o' the bow
Born of the storm-cloud.　As before, you show
Scarce recognition, no approval, some
Mistrust, more wonder at a man become
Monstrous in garb, nay—flesh disguised as well,
Through his adventure.　Whatsoe'er befell,
I followed, whereso'er it wound, that vein　　　　　*90*
You authorized should leave your whiteness, stain
Earth's sombre stretch beyond your midmost place
Of vantage,—trode that tinct whereof the trace
On garb and flesh repel you!　Yes, I plead
Your own permission—your command, indeed,
That who would worthily retain the love
Must share the knowledge shrined those eyes above,
Go boldly on adventure, break through bounds
O' the quintessential whiteness that surrounds
Your feet, obtain experience of each tinge　　　　　*100*
That bickers forth to broaden out, impinge
Plainer his foot its pathway all distinct
From every other.　Ah, the wonder, linked
With fear, as exploration manifests
What agency it was first tipped the crests
Of unnamed wildflower, soon protruding grew
Portentous mid the sands, as when his hue
Betrays him and the burrowing snake gleams through;
Till, last . . . but why parade more shame and pain?
Are not the proofs upon me?　Here again　　　　　*110*
I pass into your presence, I receive
Your smile of pity, pardon, and I leave . . .
No, not this last of times I leave you, mute,
Submitted to my penance, so my foot
May yet again adventure, tread, from source
To issue, one more ray of rays which course
Each other, at your bidding, from the sphere
Silver and sweet, their birthplace, down that drear
Dark of the world,—you promise shall return
Your pilgrim jewelled as with drops o' the urn　　　　　*120*
The rainbow paints from, and no smatch at all

Of ghastliness at edge of some cloud-pall
Heaven cowers before, as earth awaits the fall
O' the bolt and flash of doom. Who trusts your word
Tries the adventure: and returns—absurd
As frightful—in that sulphur-steeped disguise
Mocking the priestly cloth-of-gold, sole prize
The arch-heretic was wont to bear away
Until he reached the burning. No, I say:
No fresh adventure! No more seeking love   *130*
At end of toil, and finding, calm above
My passion, the old statuesque regard,
The sad petrific smile!

        O you—less hard
And hateful than mistaken and obtuse
Unreason of a she-intelligence!
You very woman with the pert pretence
To match the male achievement! Like enough!
Ay, you were easy victors, did the rough
Straightway efface itself to smooth, the gruff
Grind down and grow a whisper,—did man's truth   *140*
Subdue, for sake of chivalry and ruth,
Its rapier-edge to suit the bulrush-spear
Womanly falsehood fights with! O that ear
All fact pricks rudely, that thrice-superfine
Feminity of sense, with right divine
To waive all process, take result stain-free
From out the very muck wherein . . .

        Ah me!
The true slave's querulous outbreak! All the rest
Be resignation! Forth at your behest
I fare. Who knows but this—the crimson-quest—   *150*
May deepen to a sunrise, not decay
To that cold sad sweet smile?—which I obey.

EPILOGUE TO "ASOLANDO"

AT the midnight in the silence of the sleep-time,
   When you set your fancies free,
Will they pass to where—by death, fools think, imprisoned—
Low he lies who once so loved you, whom you loved so,
       —Pity me?

Oh to love so, be so loved, yet so mistaken!
   What had I on earth to do
With the slothful, with the mawkish, the unmanly?
Like the aimless, helpless, hopeless, did I drivel
       —Being—who?

One who never turned his back but marched breast forward,
   Never doubted clouds would break,   **10**
Never dreamed, though right were worsted, wrong would
    triumph,
Held we fall to rise, are baffled to fight better,
       Sleep to wake.

No, at noonday in the bustle of man's work-time
   Greet the unseen with a cheer!
Bid him forward, breast and back as either should be,
'Strive and thrive!' cry 'Speed,—fight on, fare ever
       There as here!'

NOTES

Love Among the Ruins. In later editions the fourteen stanzas were printed as seven by joining pairs.

    39. *caper:* a prickly south European shrub.

    65. *causeys:* causeways.

A Lovers' Quarrel.

    30. *the emperor:* Napoleon III.

    43. *table turn:* allusion to a spiritualists' seance.

Evelyn Hope.

    19. *good stars met in your horoscope:* she was born at a time when the position of the stars was favourable.

Up at a Villa—Down in the City.

    35. *cicala:* an insect which makes a whirring noise.

    39. *diligence:* stage coach.

    42. *Pulcinello-trumpet:* signal for the Punch and Judy show.

    52. *pink gauze . . . heart:* the procession of the Seven Sorrows of Our Lady.

    56. *oil . . . gate:* the 'octroi', or dues on goods entering Italian cities.

Fra Lippo Lippi. Browning's principal source for the life of Brother Lippo Lippi was Giorgio Vasari's *Lives of the Painters.*

    17. *Cosimo of the Medici:* the banker and art patron who was the virtual ruler of Florence.

    53. *Flower o' the broom:* here and at intervals Lippo breaks into a type of Florentine folk song called the 'stornello'.

    73. *Jerome:* the ascetic St Jerome (340–420).

    121. *the Eight:* magistrates who governed Florence.

    139. *Camaldolese:* monastic order founded by St Rinaldo in 1027.

    140. *Preaching Friars:* the Dominicans.

    189. *Giotto:* the early mediaeval painter noted for the purity of his religious pictures.

    235. *Brother Angelico:* (1387–1455) noted for the saintliness of his life and paintings.

    236. *Brother Lorenzo:* (c. 1370–1425) Don Lorenzo 'Monaco' ('the monk').

    277. *Hulking Tom:* Tomaso Guidi (1401–28), called 'Masaccio'.

    377. *Iste perfecit opus:* 'This man accomplished the work', or 'This man caused the work to be made'. Browning, probably wrongly, took these words in Lippo's 'The Coronation of the Virgin' in the Accademia delle Belle Arti at Florence in the former sense.

A Toccata of Galuppi's. Baldassare Galuppi (1706–85) was a famous Venetian musician. A Toccata ('touch piece') is a light, showy piece intended to exhibit virtuoso performance.

    6. *Doges . . . rings:* the annual ceremony in which the Doge, chief magistrate of Venice, threw a ring into the Adriatic to symbolize its wedding with the city.

Notes

By the Fireside.
  43. *Pella:* a village near the Lake of Orta in Piedmont.
  101. *Leonor:* the perfect wife in Beethoven's opera 'Fidelio'.
  132. *The great Word:* see Revelation, 21: 5.
  185. *chrysolite:* an olive-green precious stone, mentioned in Revelation, 21: 20.

An Epistle Containing . . . Karshish . . . Both Karshish and Abib are imaginary characters. Cf. John, 11: 1–44.
  28. *Vespasian:* the Roman emperor Vespasian invaded Jerusalem in A.D. 66, which fixes the time of the poem.
  44. *falling sickness:* epilepsy.
  50. *sublimate:* medicine produced by reducing a substance to vapour and then condensing it again.
  60. *Zoar:* a city near the Dead Sea.
  89. *conceit:* fancy.
  109. *sanguine:* active, energetic.
  fifty years of age: Lazarus would have been about sixty-five in A.D. 66. To Karshish he appears much younger.
  177. *Greek-fire:* the precursor of gunpowder.
  259. *the earthquake:* that mentioned in Matthew, 27: 51 as occurring at the time of the crucifixion.

Mesmerism.
  45. *calotypist:* photographer.
  75. *tractile:* obedient; capable of being directed.

Instans Tyrannus. ('The Threatening Tyrant'). The source is a passage from Horace's Ode on the Just Man (Od. iii. 3. 1): 'The just man, firm to his purpose, is not to be shaken from his fixed resolve by the fury of a mob laying upon him their impious behests, nor by the frown of a threatening tyrant.'

'Childe Roland to the Dark Tower Came'. *Childe:* the title given to a young, untried knight. *Edgar's song:* see *King Lear*, III, iv.
  48. *estray:* strayed animal.
  80. *colloped:* in folds.
  160. *Apollyon:* the devil. See Revelation, 9: 11.
  161. *dragon-penned:* dragon-pinioned.
  203. *slug-horn:* a battle trumpet is meant. Browning follows Chatterton's misunderstanding of O.E. 'slogan', a battle cry.

Respectability.
  15–16. *feel the Boulevard . . . light:* see the lights of the Paris boulevard.
  21. *Institute . . . Montalembert:* In that symbol of respectability, L'Institut National, the historian Guizot was obliged by protocol to welcome the author Montalembert politely, even though the two were bitter enemies.

The Statue and the Bust.
  1. *a palace in Florence . . . well:* the palace of the Riccardi (now called the Palazzo Antinori), a noble family of Florence.
  12. *Ferdinand:* Ferdinand de Medici (1549–1608), Grand Duke of Florence.

22. *encolure:* mane.

33–5. *the pile . . . overshadows one:* the Grand Duke's palace symbolically overshadows the Via Larga.

36–9. *a crime . . . cursed son:* Cosimo de Medici destroyed the Republic of Florence by seizing the government in 1434.

57. *catafalk:* here, the funeral procession, rather than the stage used for requiem masses.

94–6. *What if we break . . . morning's flowers:* the Duke invites the couple to leave Florence on the Arno for a holiday at his house in the suburb of Petraja.

169. *Robbia craft:* the work in enamelled terra-cotta relief done by the della Robbia family and their successors.

189. *the empty shrine:* the Palace of the Riccardi contained a niche which might have held such a bust as that described in the poem.

202. *John of Douay:* usually called Giovanni da Bologna (1524–1608), a famous Italian sculptor, whose equestrian statue of the Duke still stands.

234. *stamp of the very Guelph:* coin with the genuine government stamp.

250. *De te fabula:* the Horatian phrase '*Mutato nomine de te fabula narratur*': 'change the name and the story is told of you'.

How it Strikes a Contemporary.

3. *Valladolid:* the principal town of the Spanish province of that name.

19. *Moorish work:* the Moors occupied Spain long enough to leave architectural imprints.

28. *fly-leaf ballads:* printed in single sheets.

44. *Lord the King:* in later editions Browning changed such pronouns, here capitalized, to lower case, as if to obscure the originally suggested allegorical significance.

90. *the Corregidor:* the chief magistrate of the town.

115. *Prado:* the fashionable promenade of Madrid, the capital city.

The Last Ride Together.

65. *scratch his name on the Abbey stones:* honour him with a tomb in Westminster Abbey.

The Patriot.

26. *Brescia:* capital of the province of Brescia in northern Italy. In later editions Browning dropped the name (changing the line to 'Thus I entered, and thus I go'), probably to correct the impression that the poem was specifically about Arnold of Brescia.

Master Hugues of Saxe-Gotha, a purely imaginary composer. Saxe-Gotha in central Germany was the birthplace of Bach.

26. *Aloys . . . Just:* sacristan's assistants.

29. *sacrament lace:* lace on the altar linen.

39. *claviers:* keyboards.

44. *breves:* a breve is the longest note in music, formerly square in shape.

49. *shent:* rebuked.

60. *Two:* the numbers refer to the five musical phrases out of which the complex fugue is woven.

67. *discept:* contend, disagree.

79. *strepitant:* noisy.

80. *Danaides . . . Sieve:* the Danaides were the fifty daughters of Danaus who were condemned in the underworld to pour water eternally through a sieve. Hence, a never-ending argument or task.

83. *Escobar:* Escobar of Mendoza (1589–1669), a famous Jesuit casuist, condemned by the Church and attacked by Pascal.

86. *Est fuga, volvitur rota:* 'it is a flight, the wheel rolls itself round'.

100. *tickens:* a ticken is a closely woven twill fabric.

136. *meâ pœnd:* at my risk of punishment.

140. *mode Palestrina:* Giovanni P. da Palestrina (1524–94) emancipated music from the intricate pedantries of his predecessors.

Bishop Blougram's Apology. Blougram is an imaginary prelate, but Browning's conception of the character of Cardinal Wiseman was the original of the portrait. Gigadibs the journalist is likewise fictional. 'Apology' is used in the old sense of 'justification' or 'vindication'.

3. *our Abbey:* Westminster Abbey, lost by the Church of Rome at the Reformation.

6. *Pugin:* A. W. N. Pugin (1812–52), a Catholic architect who built many Gothic church buildings in England.

45. *Che ch'è:* 'what, what!', a common Italian exclamation.

54. *Count D'Orsay:* (1798–1852), a French dandy and savant.

70. *tire-room:* dressing room.

114–18. *Parma's pride, the Jerome . . . Correggio . . . Modenese:* the great painting of St Jerome by Antonio Allegri, commonly called Correggio (1494–1534), hangs in the Ducal Academy at Parma. Correggio is alleged to have studied at Modena.

317. *Hildebrand:* as Pope Gregory VII (1073–85) Hildebrand made the Church's most extreme claim to temporal power.

382–7. *Verdi . . . Rossini patient:* having written a poor opera, Verdi ignored the plaudits of the crowd and found his judgment in Rossini's silence.

412. *Schelling:* Frederick William Joseph von Schelling (1775–1854), a famous German philosopher, argued that what might seem true to the senses, or 'Understanding', might be judged false by a higher faculty, the 'Reason'.

476. *Austerlitz:* one of Napoleon's greatest victories.

517. *Giulio Romano:* Italian painter and architect (1492–1546), a pupil of Raphael's.
   Dowland: John Dowland, sixteenth-century English composer and lutenist.

520. *'Pandulph . . . cardinal':* from Shakespeare's *King John,* III, i.

534. *Gothard:* the St Gothard's pass in the Alps between Italy and Switzerland.

573. *Re-opens a shut book:* translates the Bible into the vernacular.

578. *Strauss:* David Friedrich Strauss (1808–74), who wrote the rationalistic 'Life of Jesus' (1835).

700. *Virgin's winks:* miracles generally.

704. *brother Newman:* Cardinal Newman wrote in defence of miracles.

705. *Immaculate Conception:* proclaimed dogma in 1854.

716. *King Bomba:* King puff-cheek, liar, or knave: nickname given to Ferdinand II (1810–59), King of the Two Sicilies.
lazzaroni: Naples beggars.

717. *Antonelli:* Cardinal, secretary to Pius IX.

729. *Naples' liquefaction:* the periodic liquefaction of the blood of St Jannarius, Christian martyr of the fourth century.

745. *Fichte . . . God himself:* Johann Gottlieb Fichte (1762–1814), German philosopher, argued that God is the moral order of the universe.

878. *Pastor est tui Dominus:* 'the Lord is thy shepherd'.

916. *Anacreon:* Greek poet of the sixth century B.C., famous for his drinking songs.

973–5. *in partibus . . . novel hierarchy:* a bishop 'in partibus infidelium' is bishop of a see which has fallen away from the Church. When the Pope re-established the Catholic hierarchy in England in 1850, Wiseman's title was changed from titular Bishop of Melipotamus, 'in partibus infidelium', to Archbishop of Westminster.

979. *While the great bishop rolled him out his mind:* in later editions Browning made an addition here: 'a mind/ Long crumpled, till creased consciousness lay smooth.'

1014. *studied his last chapter of St. John:* the meaning of this has been disputed. It probably means simply 'completed his personal study of the Gospels'.

Andrea del Sarto. Browning's source for his poem on this painter (1487–1531) was the first edition of *The Lives of the Painters* by Giorgio Vasari, who had been Andrea's apprentice.

15. *Fiesole:* a small cathedral town on the hills near Florence.

93. *Morello:* a mountain near Florence.

95. *Rightly traced and well ordered—what of that?* In later editions Browning added another line here: 'Speak as they please, what does the mountain care?'

104. *The Urbinate:* Raphael Sanzio (1483–1502), commonly called Raphael, was born at Urbino.

129. *Angelo:* 'Agnolo' in later editions, Michel Agnolo being the more correct form of the commoner Michaelangelo (1475–1564).

145. *the Paris lords:* representatives from the court of Francis I, King of France, Andrea's great patron, who had given him a sum of money to buy pictures while on leave in Italy. Browning adopts the story that Andrea had dishonestly spent the money on his wife and himself.

149. *Fontainebleau:* famous pleasure resort where French kings often kept court.

209. *cue-owls:* the Scops owl whose cry ('ki-ou') suggests its name.

262. *Leonard:* Leonardo da Vinci.

Old Pictures in Florence. According to Browning, this poem was
badly mishandled by the printers, and several changes were subse-
quently made in the 1863 edition.

15. *bell-tower Giotto raised:* the unfinished campanile of the Duomo
in Florence, praised by Ruskin as the building which unites
power and beauty in their highest possible relative degree.

51. *Michael:* Michaelangelo.

64. *Dellos:* Dello di Niccolo Deli, an obscure painter born towards
the end of the fourteenth century.

67. *girns:* growls or grumbles [Scot.].

69. *Stefano:* a Florentine painter of the fourteenth century whose
naturalism earned him the title 'the Ape of Nature'.

72. *Vasari:* Giorgio Vasari's *Lives of the Painters* (1550–68).

76. *its transit:* later changed to '*sic transit*' (i.e., 'sic transit gloria
mundi', 'thus passes away the glory of the world').

84. *in fructu:* 'as fruit'.

91. *And bringing your own shortcomings there:* later changed to
'Earth here, rebuked by Olympus there'.

98. *Theseus:* the statue carved by Phidias for the Parthenon, now
in the British Museum.

99. *Son of Priam:* Paris, shown kneeling and drawing a bow in one
of the famous sculptures on the island of Aegina.

102. *Niobe:* chief figure of the group of statues 'Niobe All Tears
for her Children' in the Uffizi Gallery in Florence.

103. *the Racer's frieze:* of the Parthenon, now in the British
Museum.

104. *dying Alexander:* (Paris's second name) a piece of ancient
Greek sculpture at Florence.

108. *the worsted's duty:* later changed to 'a mortal's duty'.

112. *God's own plan:* later changed to 'God's clear plan'.

135. *just (was it not?)* '*O*': Giotto once demonstrated his skill to
the Pope by drawing a perfect O with one sweep of the brush.

147. *Replied, ' Become now self-acquainters':* later changed to 'To
become now self-acquainters'.

153. *full honour and glory:* later changed to 'their guerdon and
glory'.

156. *quiddit:* Latin *quidditas*, 'a specious argument or subtlety'.

160. *our degree:* later changed to 'your degree'.

179. *Nicolo the Pisan:* Niccola Pisano, an influential early thir-
teenth-century sculptor and architect.

180. *Cimabue:* (1240–1302) Giotto's teacher.

182. *Ghiberti:* Lorenzo (1381–1455), designed and executed the
great bronze doors on the Baptistry at Florence.

198. *Ghirlandajo:* Domenico (1449–98), the Florentine painter who
was the master of Michaelangelo.
dree: endure, suffer.

199. *Such doom, that a captive's to be out-ferreted:* later changed to
'Such doom, how a captive might be out-ferreted'

201. *Bigordi:* the family name of Ghirlandajo.

202. *Sandro:* Botticelli (1447–1510).

203. *wronged Lippino:* Filippo Lippi (1460–1505), natural son of
Fra Lippo Lippi, some of whose pictures were attributed to other
artists.

204. *Fra Angelico:* (1387–1455) the great Dominican friar-painter of Florence.
205. *Taddeo Gaddi:* (1300–66) Florentine painter and architect who carried on work on Giotto's campanile.
206. *intonaco:* plaster background for fresco painting.
207. *Jerome:* St Jerome, the translator of the Scriptures into Latin.
208. *Lorenzo Monaco:* (1370–1425) Florentine monk and painter.
210. *Pollajolo:* Antonio (1429–98), Florentine goldsmith and sculptor.
215. *Alesso Baldovinetti:* (1427–99) prominent master of the Florentine Renaissance who worked in fresco and mosaic.
217. *Margheritone of Arezzo:* thirteenth-century painter, sculptor, and architect who worked in the Greek manner.
218. *barret:* usually a flat cap, but here probably a cloak.
220. *You bald, saturnine:* later changed to 'You bald, old, saturnine.'
230. *Zeno:* Greek philosopher (fl. 500 B.C.) who founded the sect of Stoics.
232. *Carlino:* sculptor and architect of the late thirteenth and early fourteenth centuries.
236. *precious little tablet:* a painting of the Last Supper, supposed to be by Giotto, which came to light while Browning was in Florence.
237. *Buonarroti:* Michaelangelo.
238. *Buried so long:* later changed to 'Was buried so long'.
241. *San Spirito:* 'Holy Spirit', a Florentine basilica containing many famous pictures.
242. *Ognissanti:* 'All Saints', another Florentine church with rare pictures.
244. *detur amanti:* 'let it be given to the one who loves it'.
245. *Koh-i-noor:* the 'mountain of light', one of the largest diamonds in the world.
246. *Jewel of Giamschid:* Byron's name for the Koh-i-noor. *Persian Sofi:* Mohammedan mystic.
249. *certain dotard:* Ferdinand, Grand Duke of Tuscany, whom Browning would like to see pitched over the Alps because of his Austrian sympathies.
255. *Radetsky:* field marshal who commanded the Austrian forces holding northern Italy in subjection.
256. *Morello:* a mountain near Florence.
257. *We'll shoot* etc.: later changed to 'This time we'll shoot better game and bag 'em hot'.
258. *No display:* later changed to 'No mere display'
259. *Witan-agemot:* gathering of wise men, the council of the Anglo-Saxon kings.
260. *'Casa-Guidi':* the name of the Browning's house in Florence. In 1851 Mrs Browning published a poem entitled 'Casa Guidi Windows', dedicated to the cause of Italian liberty.
quod videas ante: 'which see above', or 'which you may have seen before '.
261. *To ponder:* later changed to 'Shall ponder'.

263. *Lorraine:* Tuscany had come back under the control of the foreign House of Lorraine after the French occupation of 1815.
264. *Organga:* Andrea di Cione (1315–76), a painter who lived in the days when Florence was free.
266. *Say fit things:* later changed to 'Utter fit things'.
267. *set truth,* etc.: later changed to 'Feel truth at blood-heat and falsehood at zero rate'.
273. *curt Tuscan:* Tuscan is the literary language of Italy, thus freer from colloquialisms and vulgarisms than modern forms.
274. *'issimo':* the superlative ending for adjectives in Italian.
275. *half-told tale of Cambuscan:* Cambuscan is the hero of Chaucer's 'Squire's Tale', which was left unfinished.
276. *alt altissimo:* later changed to 'alt to altissimo', 'high to the highest'.
277. *beccaccia:* woodcock.
278. *the Duomo's fit ally:* Giotto's campanile is a fit ally for the cathedral.
279. *braccia:* cubits; Giotto's plans called for a spire fifty cubits high.
285. *'God and the People':* Mazzini's motto.
287. *Foreseeing the day,* etc.: later changed to 'At least to foresee that glory of Giotto'.

In a Balcony.
    412. *baladine:* dancer.

Saul. The first nine sections of the present text of this poem were published as a fragment in Browning's *Dramatic Romances* in 1845, but the complete text of the poem, with the ninth section considerably revised, first appeared in *Men and Women*. The principal source is I Samuel, 16: 14–23.
    1. *Abner:* Saul's uncle and the commander of his army.
    31. *king-serpent:* boa-constrictor.
    45. *jerboa:* the jumping hare, a small rodent.
    65. *male-sapphires:* the star-stone, a semi-transparent sapphire.
    188. *paper reeds:* a plant of the sedge family from which papyrus was made.
    203. *Hebron:* a mountain in Judea, south-west of Jerusalem.
    204. *Kidron:* a brook east of Jerusalem.
    213. *error:* Saul had lost God's favour by refusing to exterminate the Amalekites.
    291. *Sabaoth:* armies.
    292. *and why am I loth:* in later editions this was corrected to 'Why am I not loath'.

'De Gustibus——'. The title is from the Latin proverb *de gustibus non disputandum est,* 'there is no use disputing tastes'.
    22. *cicalas:* locusts.
    35. *The king:* Ferdinand II of Naples, descended from the Spanish branch of the Bourbon family.
    36. *liver-wing:* right arm.
    40. *Queen Mary's saying:* the Queen was so grieved when the English lost Calais to the French in 1558 that she said 'Calais' would be found written on her heart when she died.

46. *So it always was, so it still shall be:* changed in 1863 to 'So it always was, so shall ever be!'

Protus. The poem has no historical foundation.
   4. *Loric:* breastplate, corselet.
   10. *Byzant:* Byzantium, i.e., Constantinople.
   36. *Pannonian:* Pannonia was a country north-west of Greece.
   53. *Thrace:* a region north-east of Macedonia, now Bulgaria.

Holy-Cross Day. The Festival of the Exaltation of the Holy Cross falls on 14 September annually. It commemorates the alleged miraculous appearance to the Emperor Constantine of the cross in the sky.
   52. *the Corso:* one of the chief streets of Rome.
   66. *Ben Ezra's Song of Death:* Abraham Ben Meir Ezra (1090–1168), also called Abenezra, or Ibn Ezra, a mediaeval Jewish philosopher, astronomer, physician, poet and commentator on the Old Testament. There is no known source for the 'Song of Death' which Browning pretends to quote here.

The Guardian Angel. The picture so entitled ('L'Angelo Custode') by the Italian painter known as 'Guercino' ('the squinter'), Giovanni Francesco Barbieri (1590–1666) is in the Church of St Augustine at Fano, a small city on the Adriatic.
   37. *Alfred, dear friend:* Alfred Domett, a boyhood friend of Browning's, described in the poem 'Waring' in *Dramatic Lyrics,* (1842).
   46. *My angel:* Mrs Browning.
   55. *the Wairoa:* a river in New Zealand, to which Domett had emigrated.
   56. *Ancona:* a province of Italy where Browning wrote this poem after his visit to Fano.

Cleon. Both the writer of the supposed letter, the philosopher and poet Cleon, and the recipient, the emperor Paulus, are fictitious. The quotation in the sub-title is from Acts, 17 : 28.
   1. *the sprinkled isles:* the Sporades, off the Greek coast.
   4. *his Tyranny:* a tyrant in the old Greek sense was one who had seized rule by usurpation, not necessarily a cruel ruler.
   51. *phare:* lighthouse.
   53. *Pœcile:* a portico at Athens covered with paintings of historical and religious subjects.
   59. *moods:* ancient Greek scale system in music.
   82–3. *rhomb . . . lozenge . . . trapezoid:* four-sided figures which combine to form a picture.
   139. *Terpander:* a Greek musician of the seventh century B.C., the father of Greek music.
   140. *Phidias:* the greatest of Greek sculptors (fifth century B.C.).
   339. *Paulus:* St Paul.

The Twins. The source of the poem is No. 316, 'On Justification', from Martin Luther's *Table Talk*.
   16. *Date:* 'give'. *Dabitur:* 'it shall be given unto you'.

Notes

Popularity.

18–20. *'Others give best . . . till now'*: see John, 2 : 1–10.

26. *Tyrian shells*: the genera Murex and Purpura secrete a liquid used by the ancients to make royal purple dye.

29. *Astarte*: the Roman form of 'Ashtoreth', the Phœnecian goddess of love.

41–2. *Solomon . . . cedar house*: see I Kings, 6–7.

44. *the Spouse*: Pharaoh's daughter.

The Heretic's Tragedy. The Latin names are the titles of popular songs to be used in the Church service. *Hock-tide*: Hock Tuesday is the second Tuesday after Easter. *Rosa Mundi*: 'Rose of the World'. *Seu, fulcite me floribus*: 'Support me with flowers'. *Cantuque Virgilius*: a Virgil in song. *Gavisus eram*: 'I was glad' (Psalm 122). *Jessides*: the son of Jesse.

1. *The Abbot Deodaet*: a fictitious churchman.

9. *plagal-cadence*: the final tonic chord immediately preceded by the subdominant.

12–16. *John, Master . . . Pope Clement*: Jacques du Bourg-Molay, the last grandmaster of the Knights Templars, was burnt at Paris in 1314 following the suppression of the order which had been accused of unmentionable sins and of betraying Christianity to the Moslems. Aldabrod seems to be fictitious. Pope Clement V (1305–14) condemned the order.

20. *clavicithern*: a keyboard instrument similar to a harpsichord.

32. *bavins*: faggots of wood used for kindling.

39. *'Laudes'*: a Catholic service associated with Matins.

53. *Salvâ reverentiâ*: 'saving reverence', an apologetic expression.

65. *Sharon's rose*: see Song of Solomon, 2:1. The rose was the symbol of secrecy.

72. *When Paul once reasoned of righteousness*: see Acts, 24:25.

Two in the Campagna. The Campagna is the country region surrounding Rome, containing many ancient ruins; mainly pasture-land at the time of the poem.

A Grammarian's Funeral.

50. *gowned him*: assumed the academic gown, i.e., became a scholar.

86. *Calculus*: the stone: a concretion in some part of the body.

88. *Tussis*: a cough.

95. *hydroptic*: thirsty.

129–31. *Hoti . . . Oun . . . enclitic De*: Greek particles meaning 'that', 'therefore', and 'toward'; thus, difficult points in Greek grammar which the scholar settled.

Another Way of Love.

19. *Eadem semper*: 'always the same'

'Transcendentalism'.

12. *six-foot Swiss tube . . . bark*: a wooden megaphone.

22. *Swedish Bœhme*: later corrected to 'German Boehme' when Browning was reminded of his error. Jacob Boehme was a German mystical philosopher (1575–1624).

30. *that tough book:* presumably Boehme's *De Signatura Rerum,* in which he recorded a mystical experience which enabled him to experience the inner being of all living things, such as flowers and grass.

37–8. *him of Halberstadt/ John:* Johannes Gleim, or Johannes Teutonicus, a mediaeval poet and scientist who was supposed to possess a 'vegetable stone' which made plants grow at his will.

One Word More. 'E. B. B.' was Elizabeth Barrett Browning, the poet's wife.

9. *but One:* Margherita (La Fornarina), the baker's daughter to whom Rapahel was devoted throughout his life.

21–4. *Madonnas . . . in the Louvre:* various famous madonnas by Raphael, the last named probably being 'La Belle Jardinière'.

27. *Guido Reni* (1575–1642), an Italian painter who kept a book of a hundred designs drawn by Raphael.

37. *his left hand in the hair o' the wicked:* see *Inferno,* Canto 32.

49. *'Then I stopped my painting':* see Dante's *Vita Nuova,* Chapter 35.

57. *Bice:* contracted form of Beatrice.

74. *He who smites the rock:* see Exodus, 16–19 and Numbers, 12 and 20.

95. *Egypt's flesh-pots:* see Exodus, 16: 3–4.

97. *Sinai-forehead's cloven brilliance:* see Exodus, 19 and 35.

101–2. *Jethro . . . bondslave:* Moses married both Jethro's daughter Zipporah and a slave girl.

120. *Lines I write . . . the last time:* as promised, Browning used the unrhymed trochaic pentameter only for this poem.

136. *Karshish:* printed mistakenly as 'Karshook' in the first edition, a mistake which was changed as soon as possible. Browning was thinking of his uncollected poem 'Ben Karshook's Wisdom'.

146. *the thrice-transfigured:* reference to the three phases of the moon, new, old, and full.

163. *Zoroaster:* founder in the sixth century B.C. of the Persian religion which worships the heavenly bodies, seeing God as light.

165. *Keats:* his poem 'Endymion' concerns love between a mortal and the moon-goddess.

173–9. *seen by Moses . . . saw God also:* see Exodus, 24: 9–10.

Johannes Agricola in Meditation. In *Dramatic Lyrics* of 1842 this poem was linked with 'Porphyria's Lover' as 'Madhouse Cells, I and II', but this title was dropped and the two poems separated in 1863. On its first publication in 1836 'Johannes Agricola' was prefaced by the following note: 'Antinomians, so denominated for rejecting the Law as a thing of no use under the Gospel dispensation: they say, that good works do not further, nor evil works hinder salvation; that, the child of God cannot sin, that God never chastiseth him, that murder, drunkenness, etc. are sins in the wicked but not in him, that the child of grace being once assured of salvation, afterwards never doubteth . . . that God doth not love any man for his holiness, that sanctification is no evidence of justification, etc. Potanus, in his

Catalogue of Heresies, says John Agricola was the author of this sect, A.D. 1535.—*Dictionary of all Religions*, 1704.'

My Last Duchess. When this poem was first published in *Dramatic Lyrics* in 1842 it was called 'I. Italy' and followed by 'II. France', the poem later called 'Count Gismond' when Browning later broke up this grouping.

    3. *Frà Pandolf:* an imaginary monastic artist.

    56. *Claus of Innsbruck:* a fictional artist.

Pictor Ignotus. First published in *Dramatic Romances* in 1845. The title is Latin for 'Artist Unknown'.

The Bishop Orders his Tomb. First published in 1845. 'Saint Praxed is an anglicization of the Church of Santa Prassede (a saint whom Browning mistakenly took to be masculine), called 'the Garden of Paradise' because of its ornate richness.

    1. *Vanity, saith the preacher:* see Ecclesiastes, 1: 2.

    31. *onion-stone:* an inferior marble which peels.

    41. *olive-frail:* rush basket.

    46. *Frascati:* a beautiful spot in the Alban Hills near Rome.

    51. *a weaver's shuttle:* see Job, 7: 6.

    54. *antique-black:* Nero antico, a very costly stone.

    77. *Tully's:* Cicero's, the purest classical style.

    79. *Ulpian:* A Roman jurist, writer of a later, less pure Latin than Cicero's.

    99. *Elucescebat:* 'he was illustrious', in Ulpian's style, instead of the classical *elucebat*.

    108. *Term:* small statue on a pedestal.

Meeting at Night and *Parting at Morning*. Originally published as 'Night' and 'Morning' in *Dramatic Romances and Lyrics*, 1845.

Caliban upon Setebos. First published in *Dramatis Personae* in 1864. Browning's elaboration of Caliban in Shakespeare's *The Tempest*, where at I, ii, 375 Caliban's mother Sycorax ('his dam') is said to have worshipped Setebos (presumably the god of the Patagonians described in Richard Eden's *History of Travaile*, 1577). 'Natural theology' is the interpretation of God's character from the evidence found in nature; the *Bridgewater Treasties* of 1833–40 were a famous Victorian example. The motto of the poem is from Psalms, 50: 21.

    7. *pompion-plant:* a wild vine of the pumpkin species.

    71. *bladdery:* bubbly.

    148. *hips:* fruit of wild rose.

    156–7. *oncelot* and *ounce:* mountain leopard.

    229. *urchin:* hedgehog.

    294. *Will let these quails fly . . . so he may 'scape:* see Numbers, 12: 29–35.

Confessions. First published in *Dramatis Personae* in 1864.

Apparent Failure. First published in *Dramatis Personae* in 1864.

    3. *the baptism of your Prince:* the son of Napoleon III was baptized in 1856.

    7. *the Congress:* the Imperial Congress in 1856 to conclude the Crimean War.

12. *Petrarch's Vaucluse:* a village in southern France near the source of the Sorgue where Petrarch lived for a time.
46–7. *red in vain. Or black:* allusion to the gambling game 'Rouge et Noir'.

Numpholeptos: First published in *Pacchiarotto* in 1876. The title means 'caught or entranced by a nymph'. Nymphs (the spelling in the title is due to Browning's theories about the correct transliteration of Greek letters) were semi-divine maidens in Greek mythology. Since the nymph is not human, she can feel no kindred feeling for the nympholept; hence nympholepsy means by extension 'ecstasy inspired by a desire for the ideal or unattainable'.

20. *the Spirit Seven:* see Revelations, 3: 1.
61–4. *from your midmost home rays forth . . . shaft upon coloured shaft:* the imagery of the poem is based upon the breaking up of pure white light into the coloured rays of the solar spectrum, a ray of white light, being composed of the seven primary colours, being divisible by a prism into these seven colours. The nymph dwells in pure white light; her mortal lover is condemned to the realm of the broken coloured rays.

'Epilogue to Asolando'. The last poem in Browning's final volume, *Asolando: Fancies and Facts*, published on the day of his death in 1889. The title of the volume is a play upon 'Asolo', the small city near Venice which Browning had always loved.

INDEX OF FIRST LINES

NOTES